20x40 DRESSAGE TEST PLANNER

CREATED BY HOW TO DRESSAGE
HowToDressage.com

Copyright © 2019 by Rosanna Sunley T/A How To Dressage (**HowToDressage.com**)

All rights reserved

ISBN: 9781073009787

No part of this book may be reproduced in any form or by any electronic or mechanical means, including information storage and retrieval systems, without written prior notice from the author, except for the use of brief quotations in a book review.

Disclaimer of liability
The author(s) shall have neither liability or responsibility to any person or entity with respect to any loss or damage caused or alleged to be caused directly or indirectly by the information contained in this book. While the book is as accurate as the author(s) can make it, there may be omissions and inaccuracies.

Requests to publish work from this book should be sent to:
hello@howtodressage.com

Use this workbook to help you create your own dressage floorplans, choreograph dressage to music routines, and help you memorize dressage tests.

If you want more exercises ideas, check out our BIG Book of Dressage Exercises on Amazon.

CONTENTS

EXERCISE NAME	PAGE NUMBER
....	....
....	....
....	....
....	....
....	....
....	....
....	....
....	....
....	....
....	....
....	....
....	....
....	....
....	....
....	....
....	....
....	....
....	....
....	....
....	....
....	....
....	....
....	....
....	....

EXERCISE NAME	PAGE NUMBER

EXERCISE NAME	PAGE NUMBER
EXERCISE NAME	PAGE NUMBER

EXERCISE NAME	PAGE NUMBER

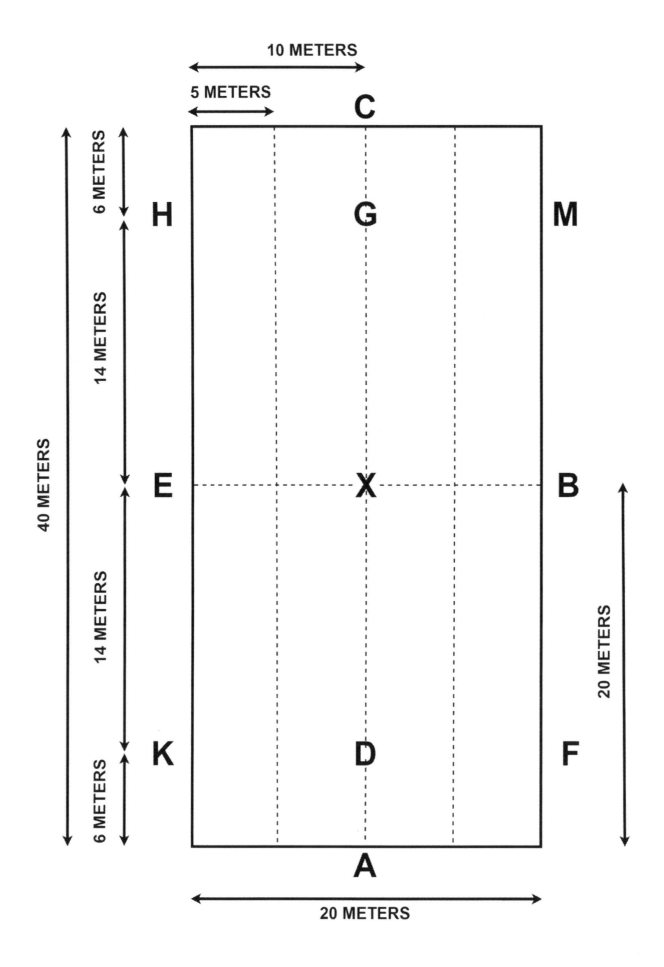

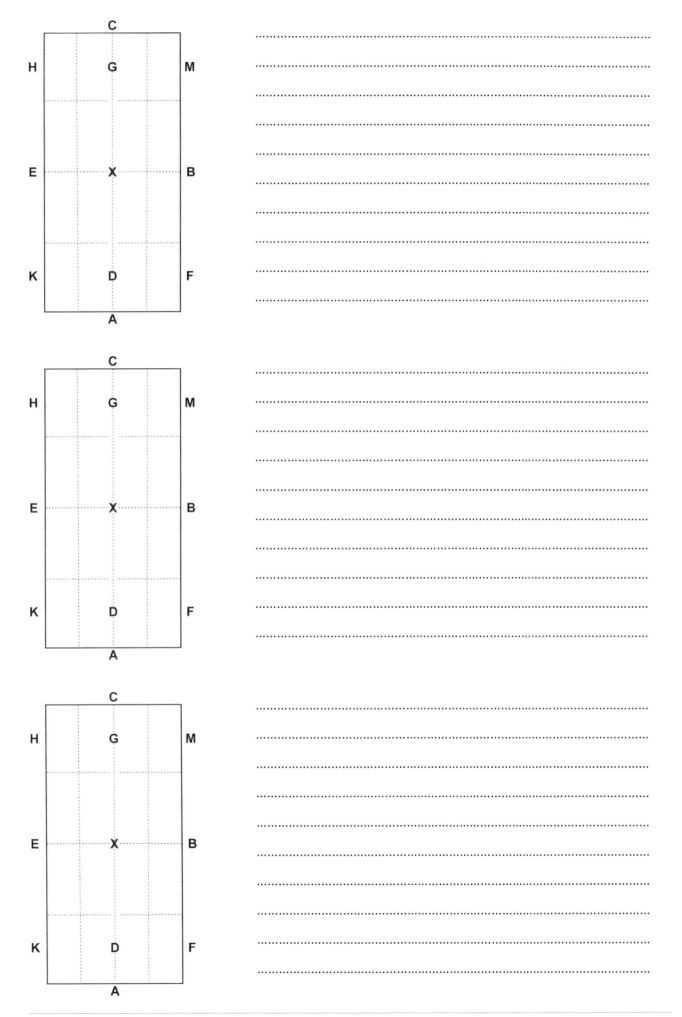

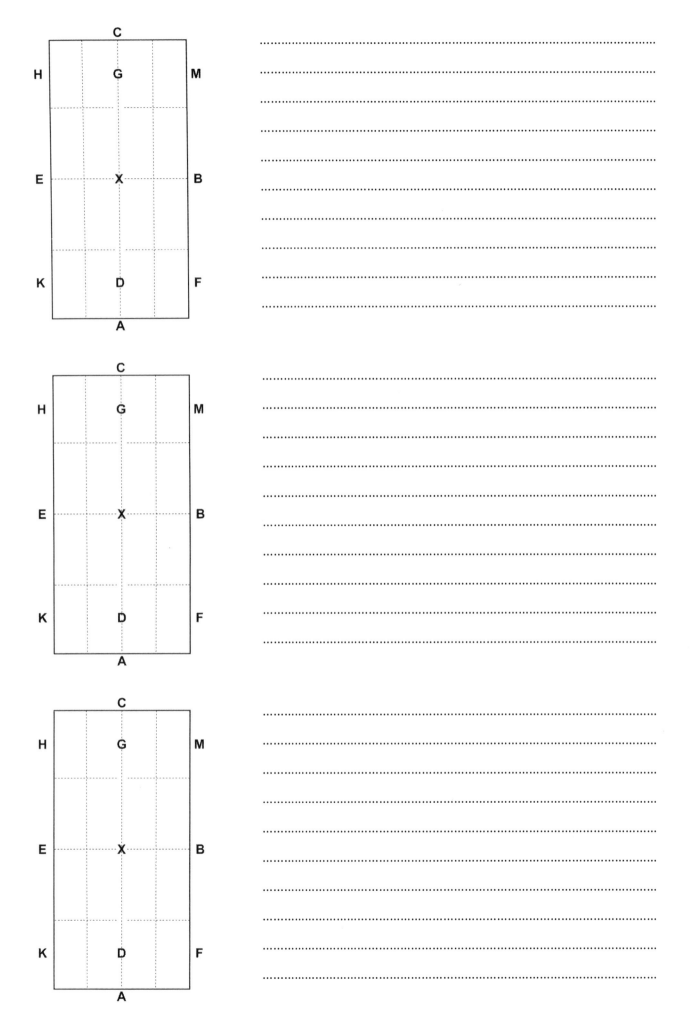

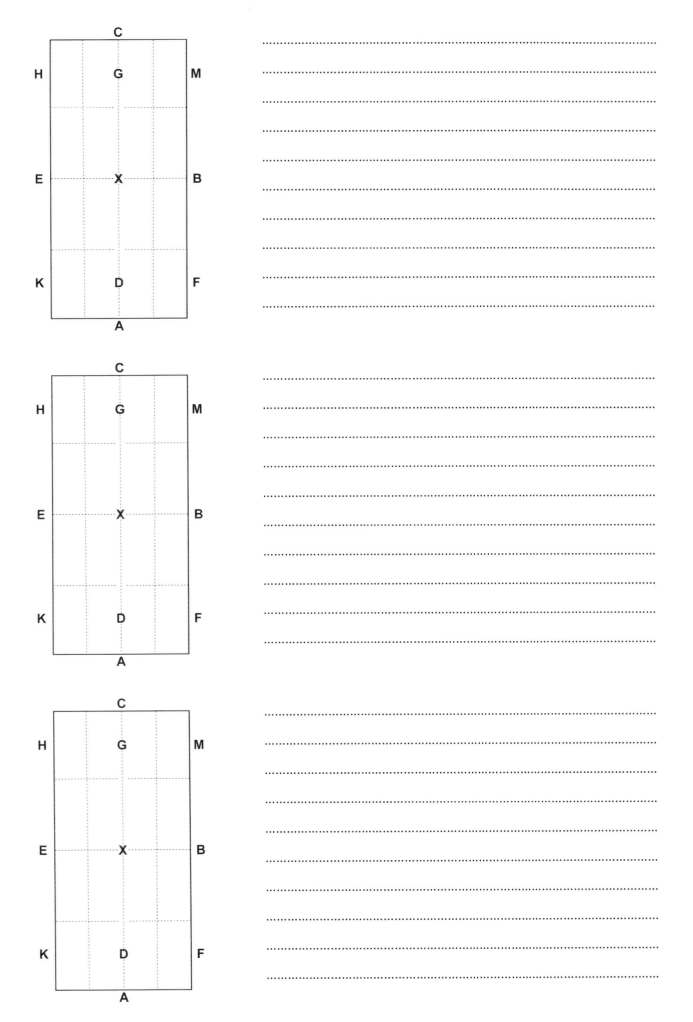

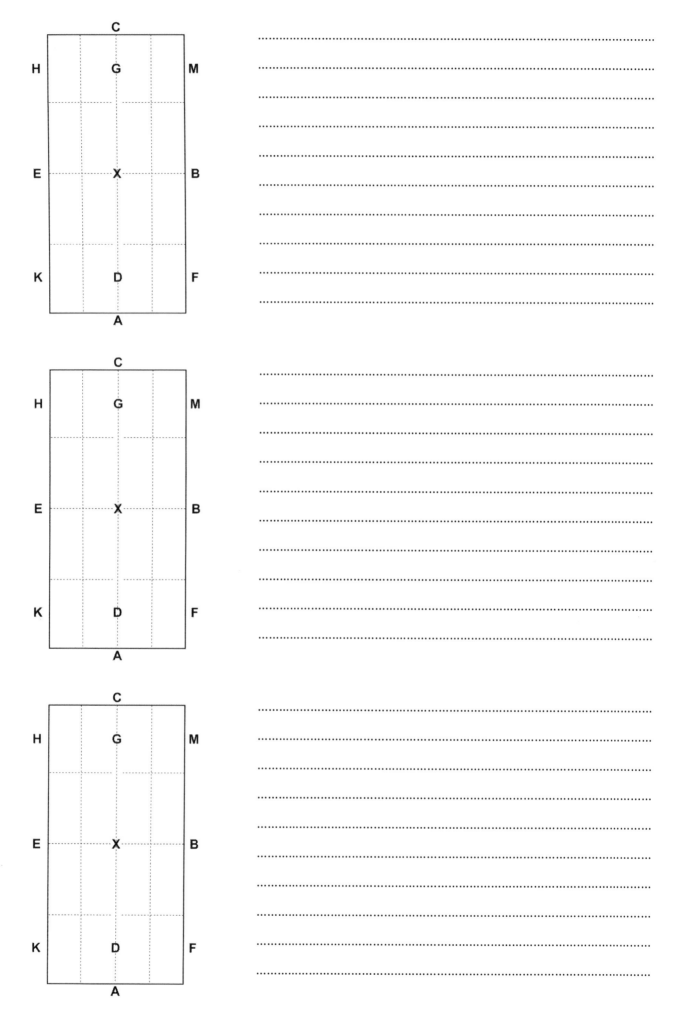

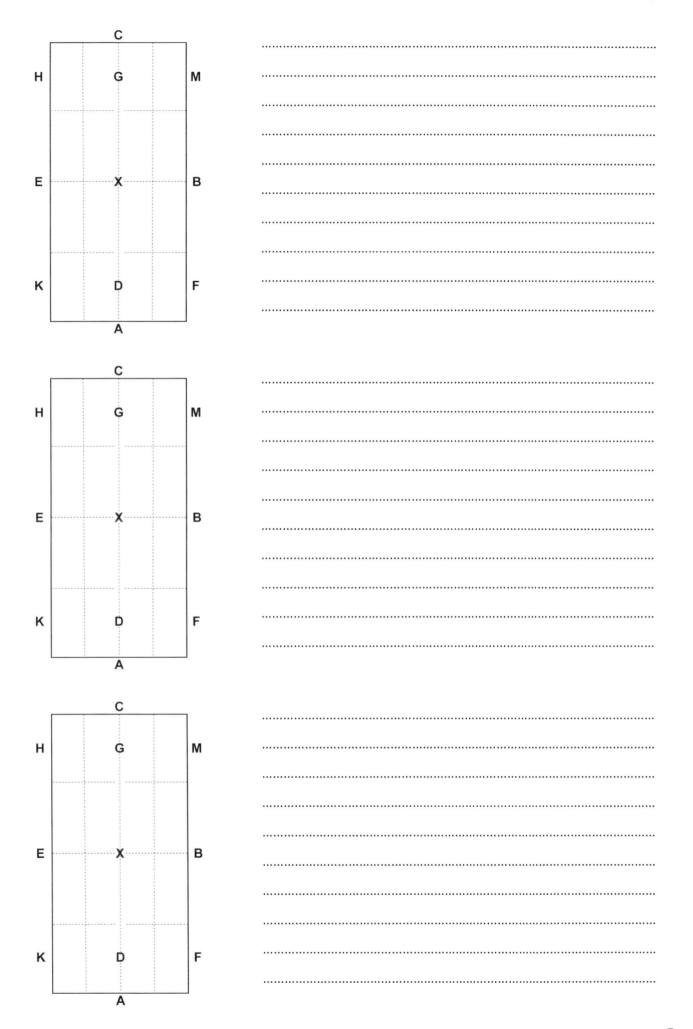

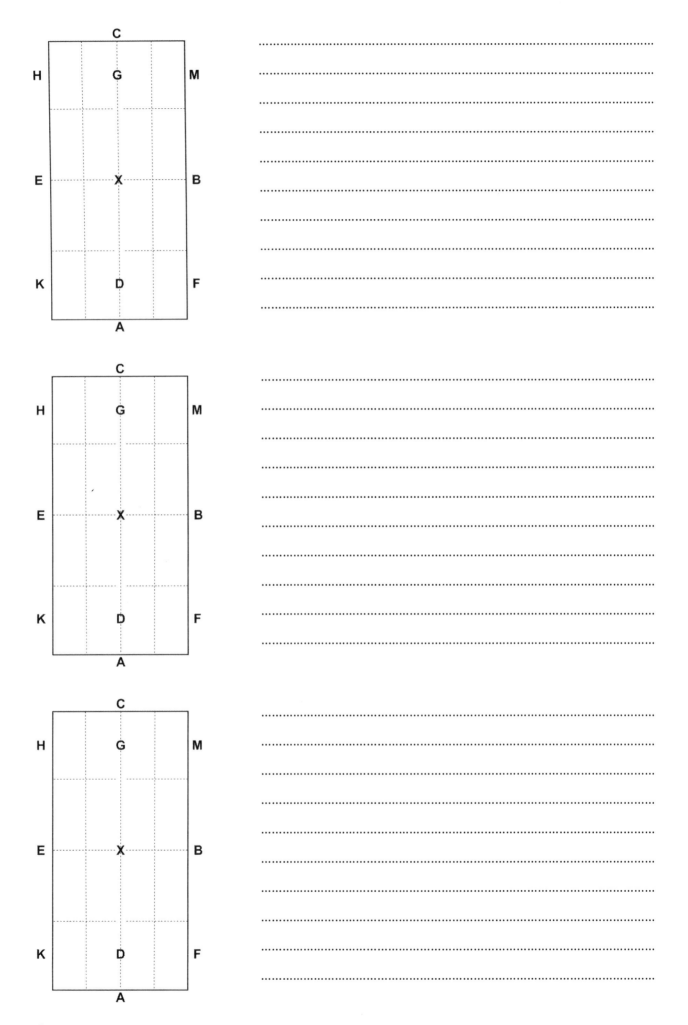

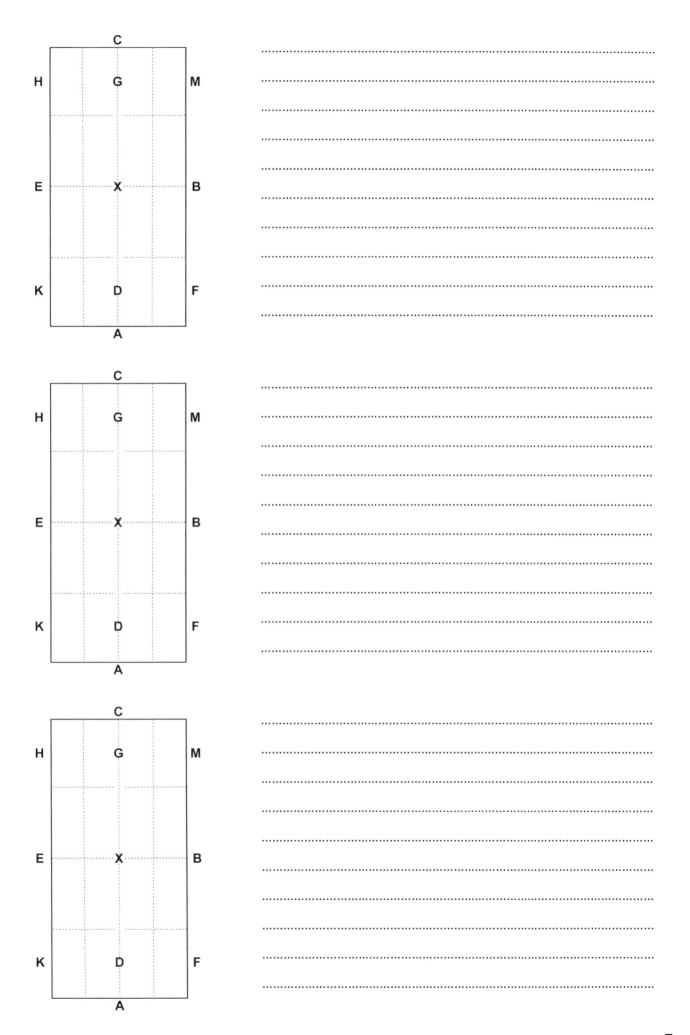

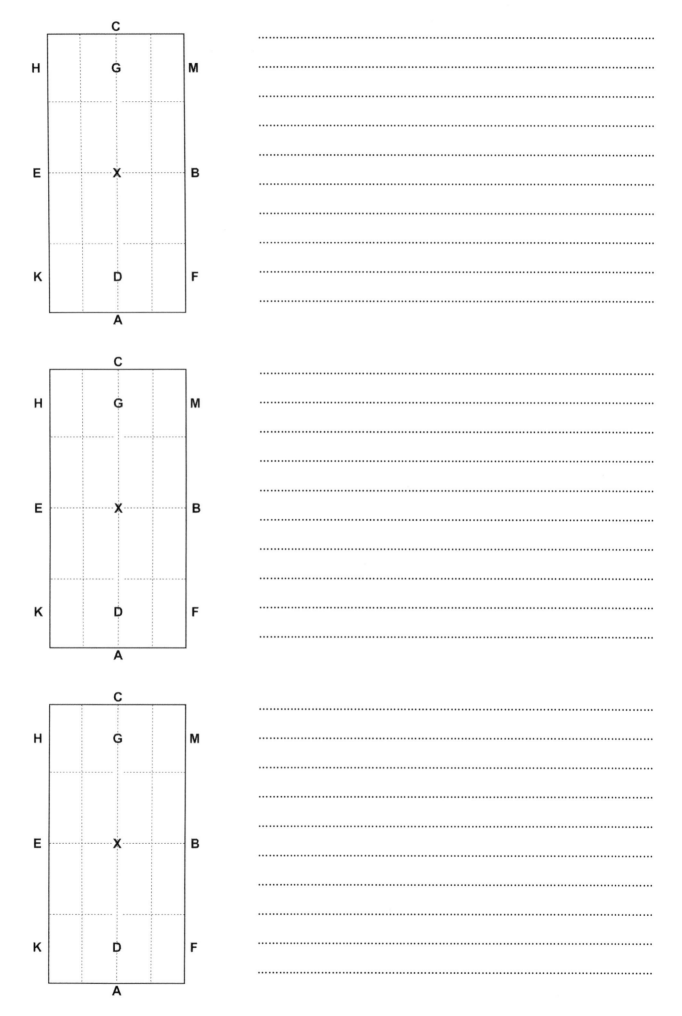

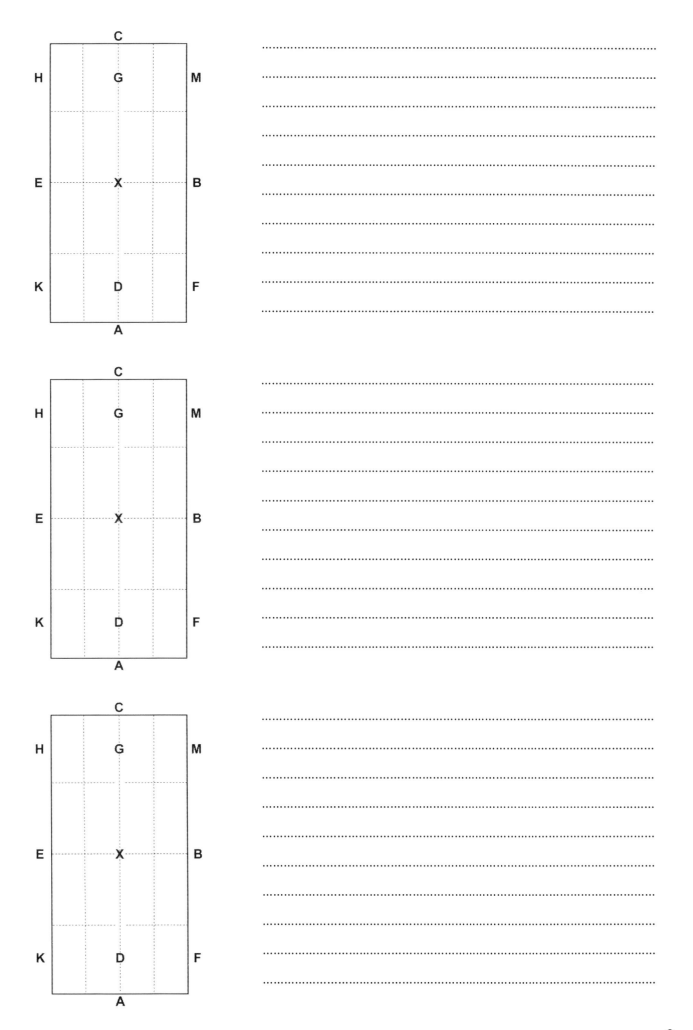

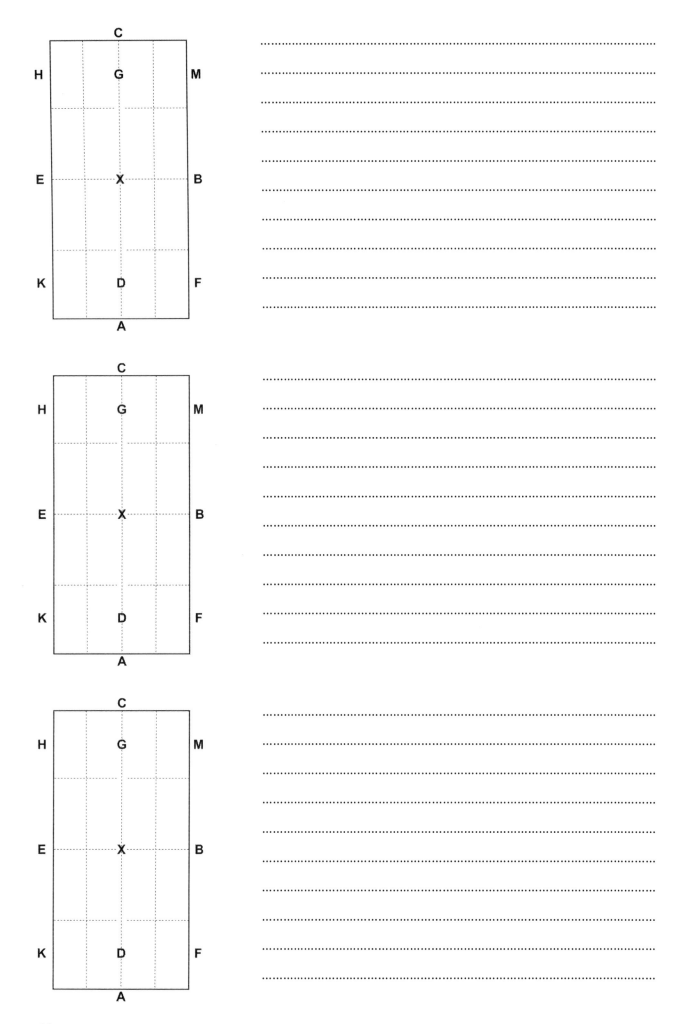

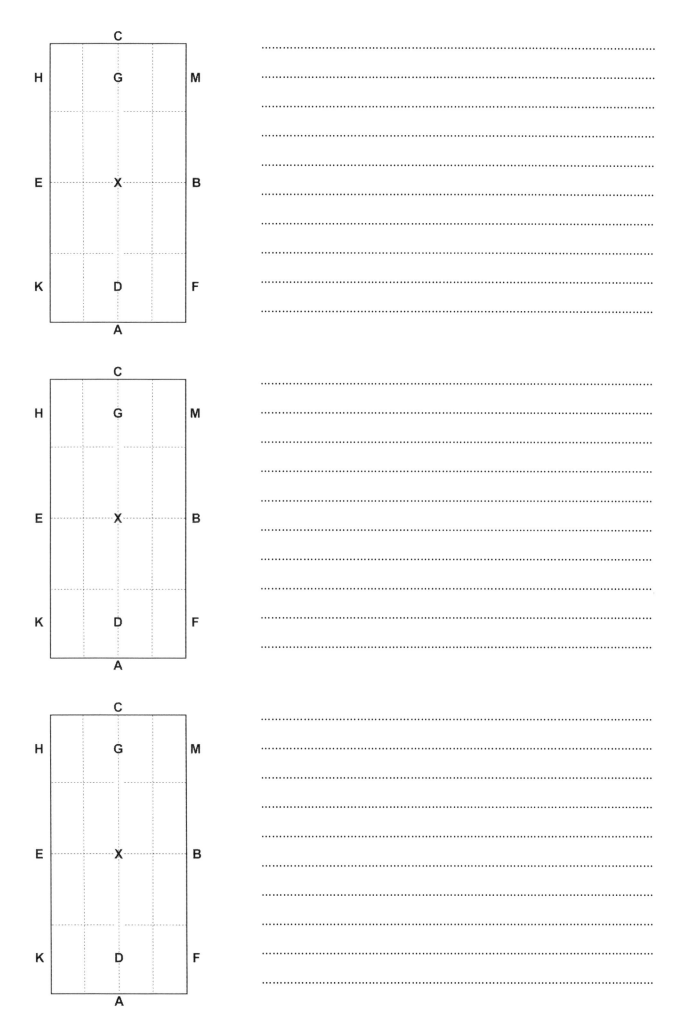

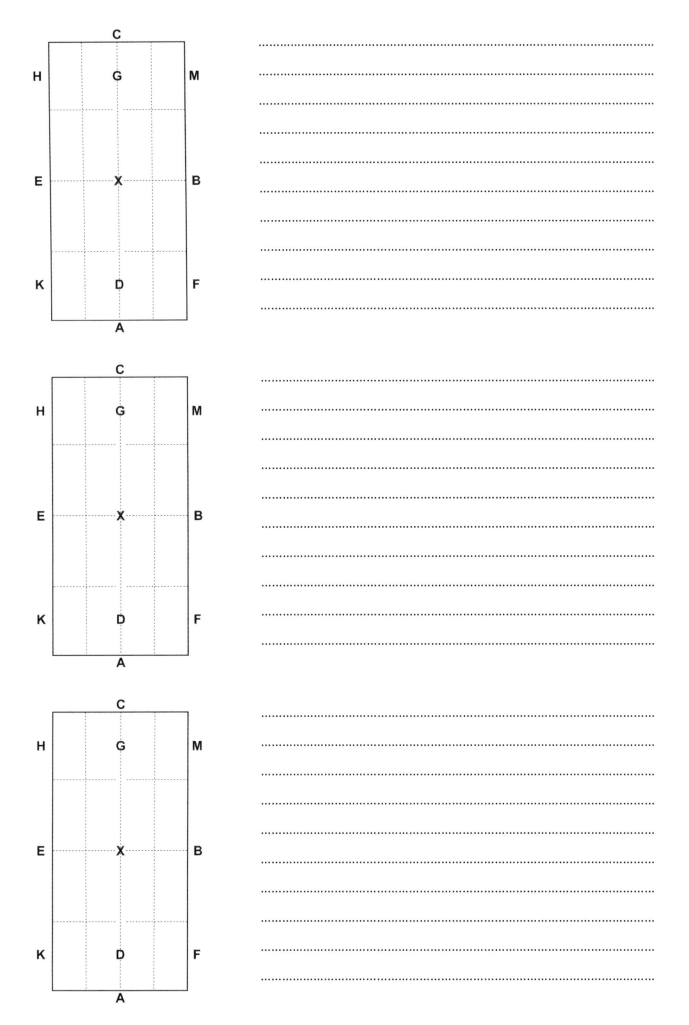

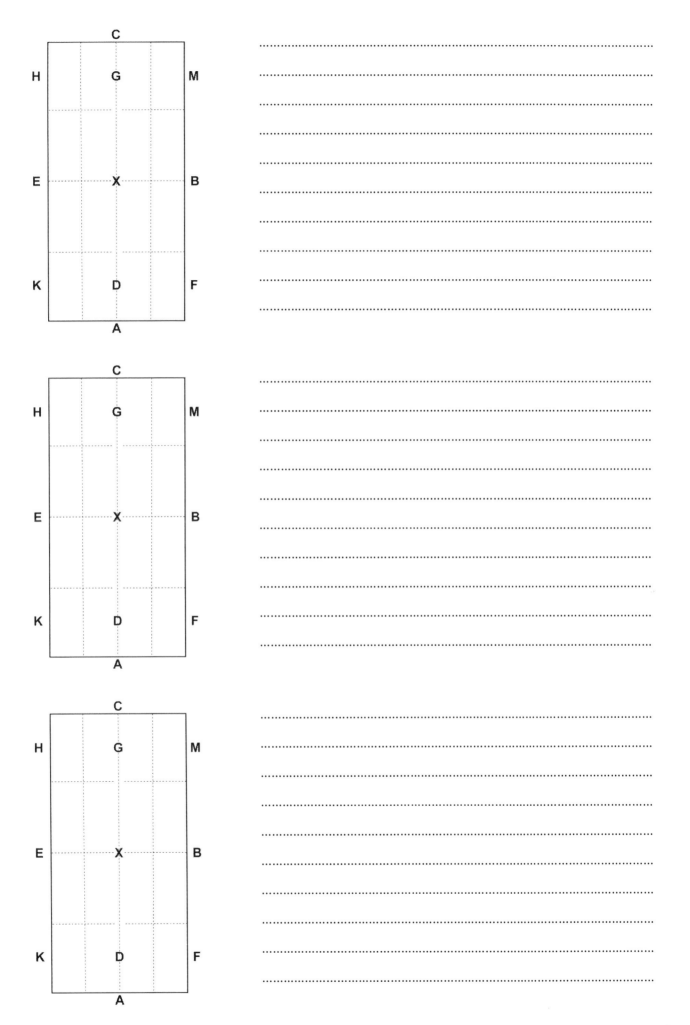

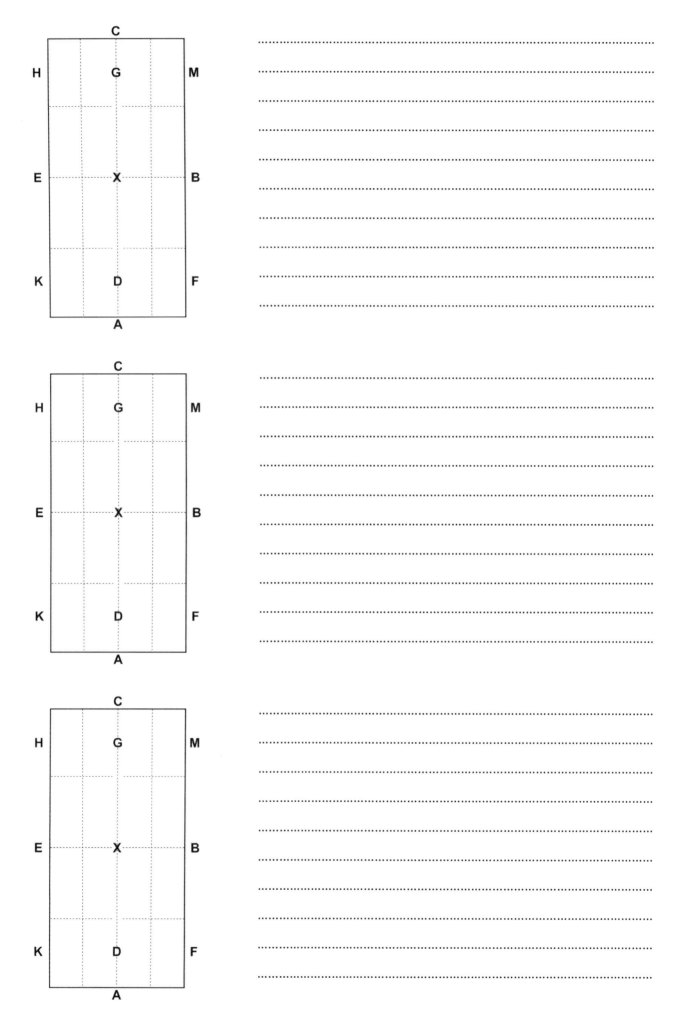

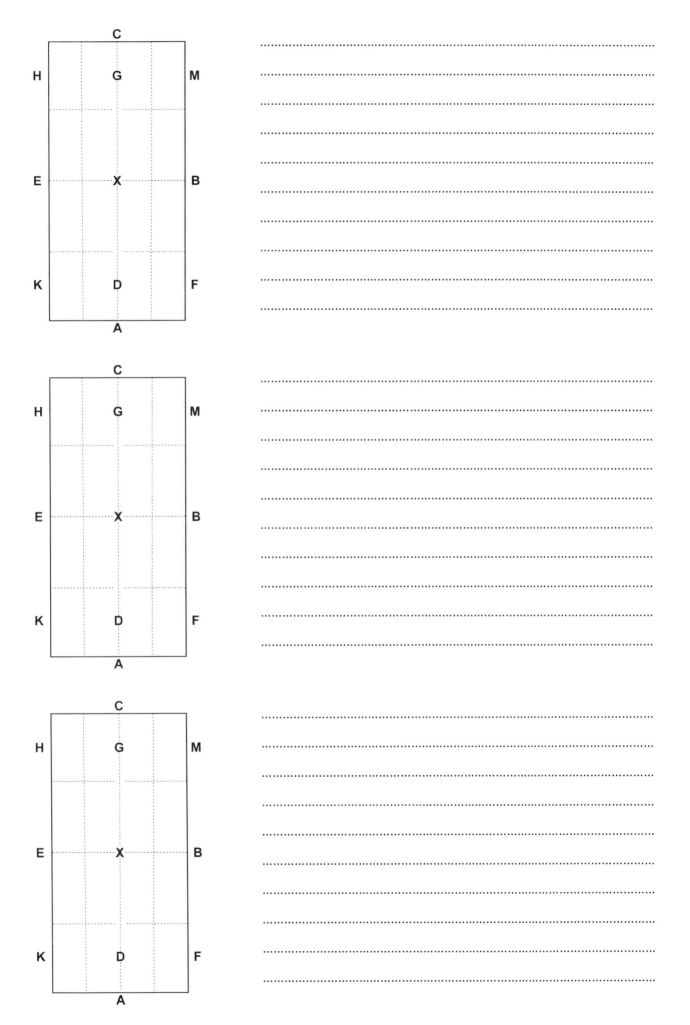

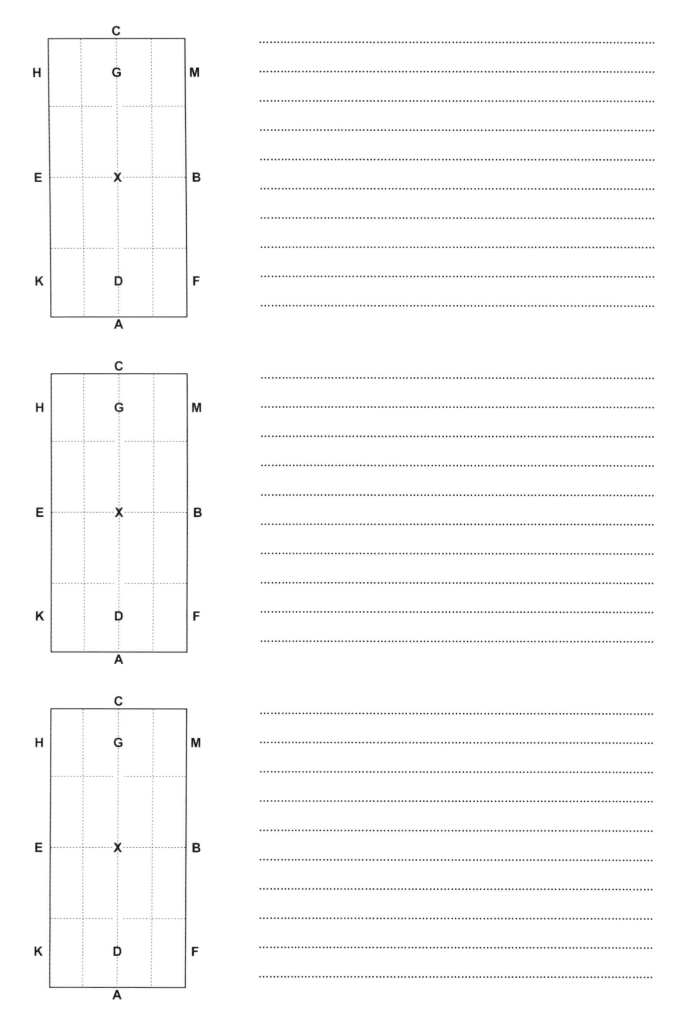

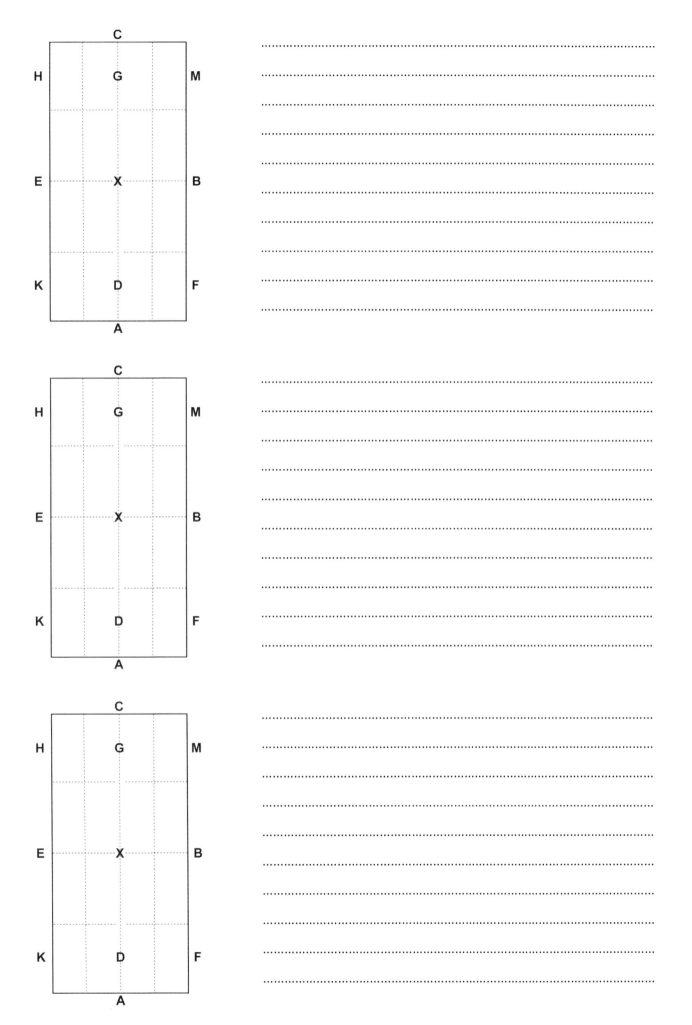

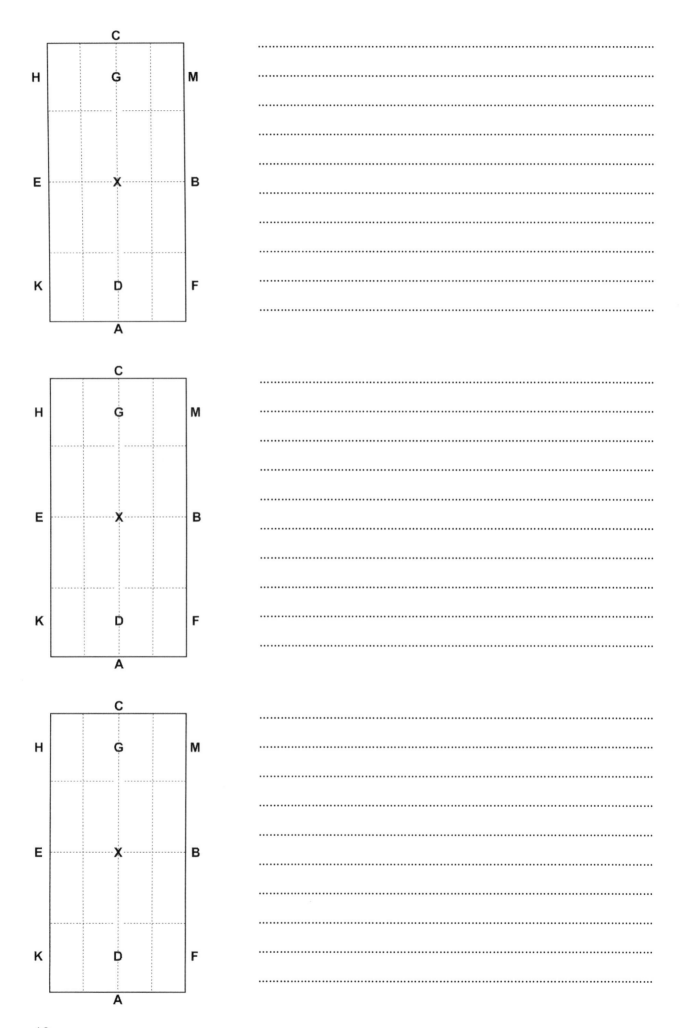

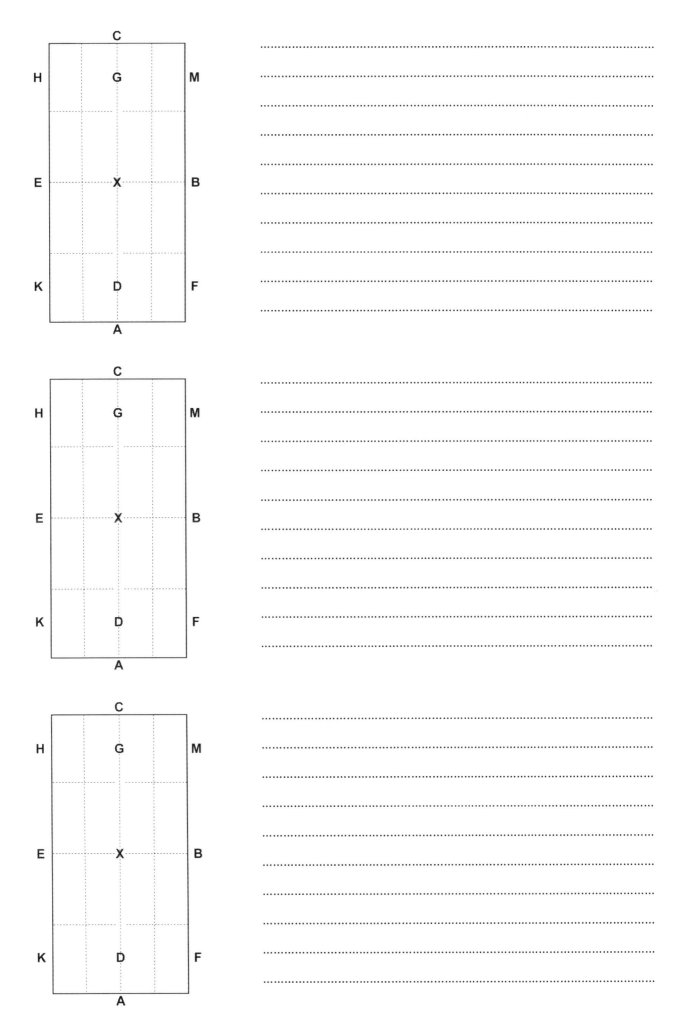

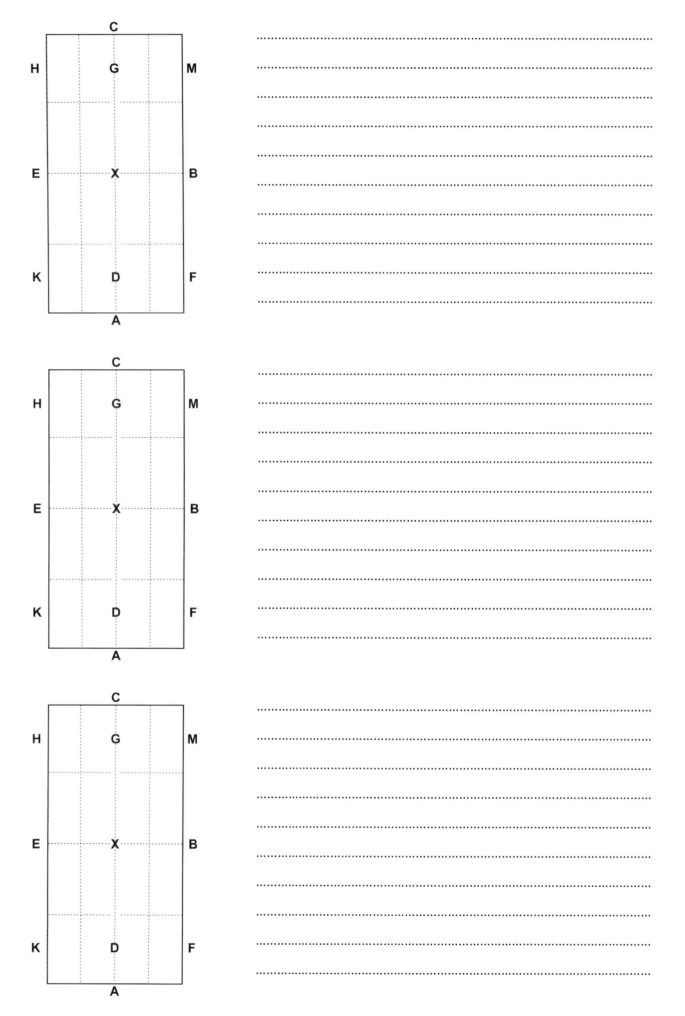

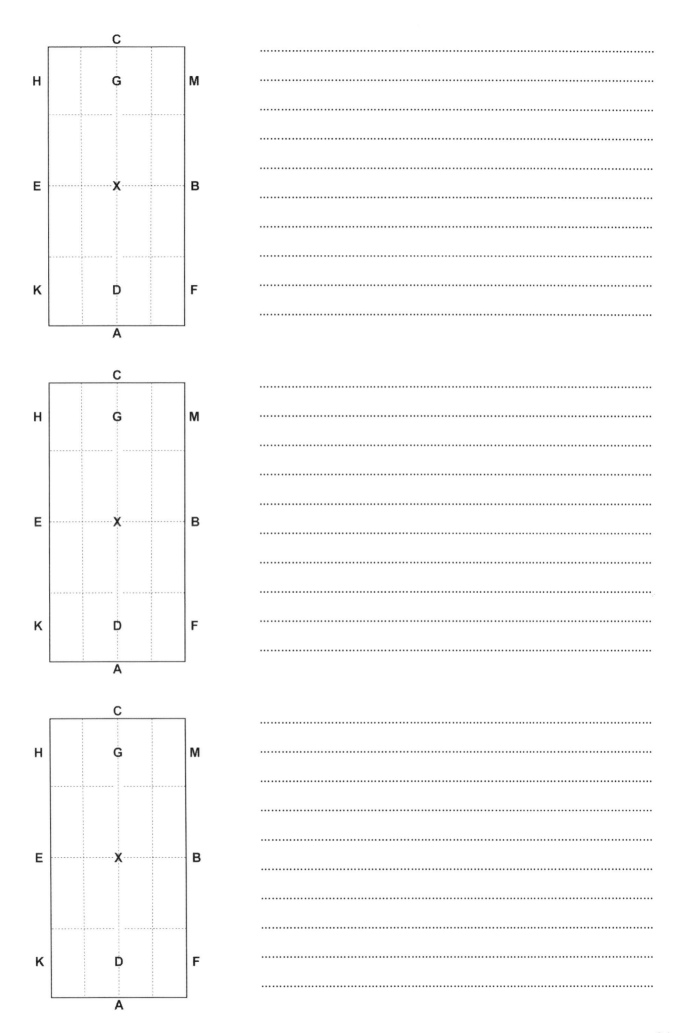

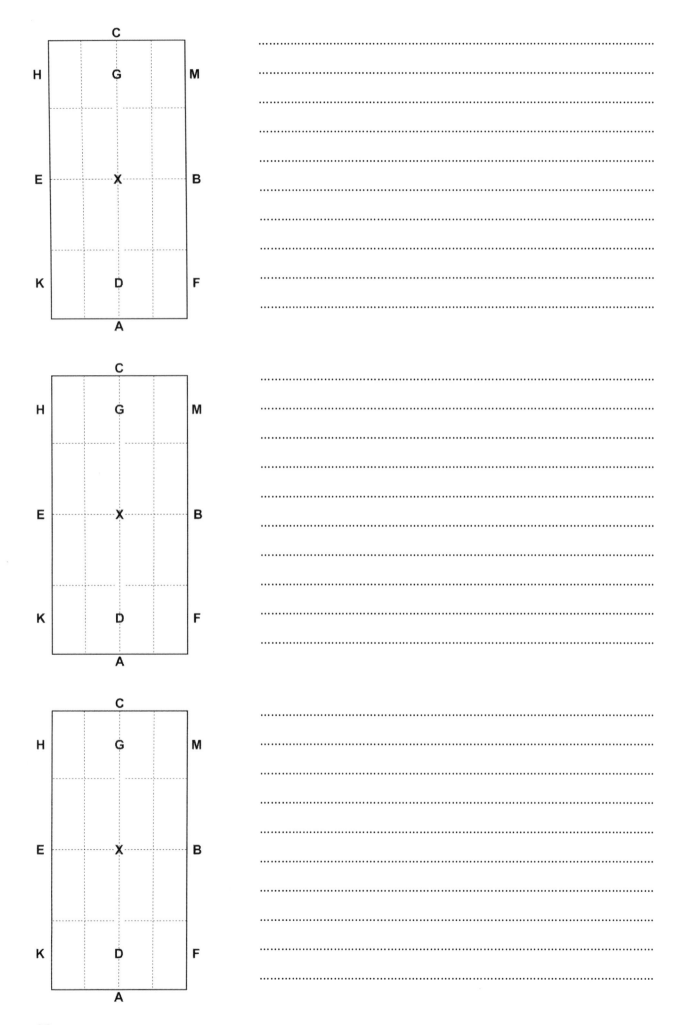

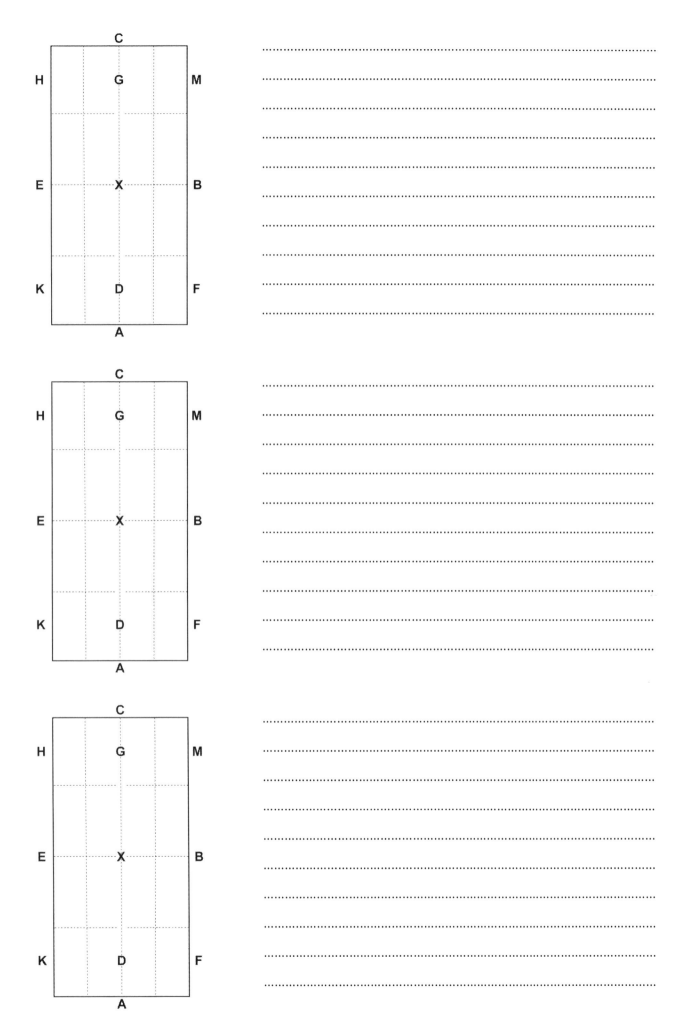

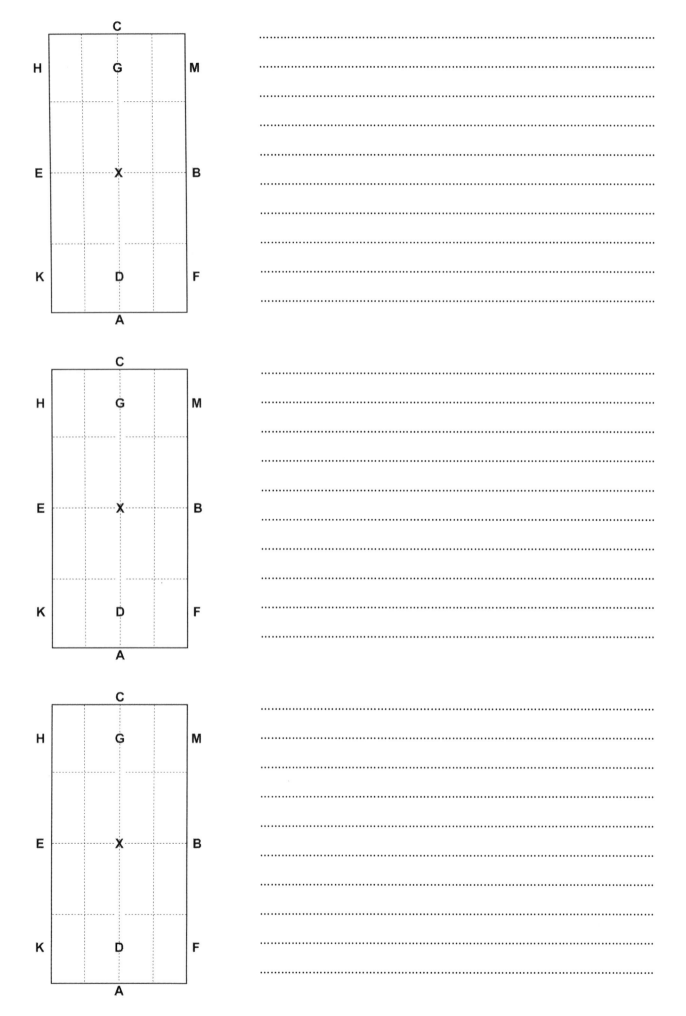

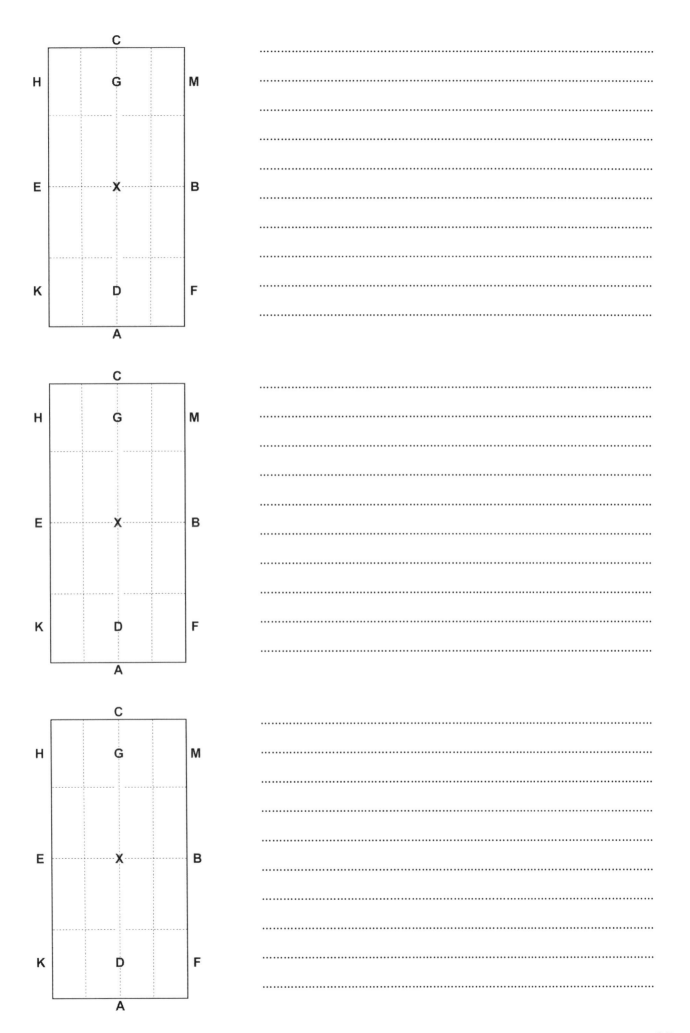

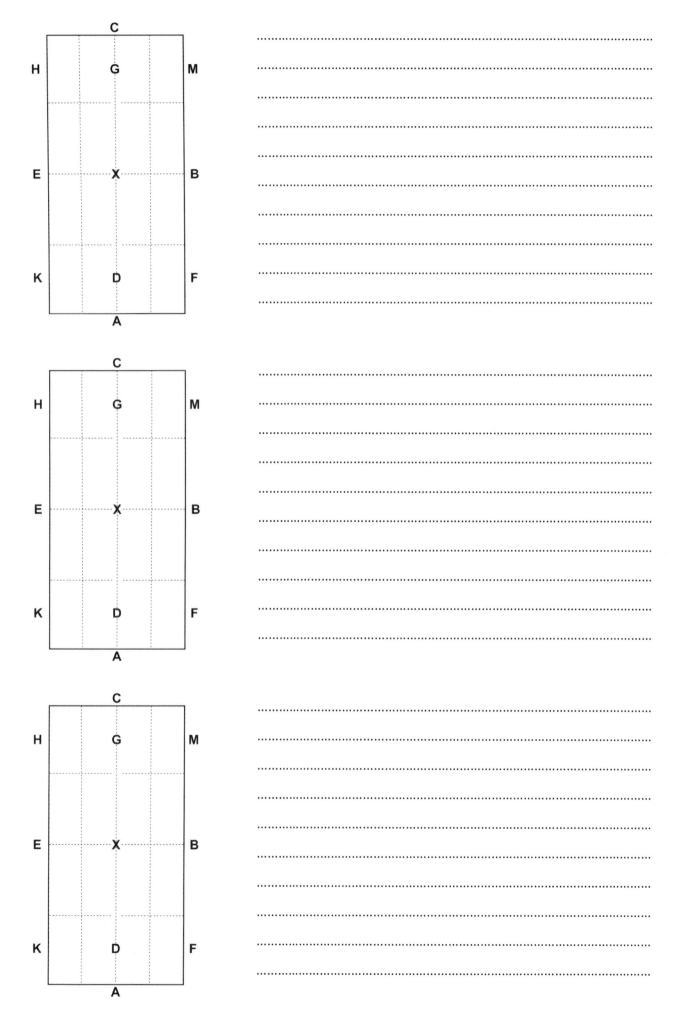

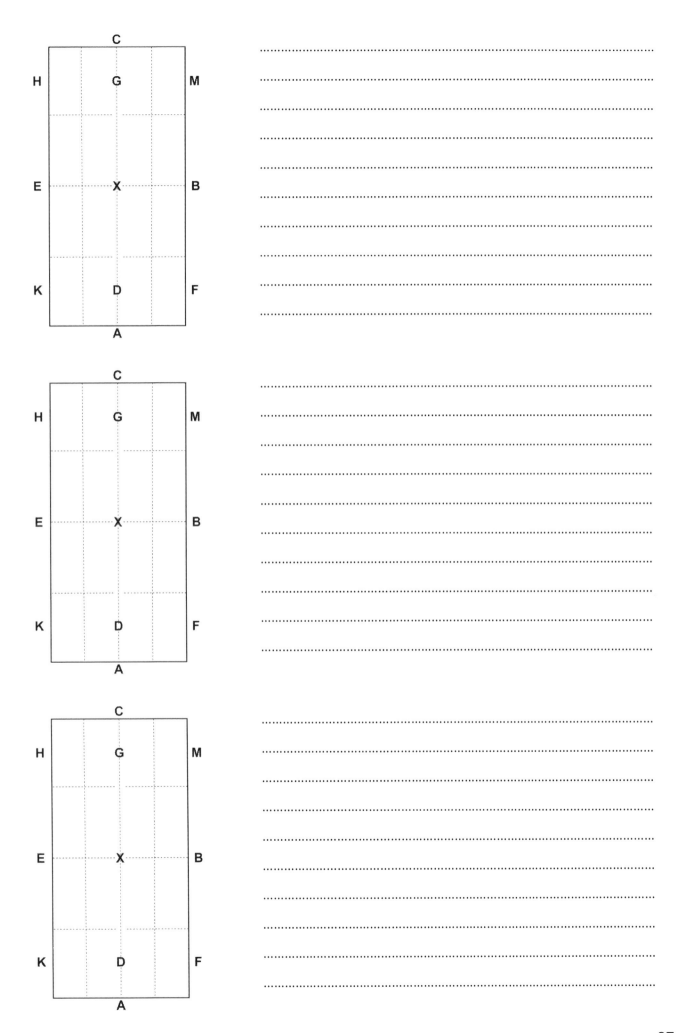

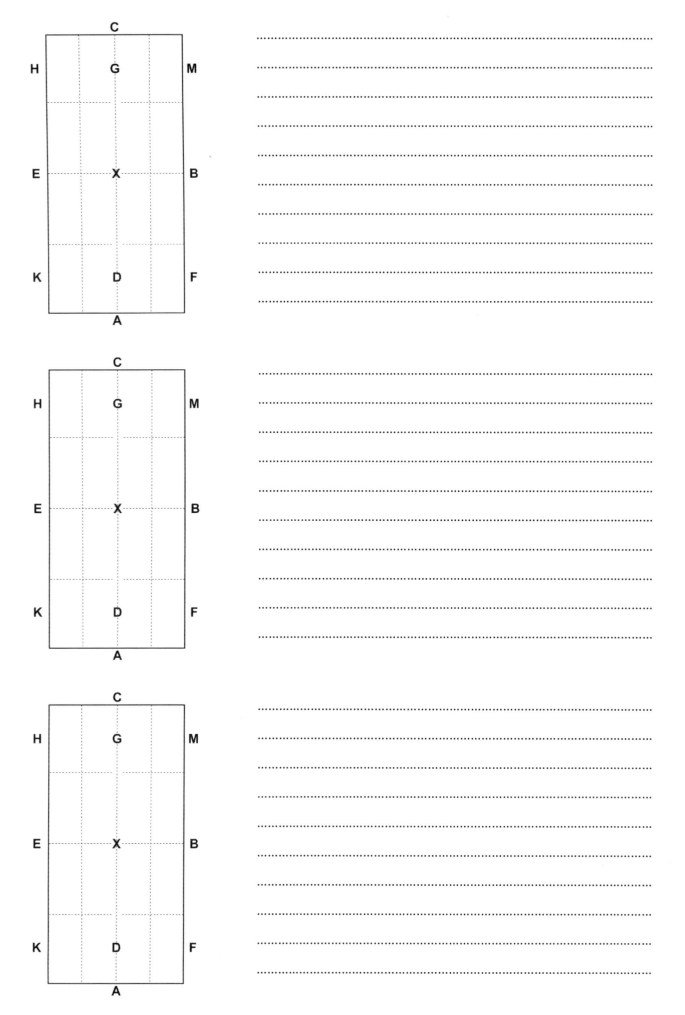

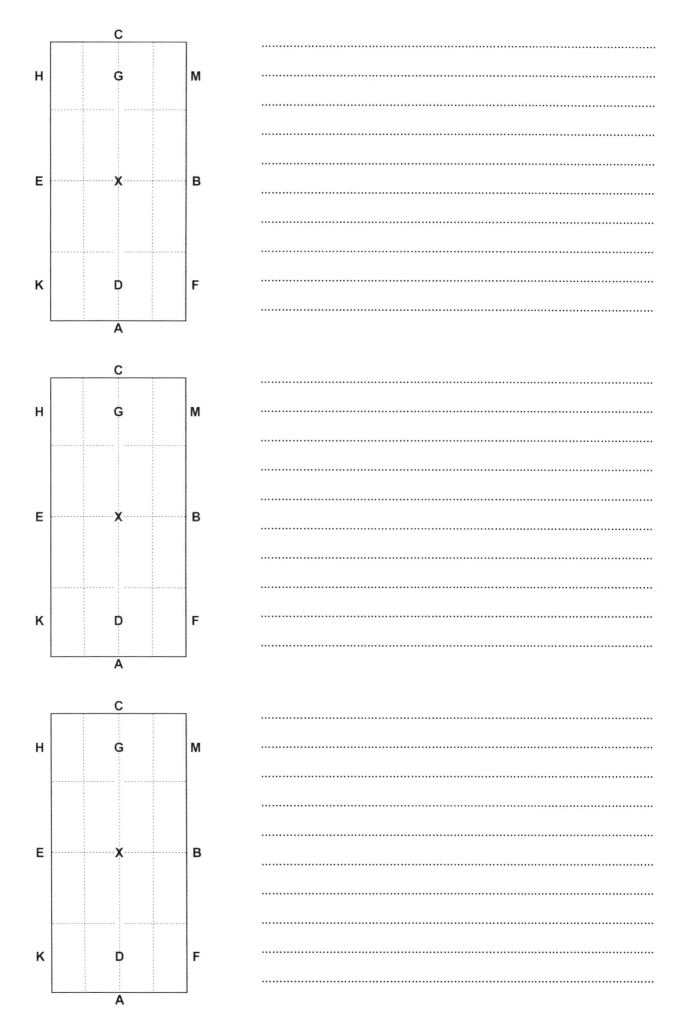

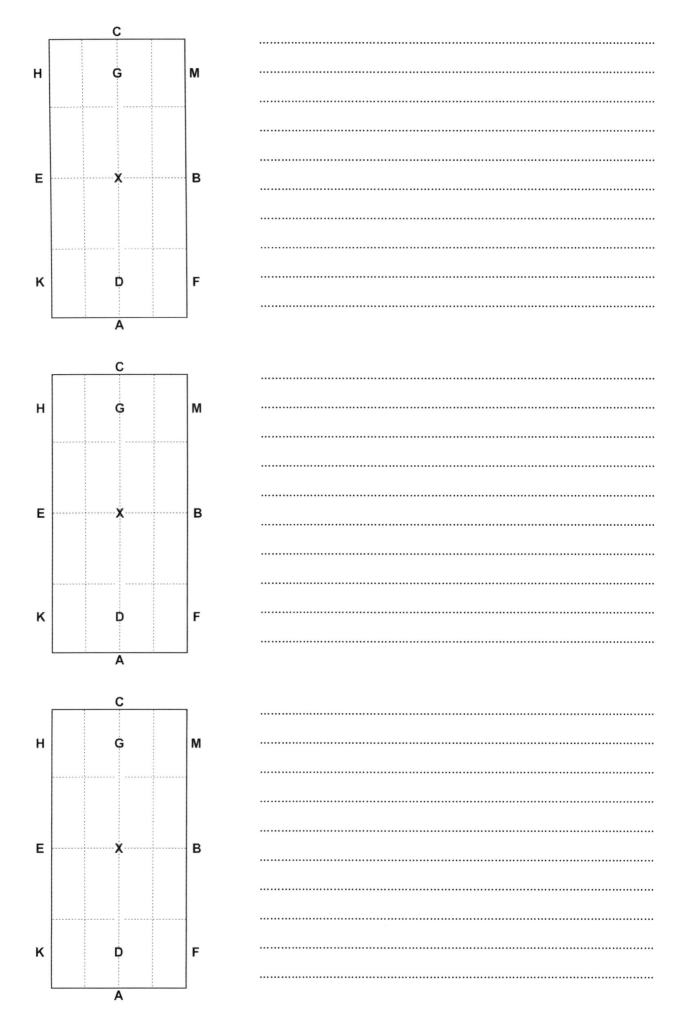

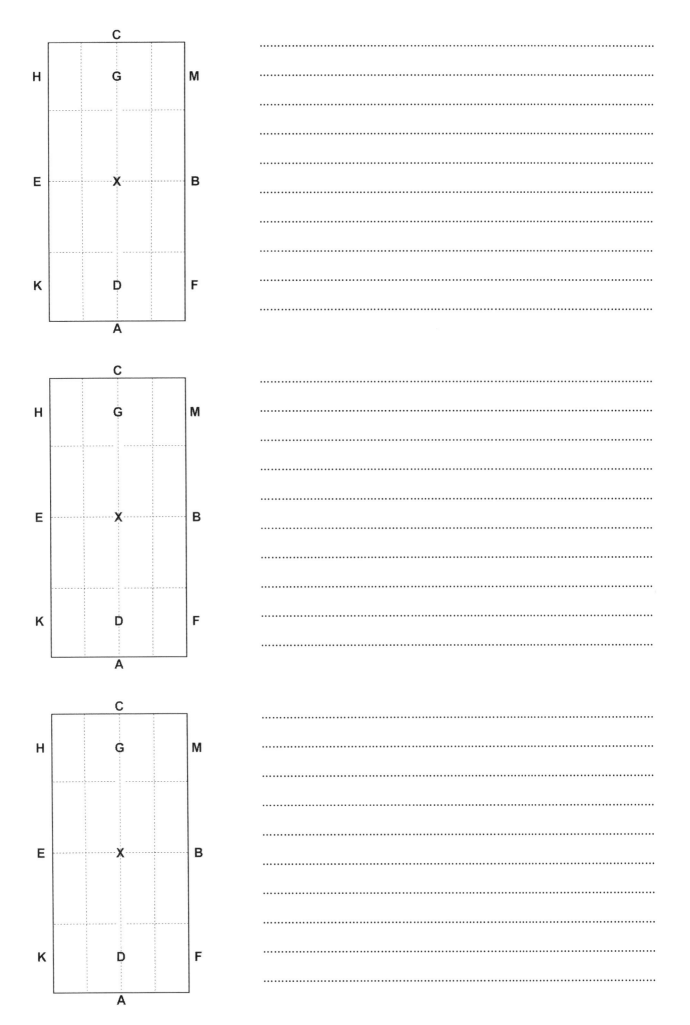

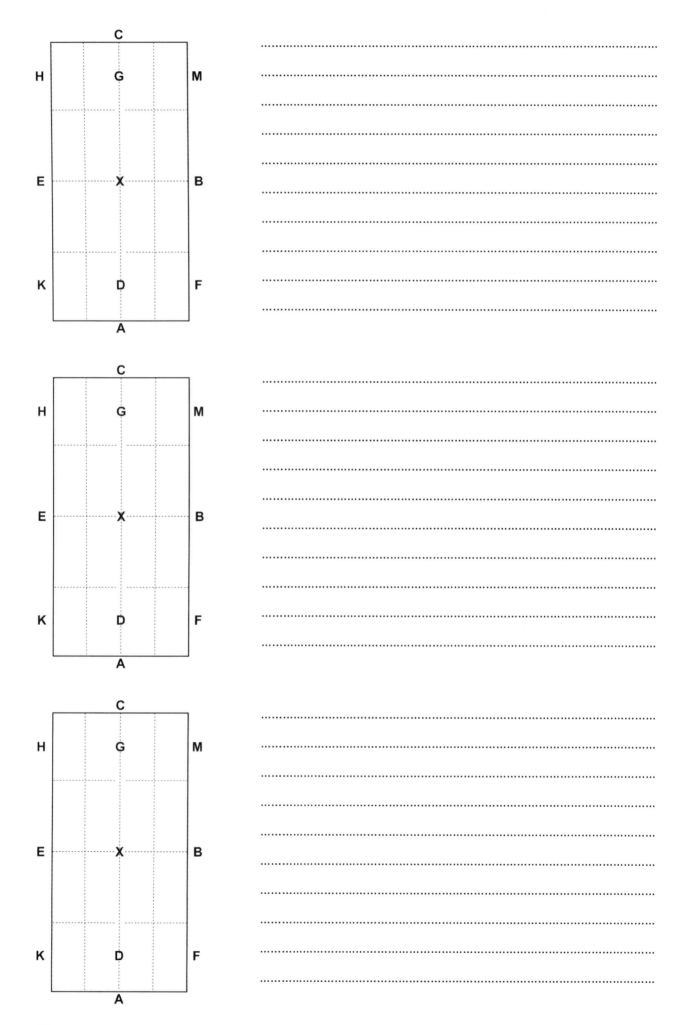

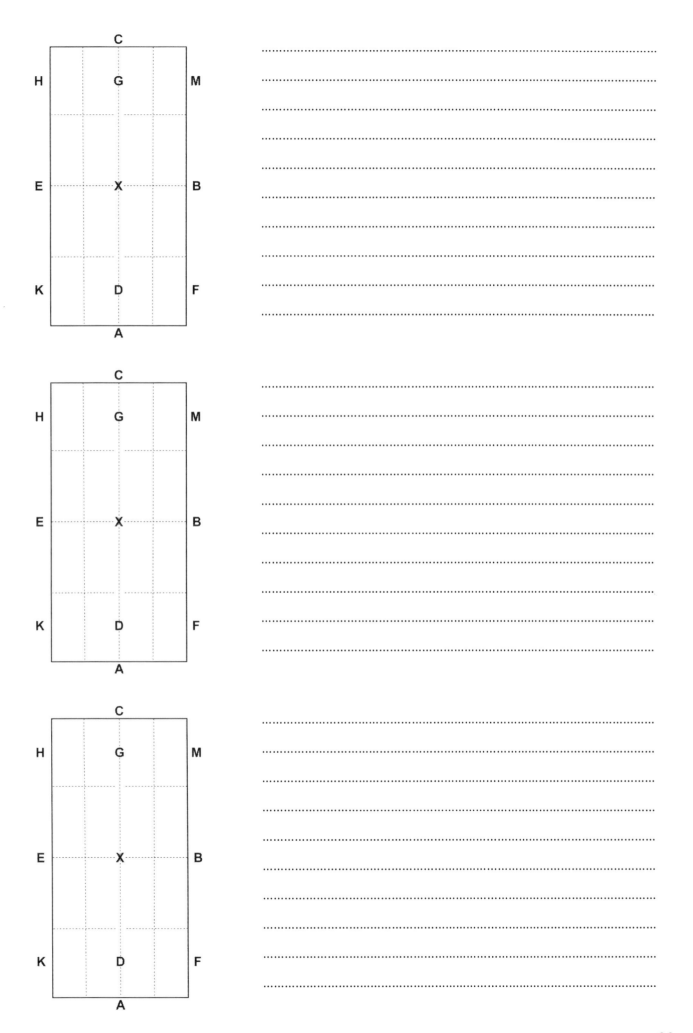

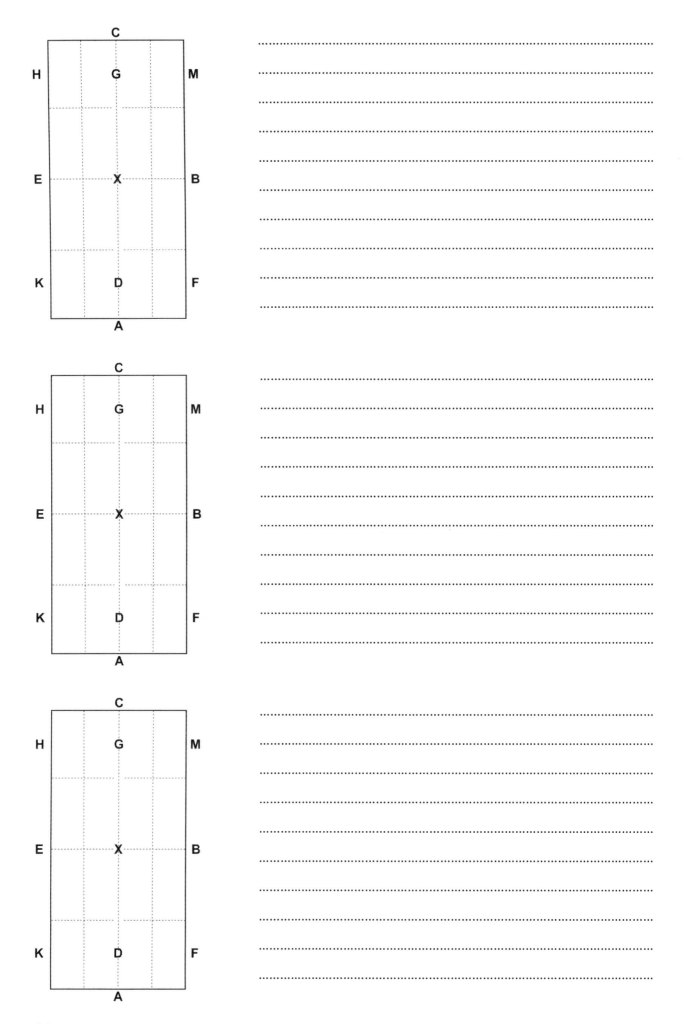

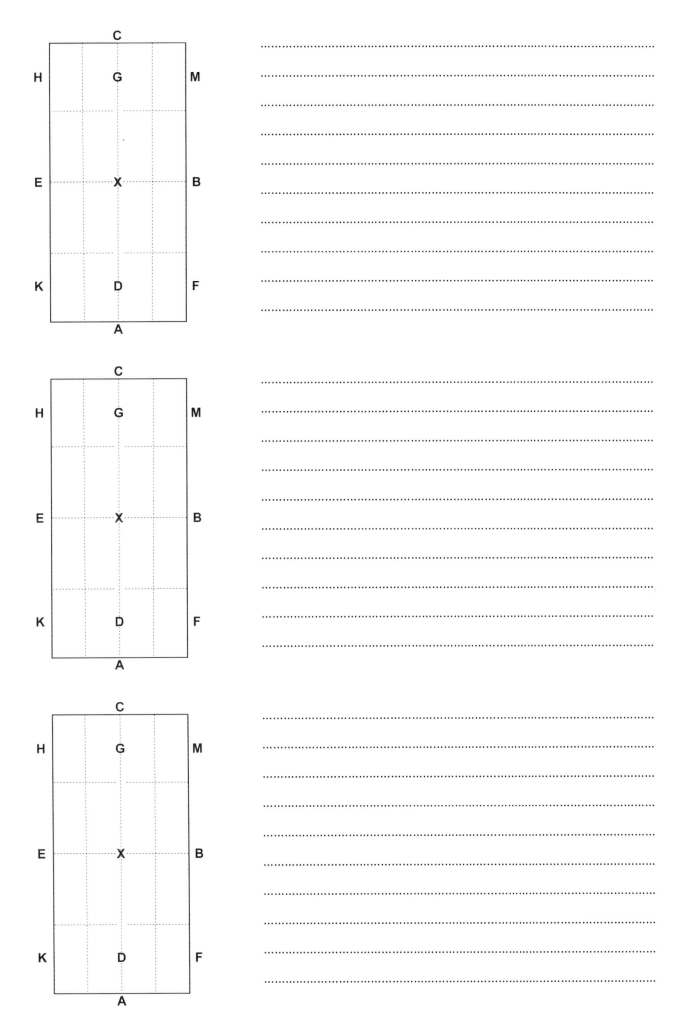

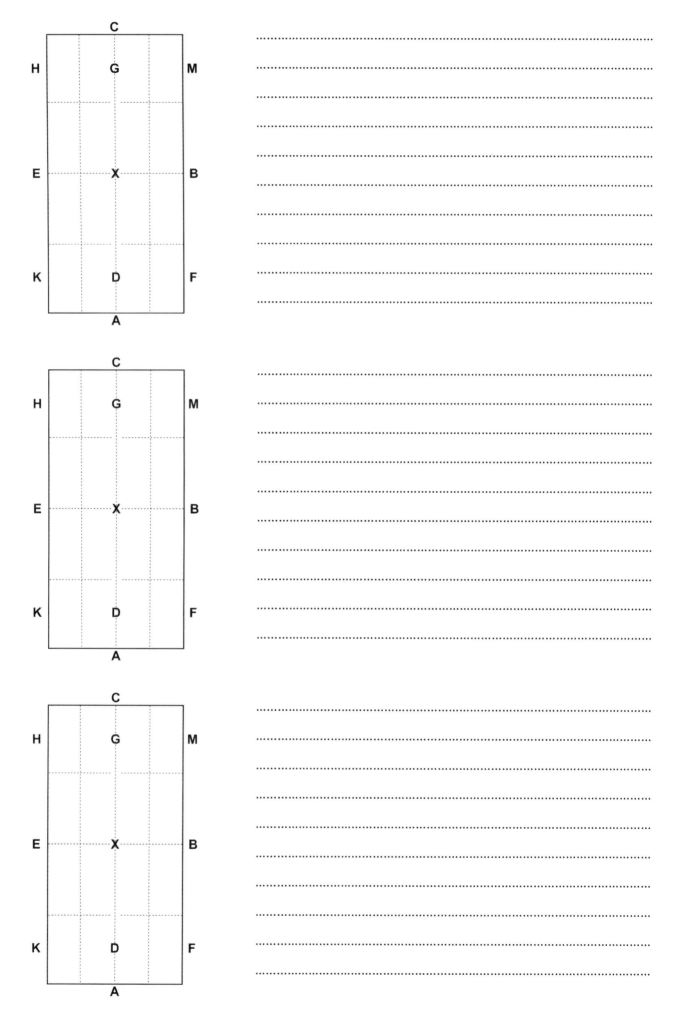

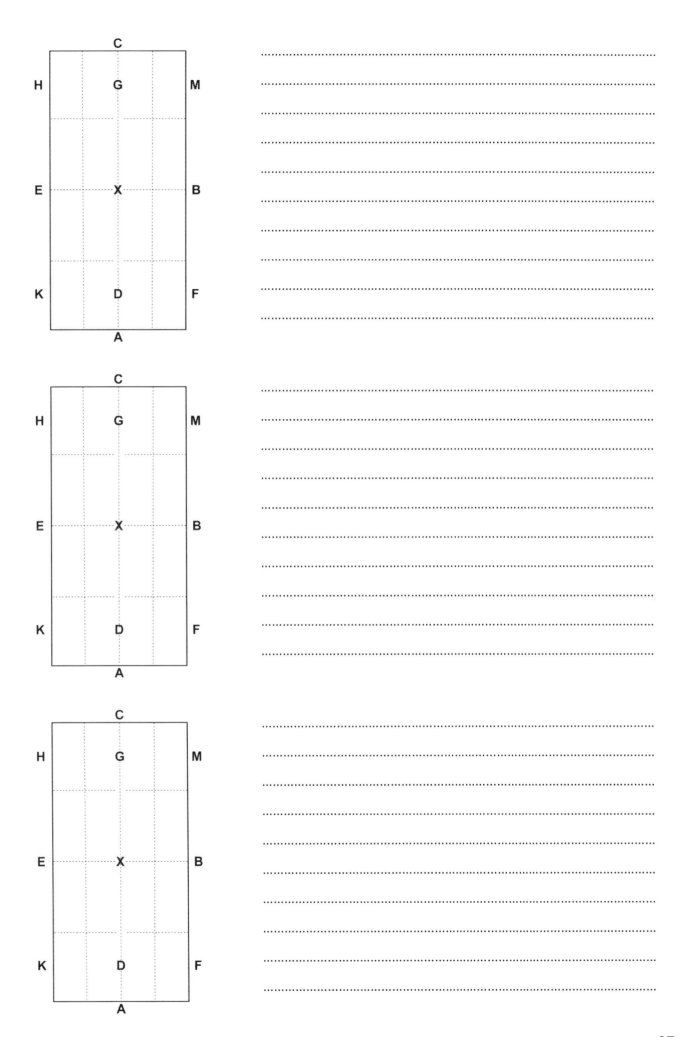

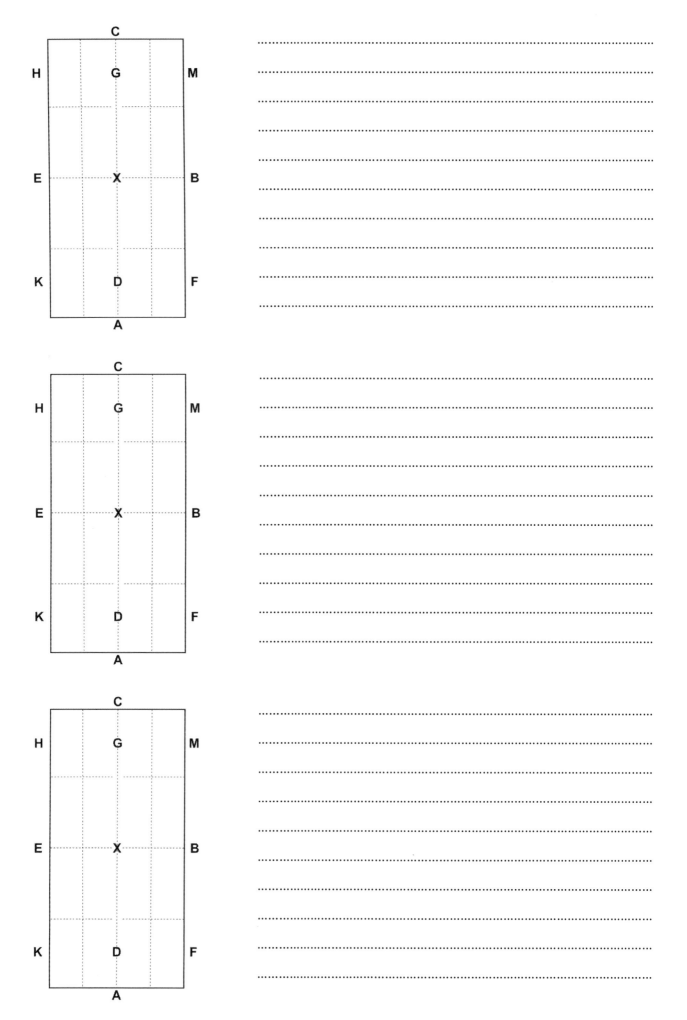

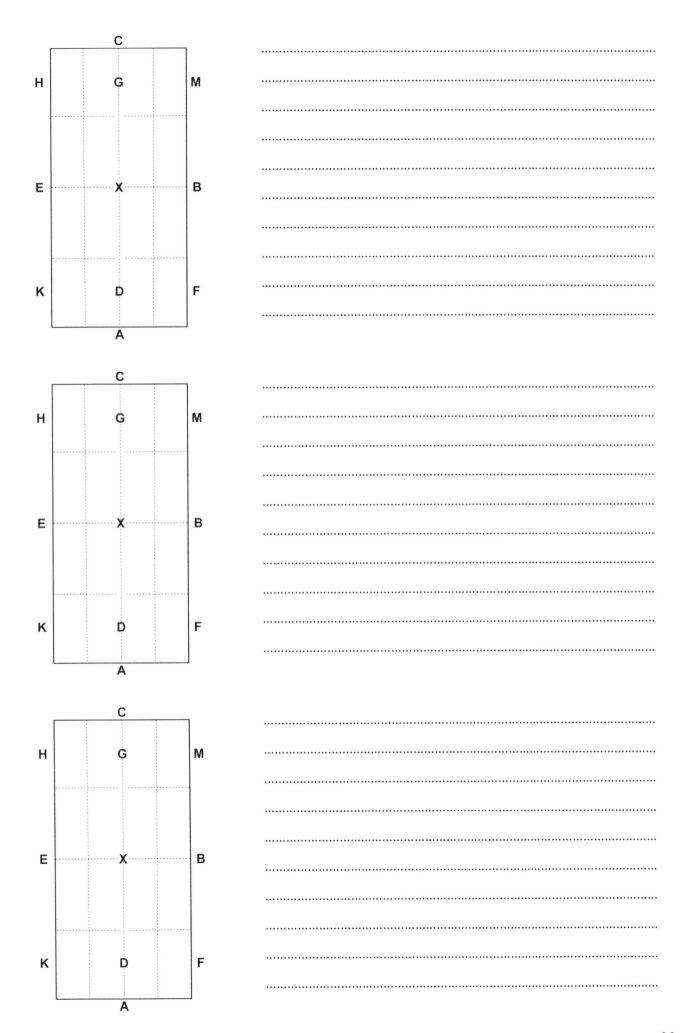

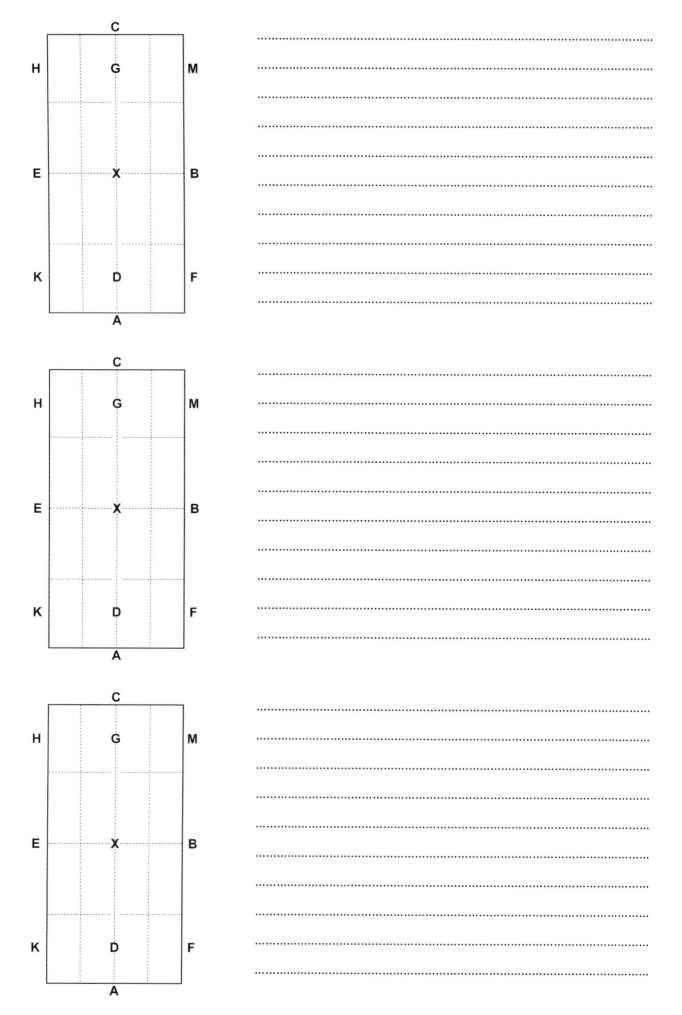

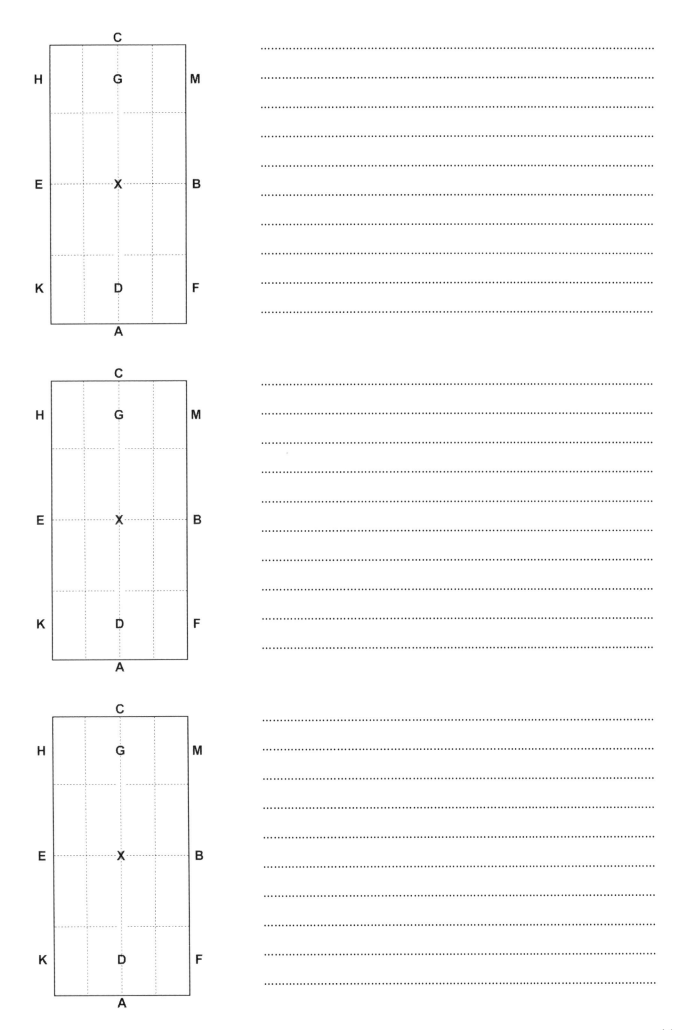

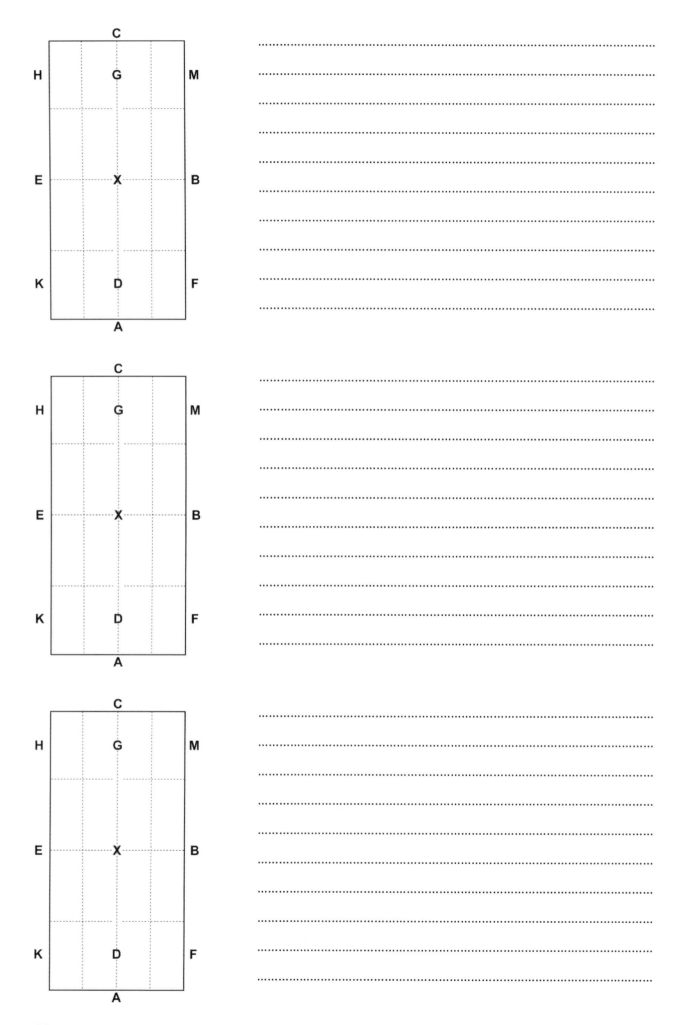

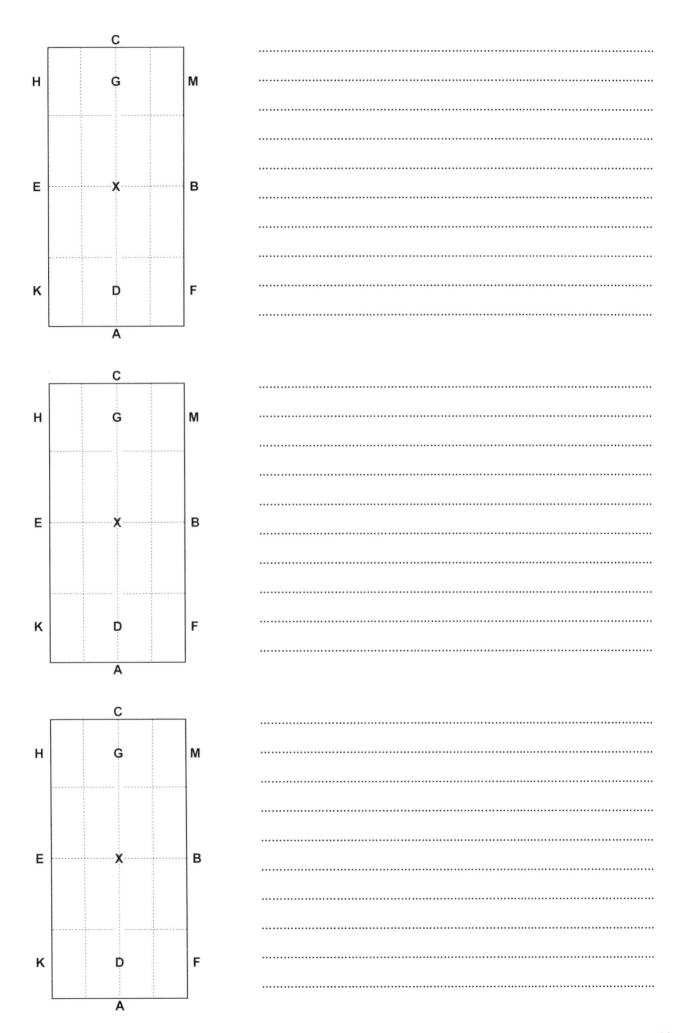

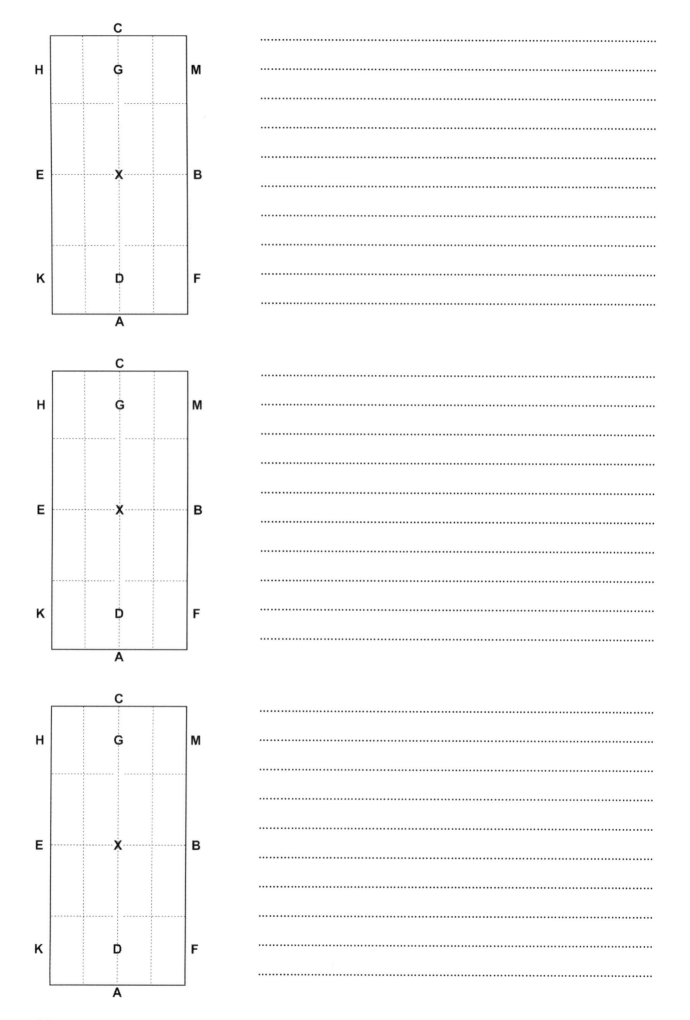

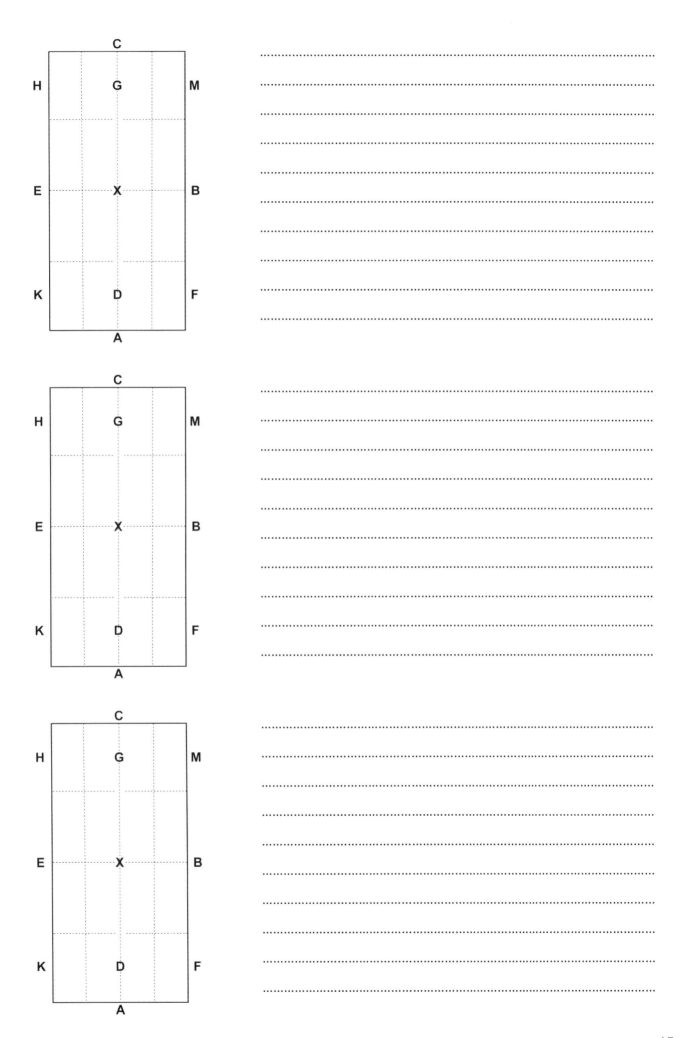

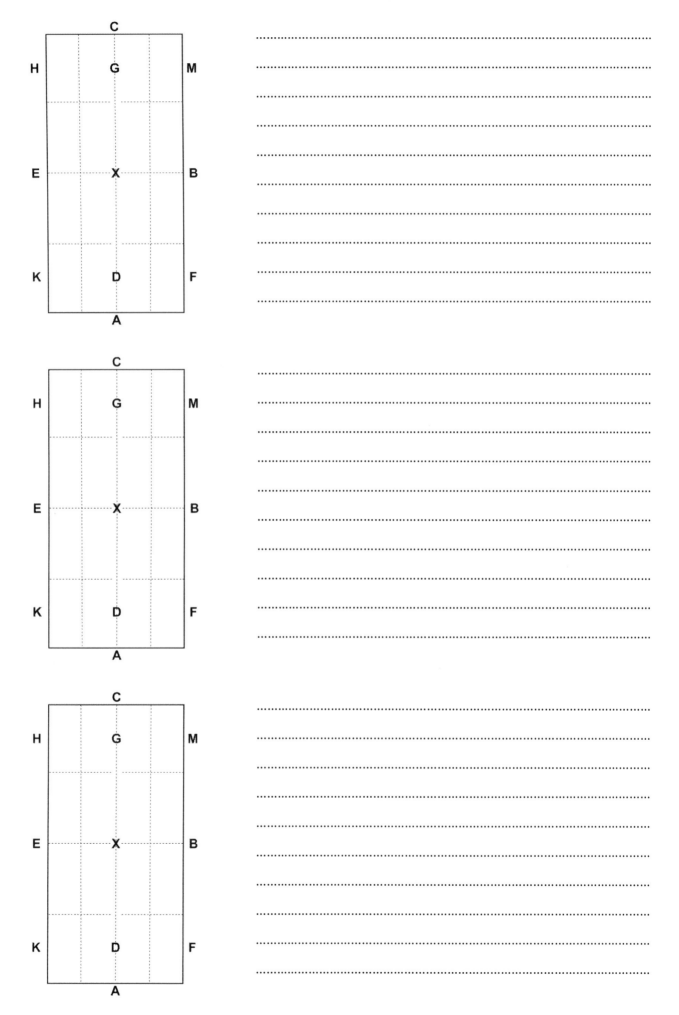

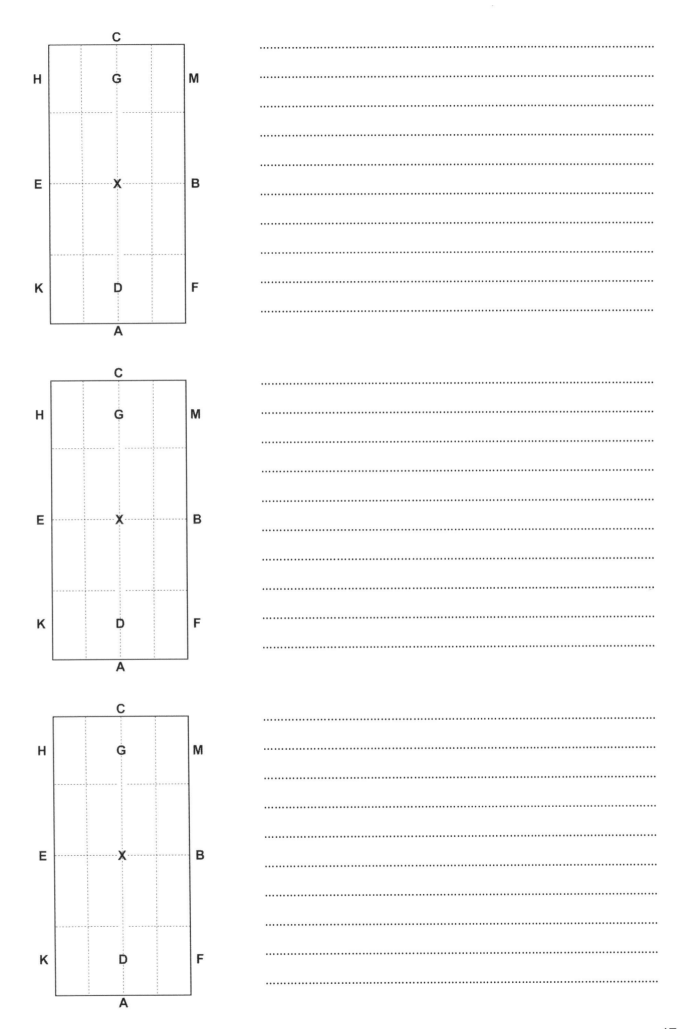

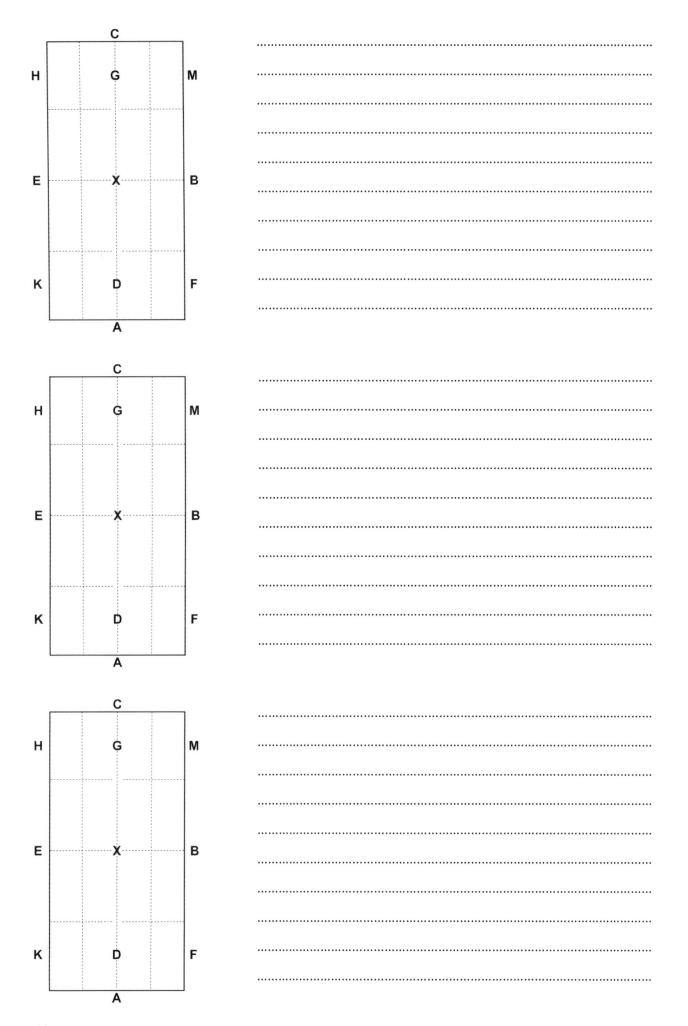

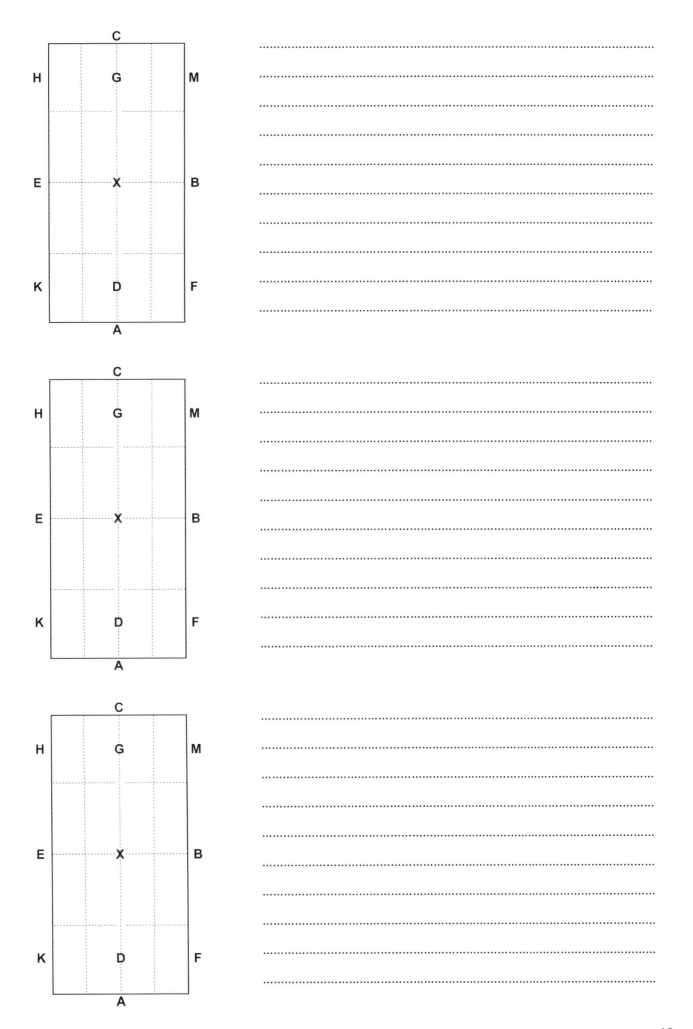

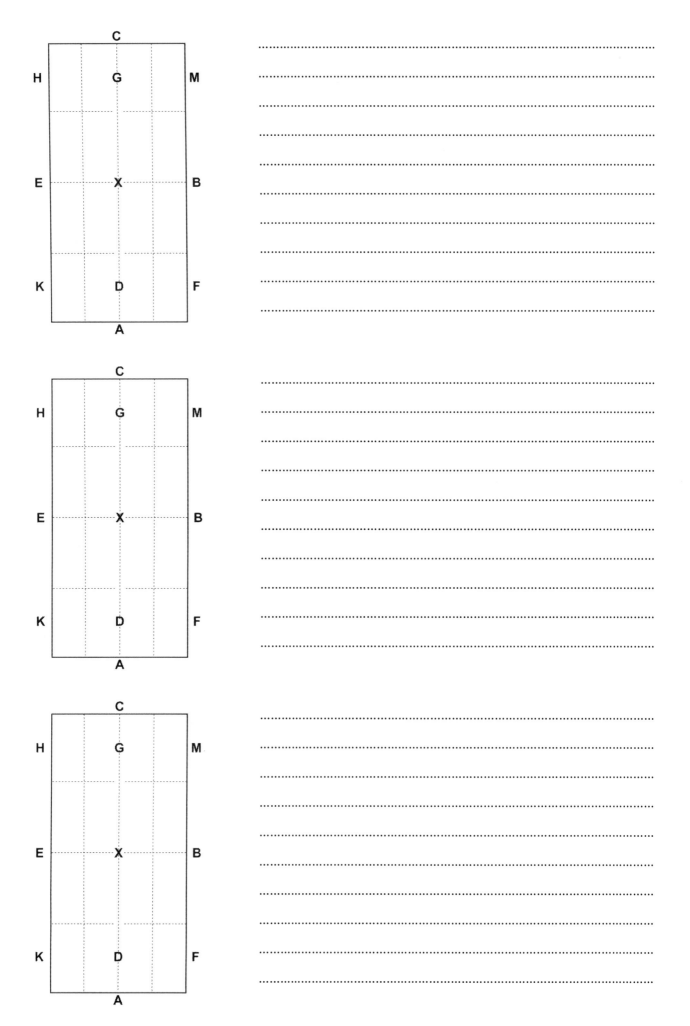

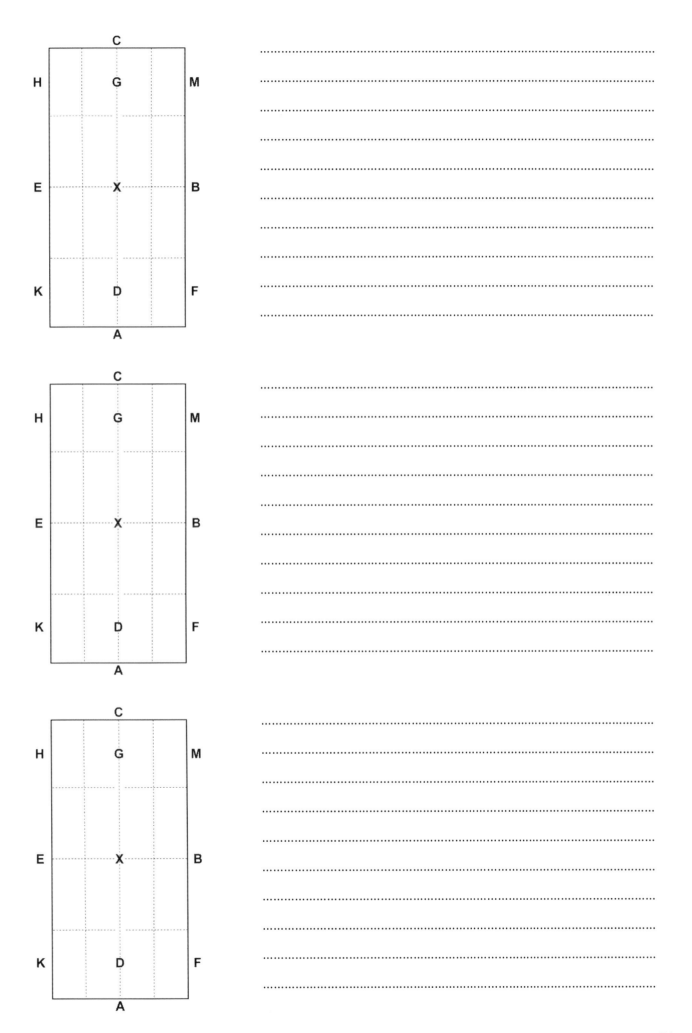

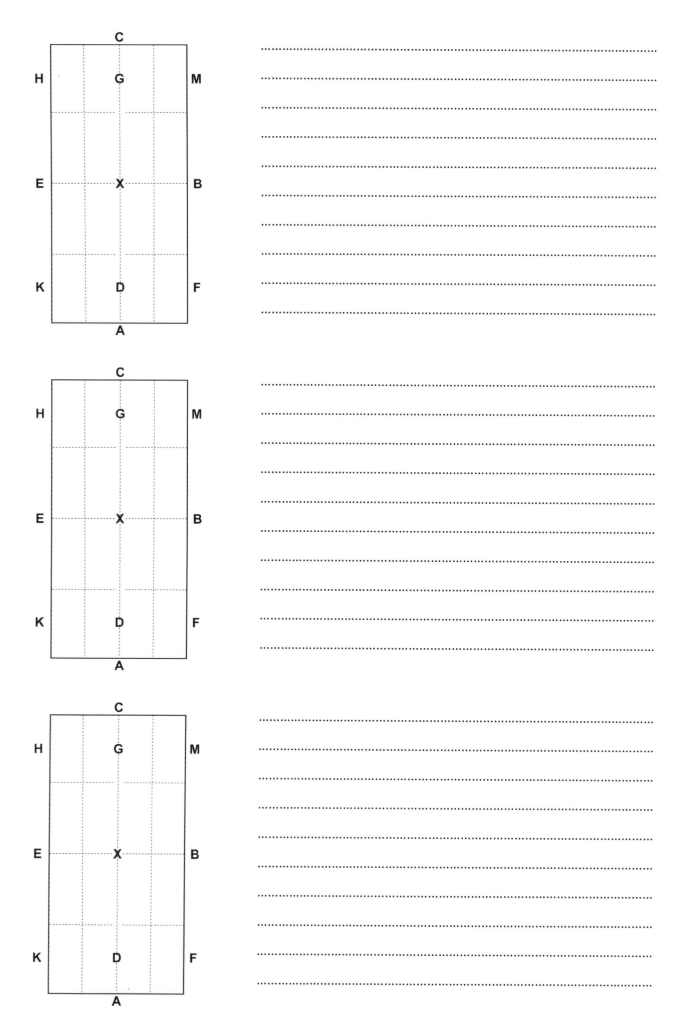

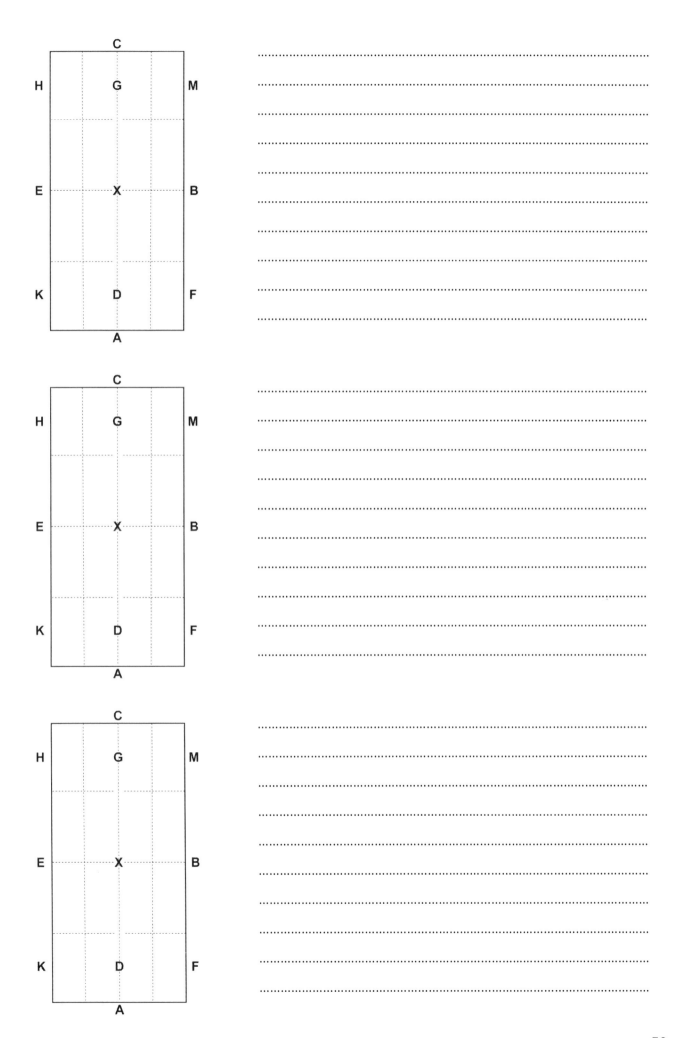

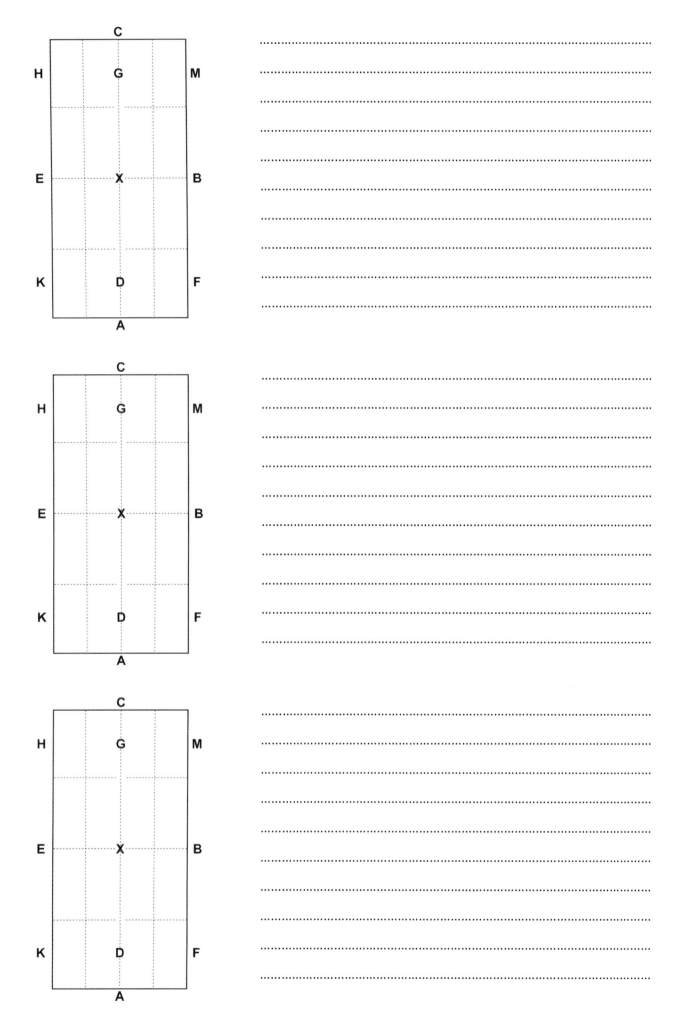

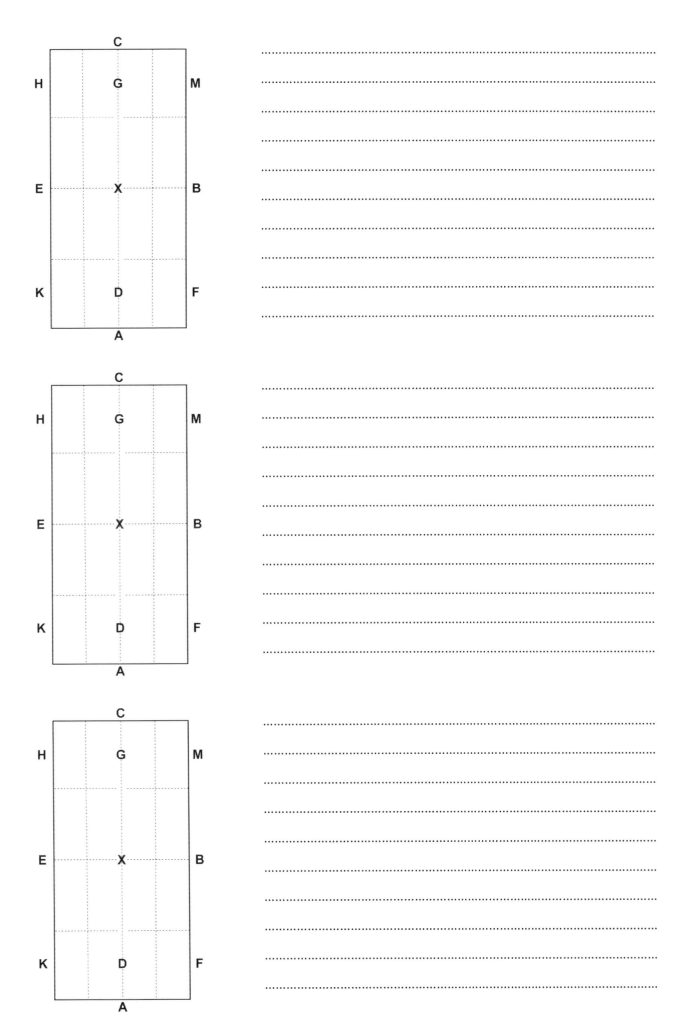

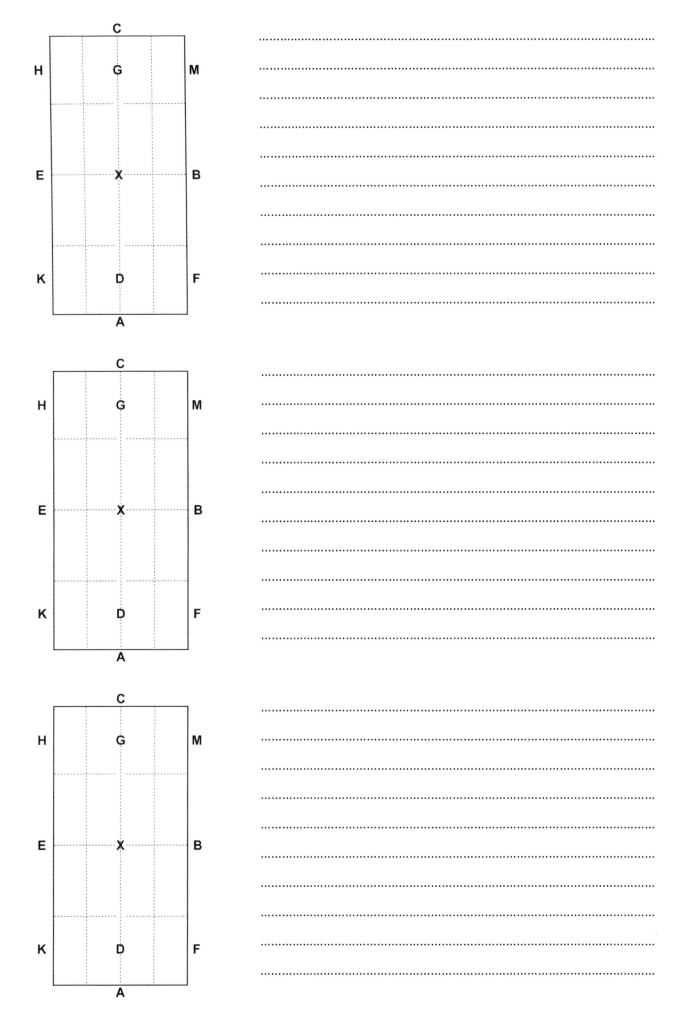

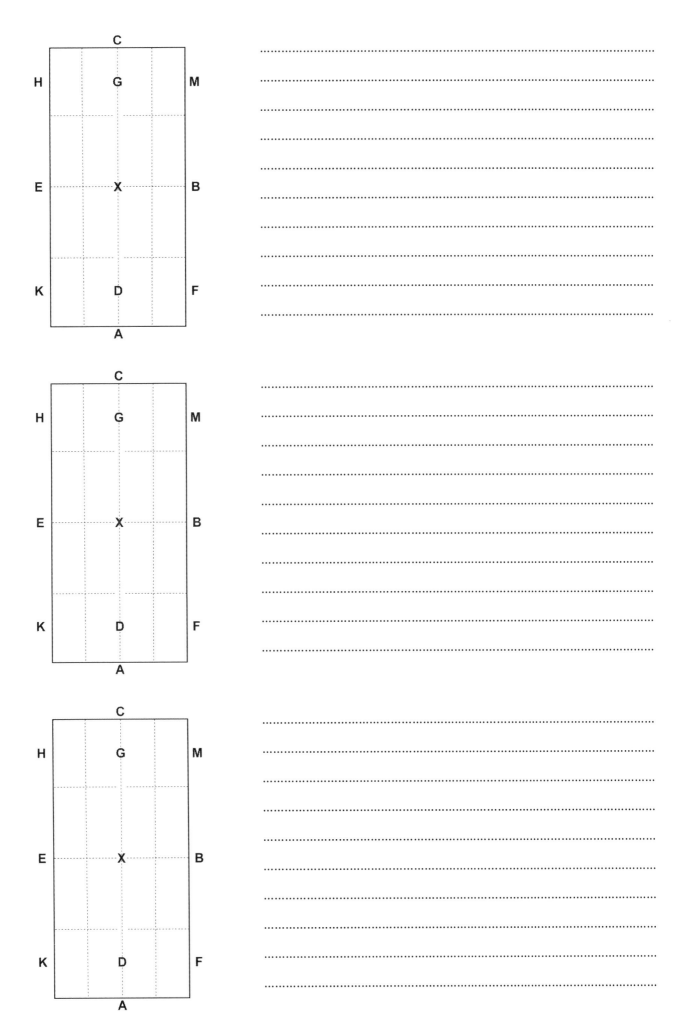

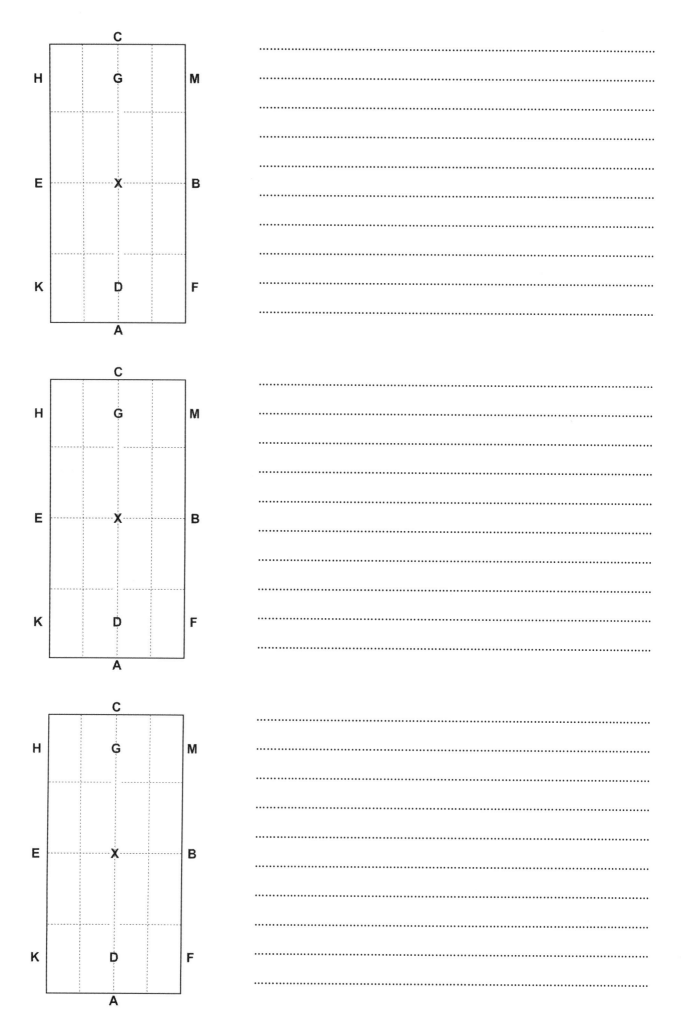

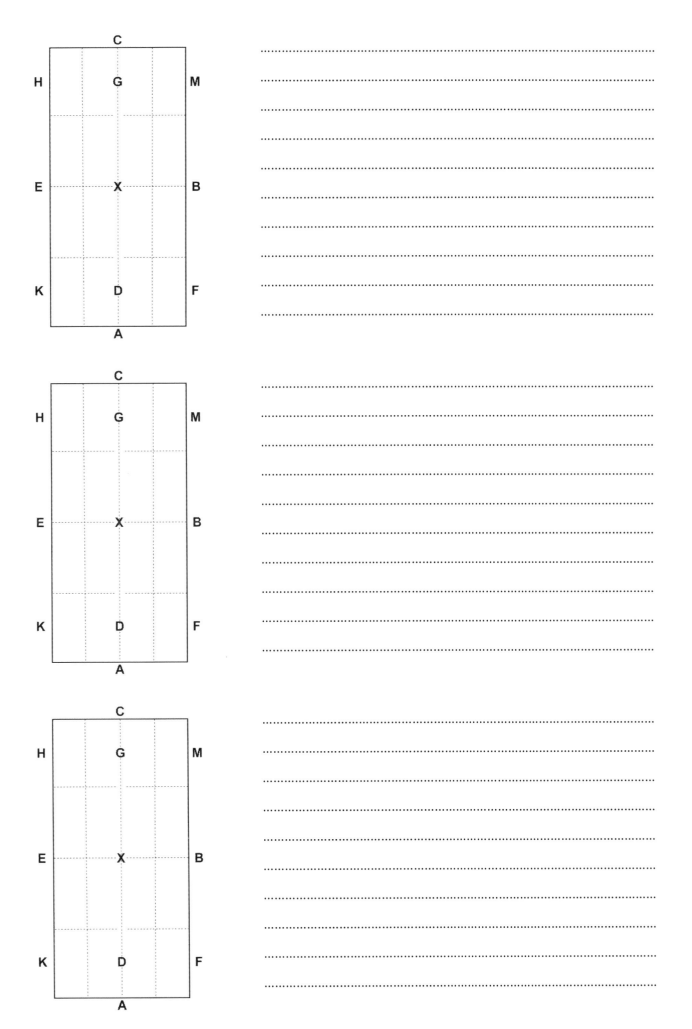

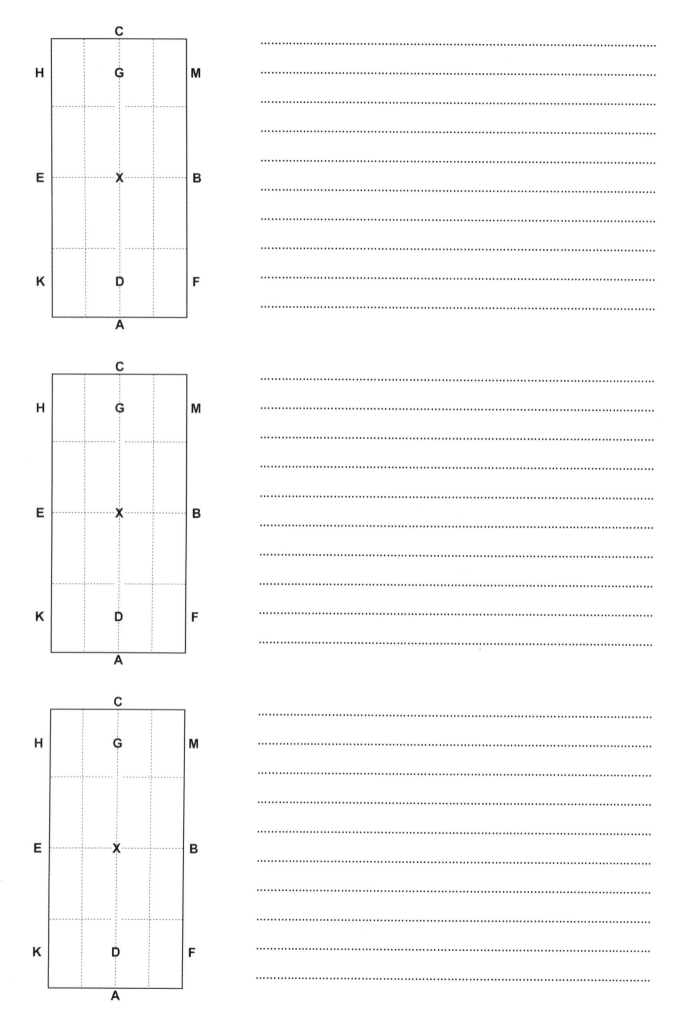

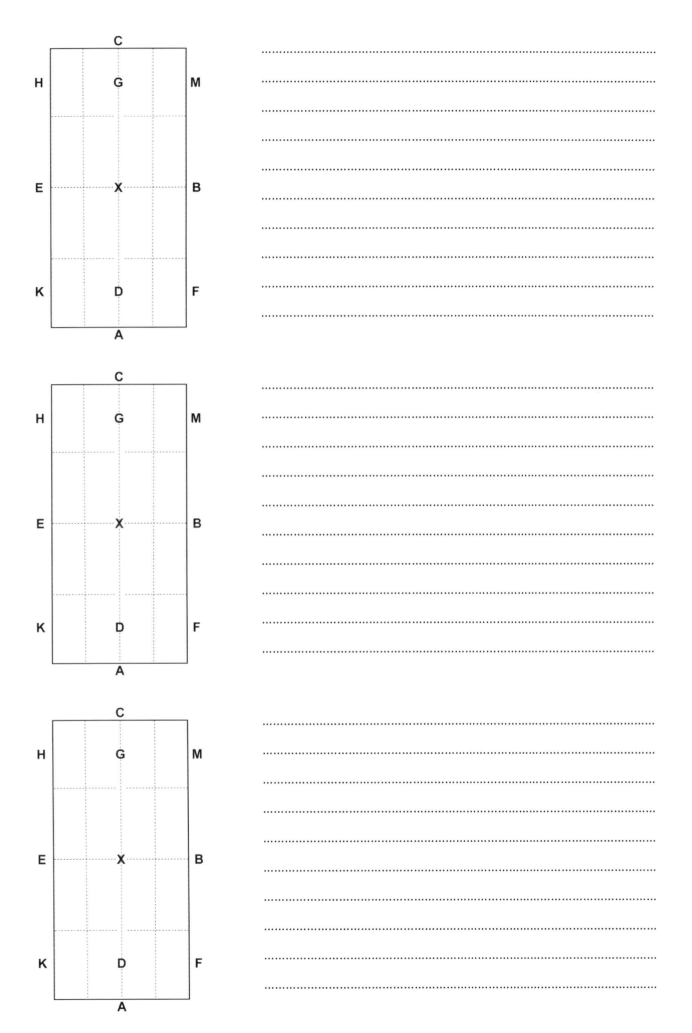

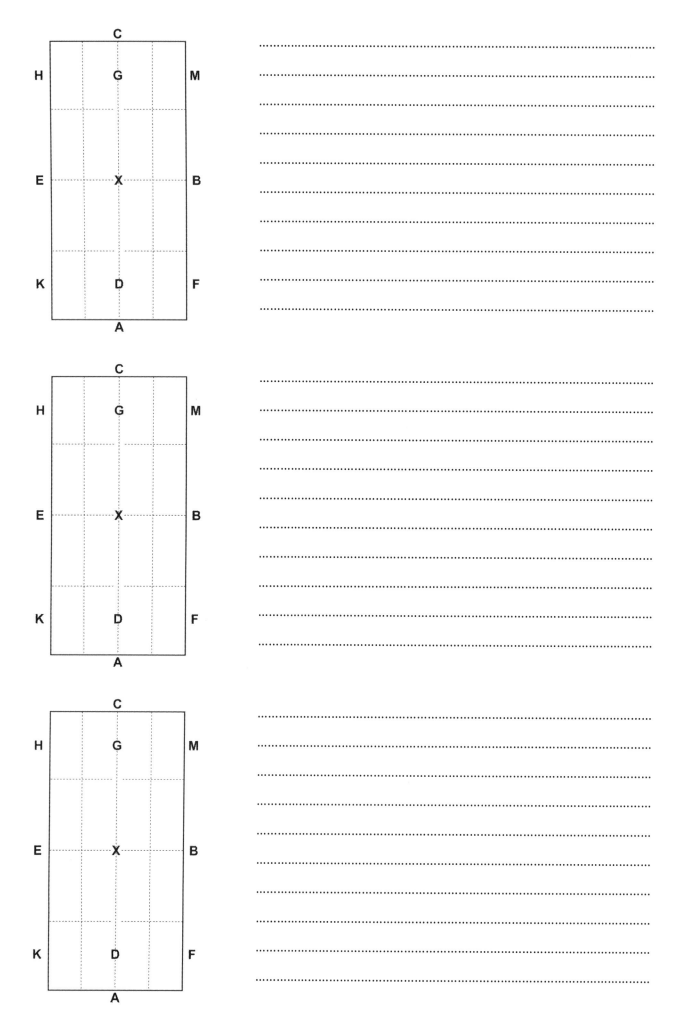

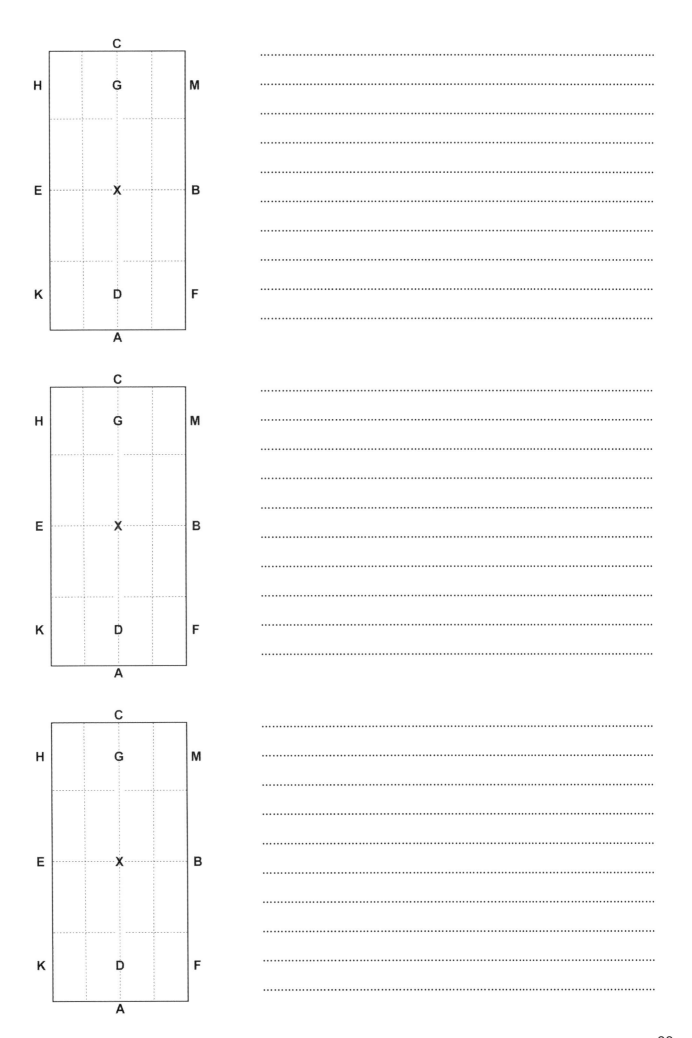

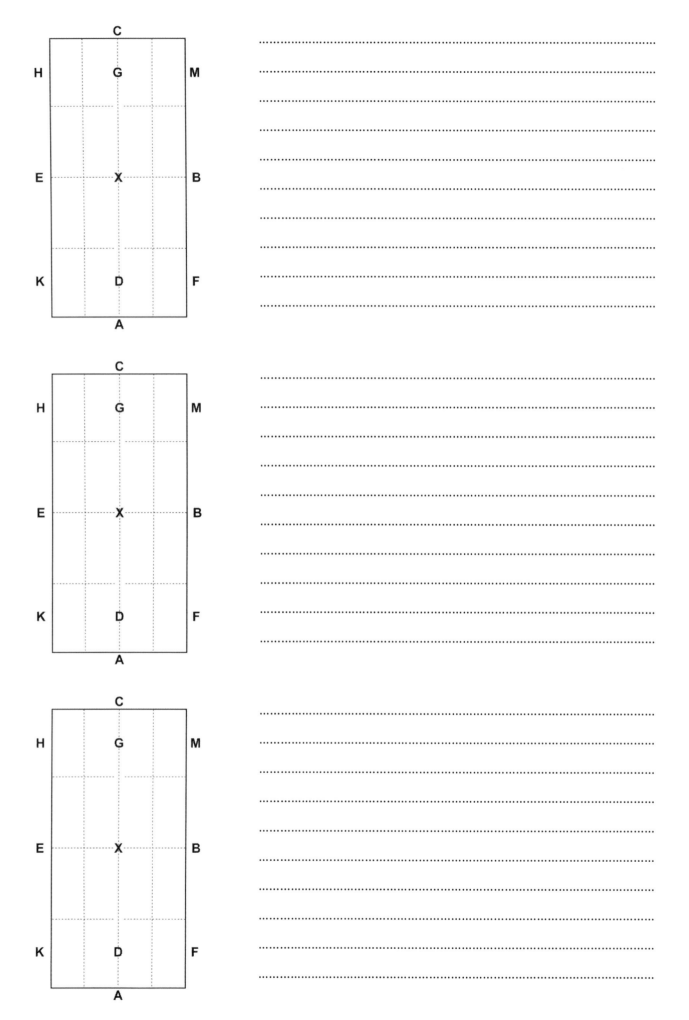

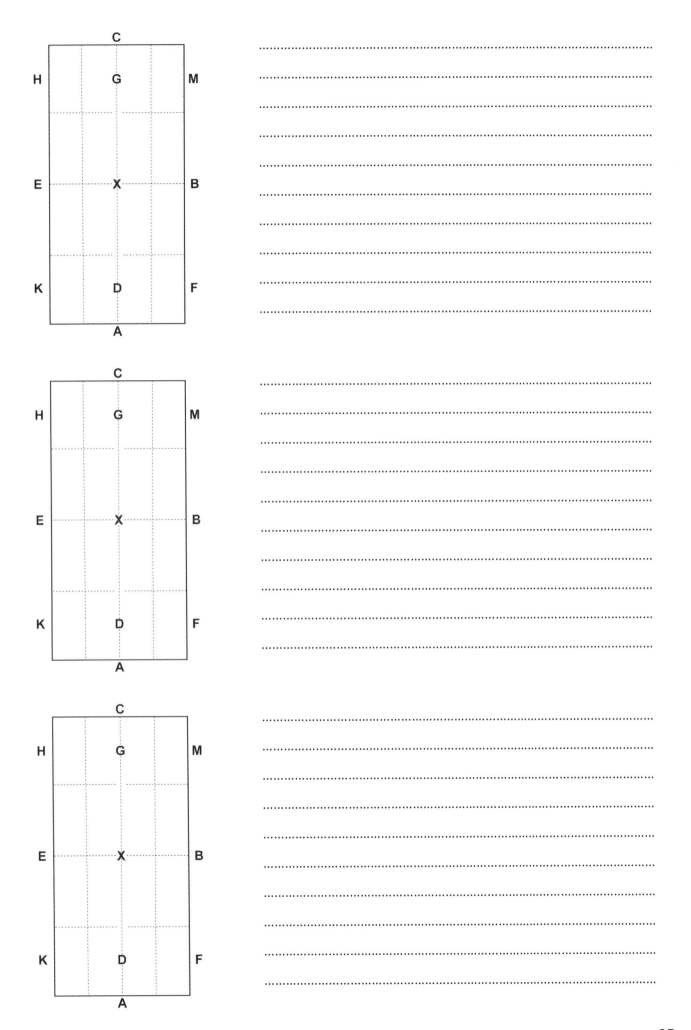

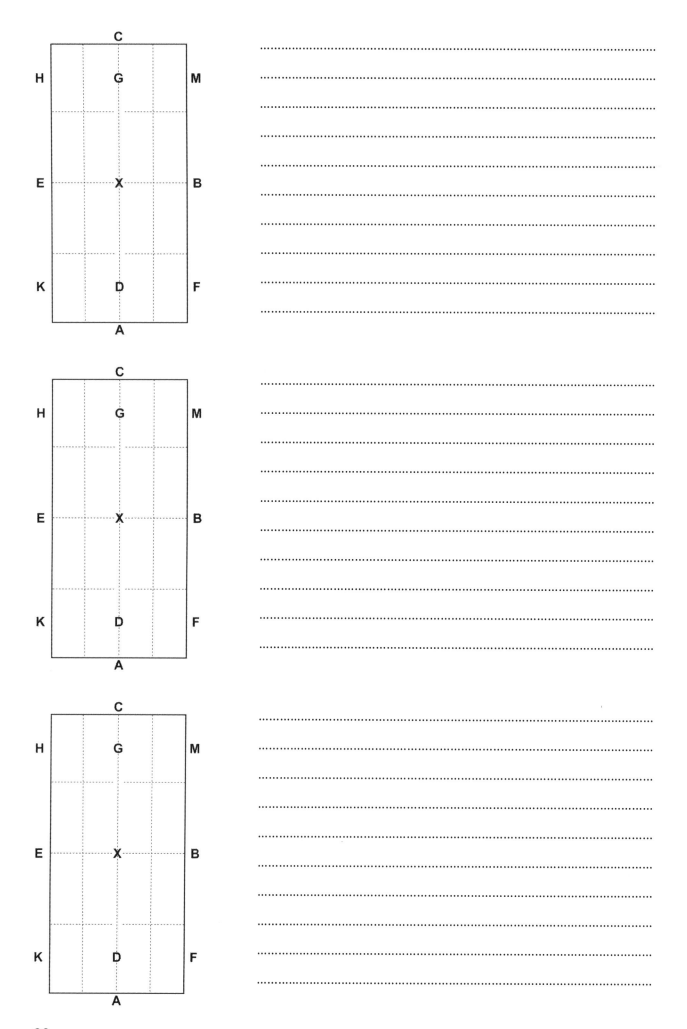

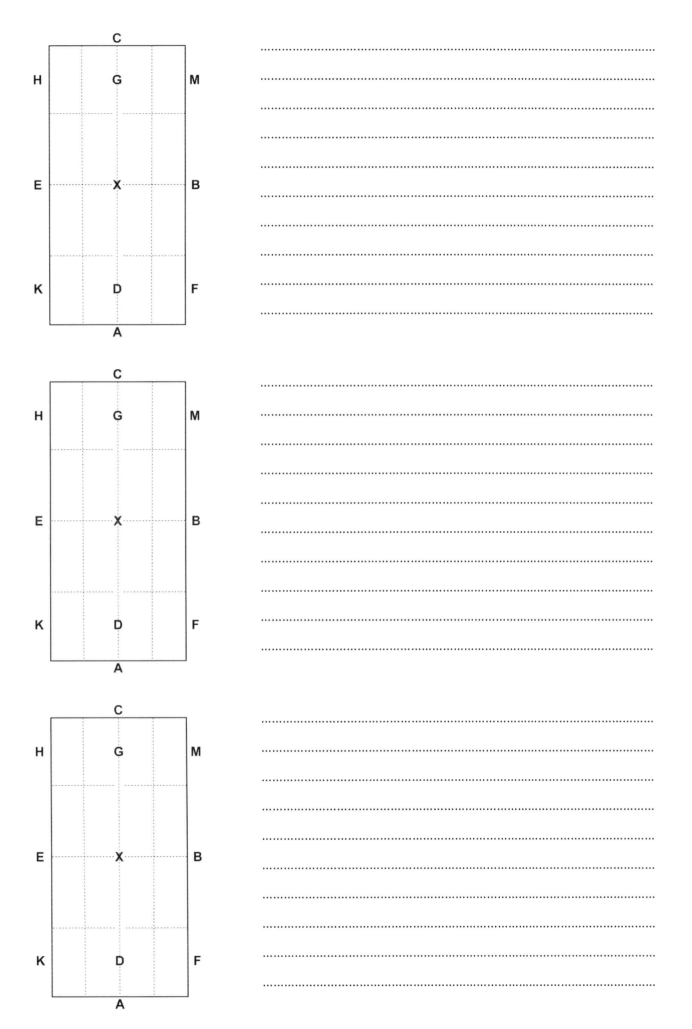

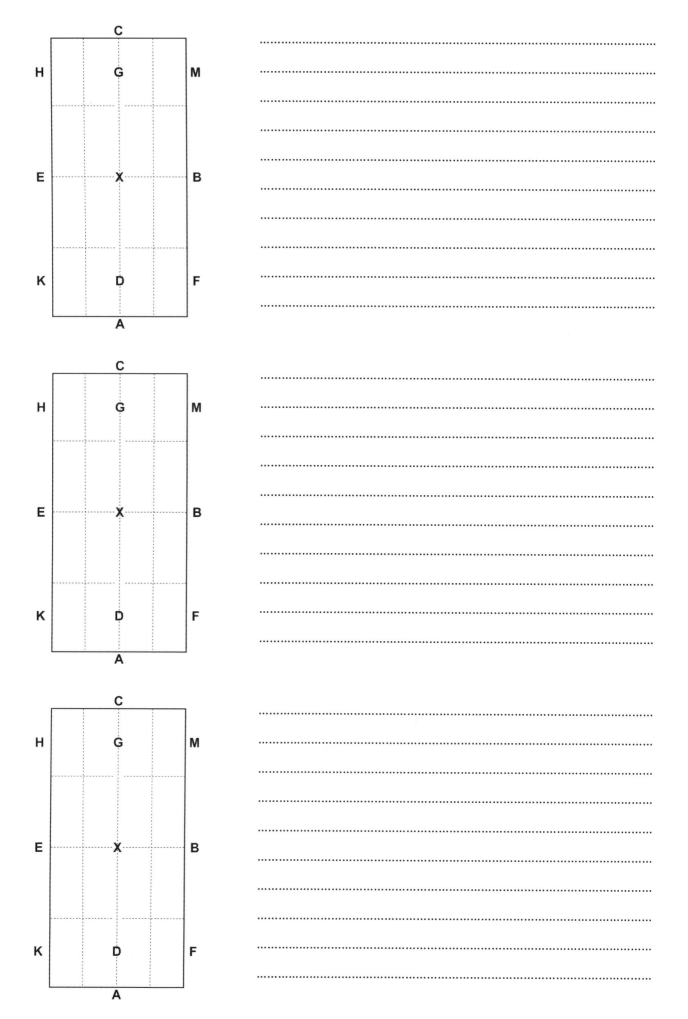

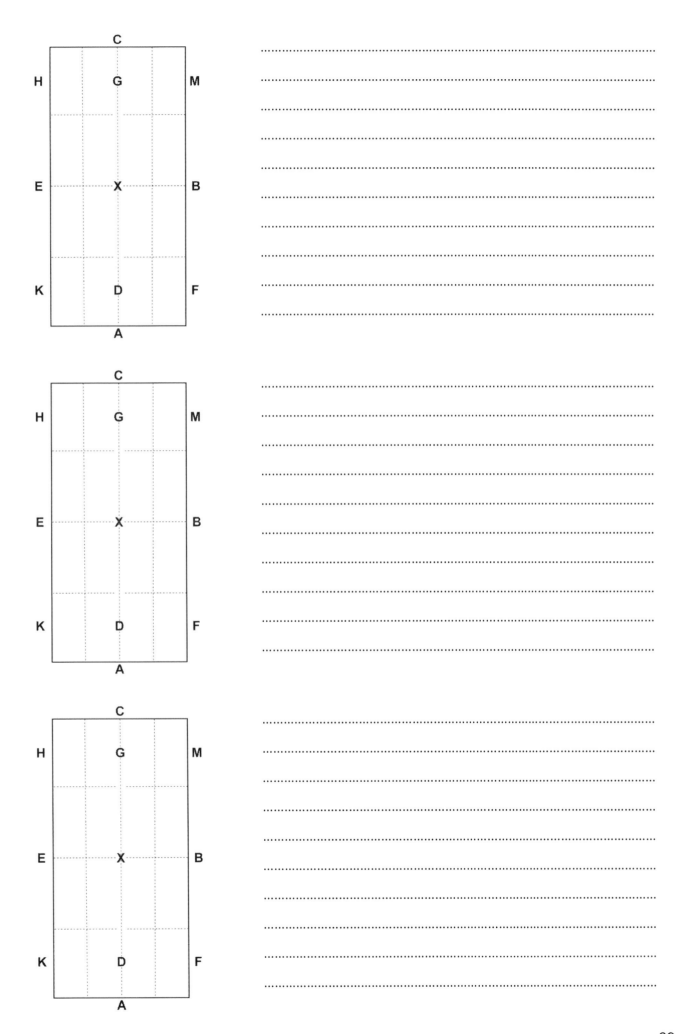

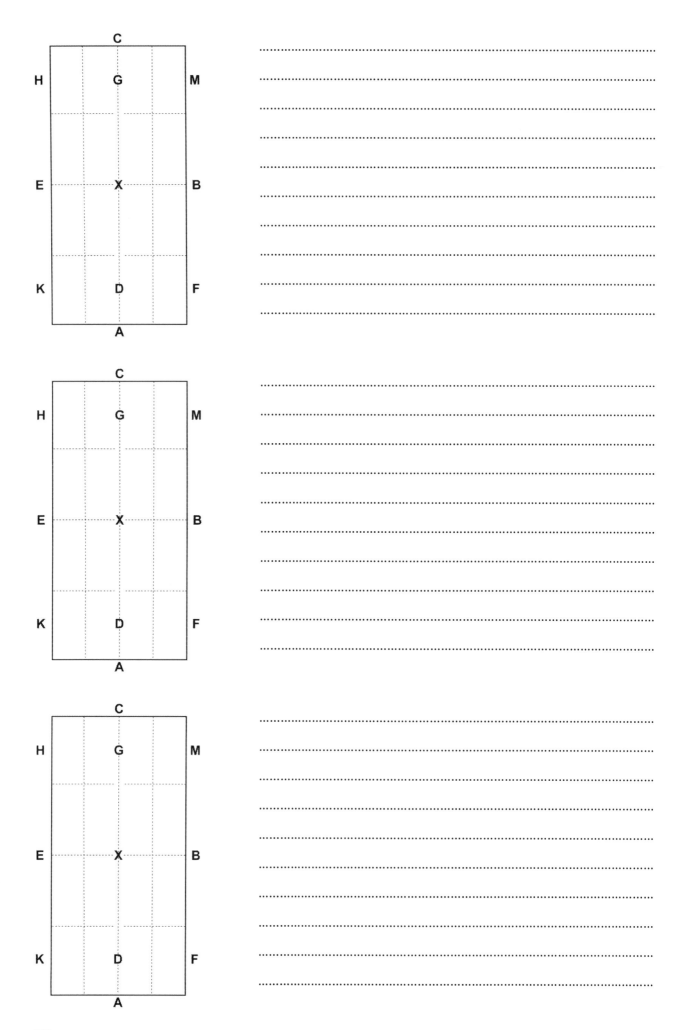

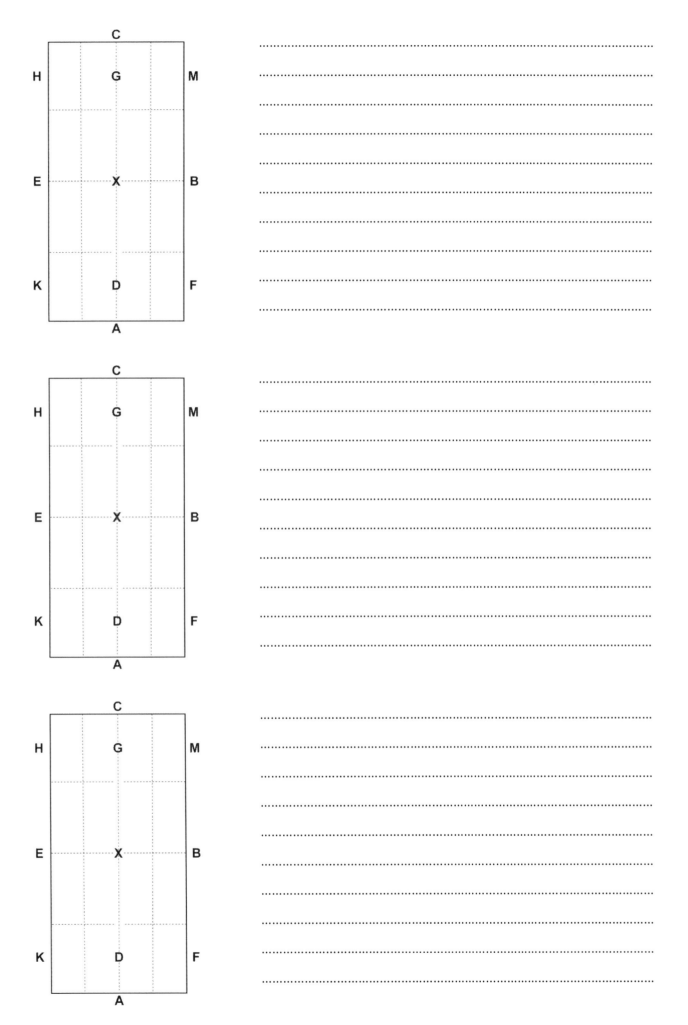

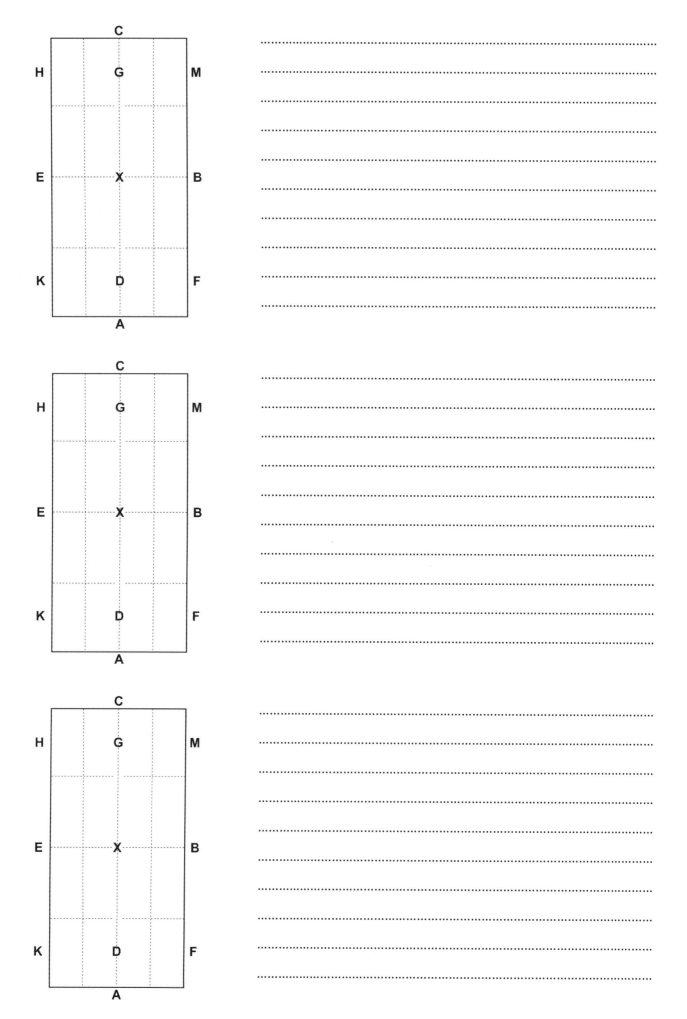

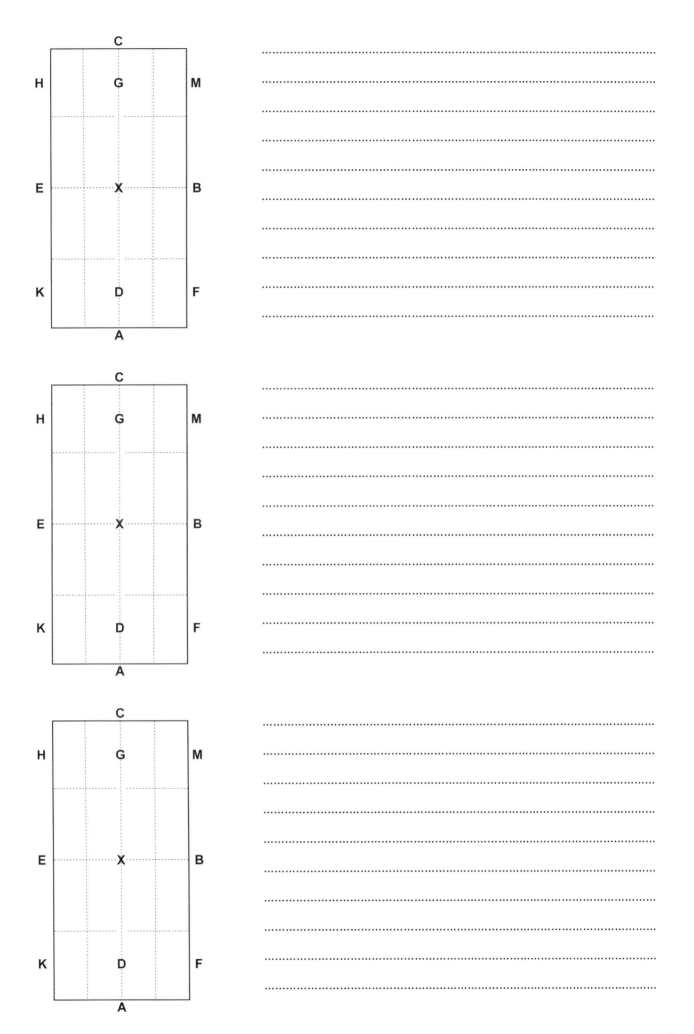

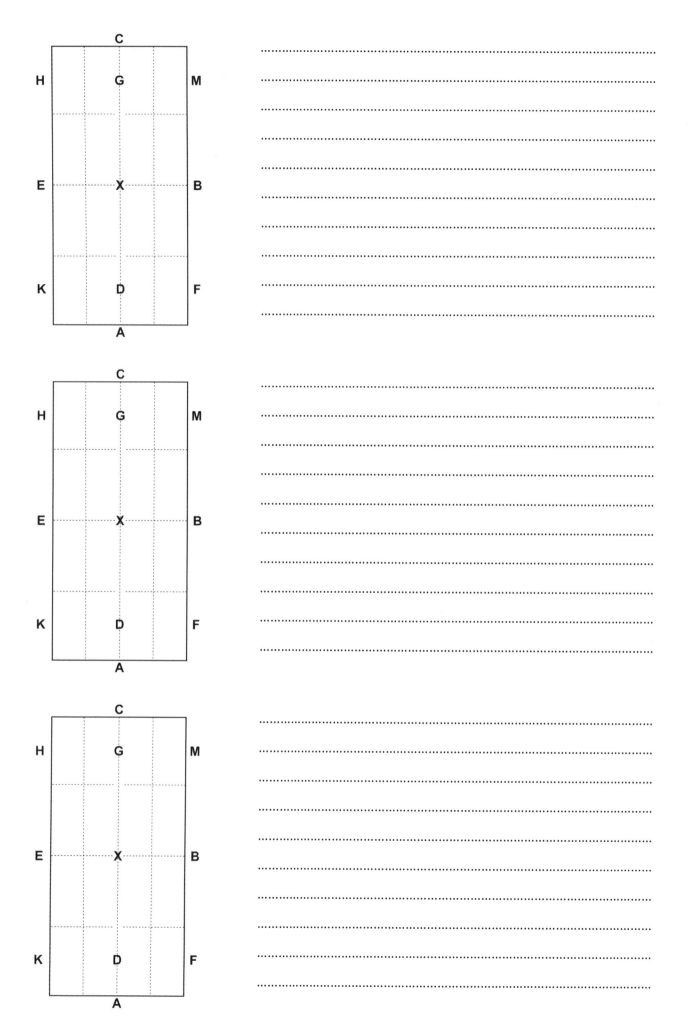

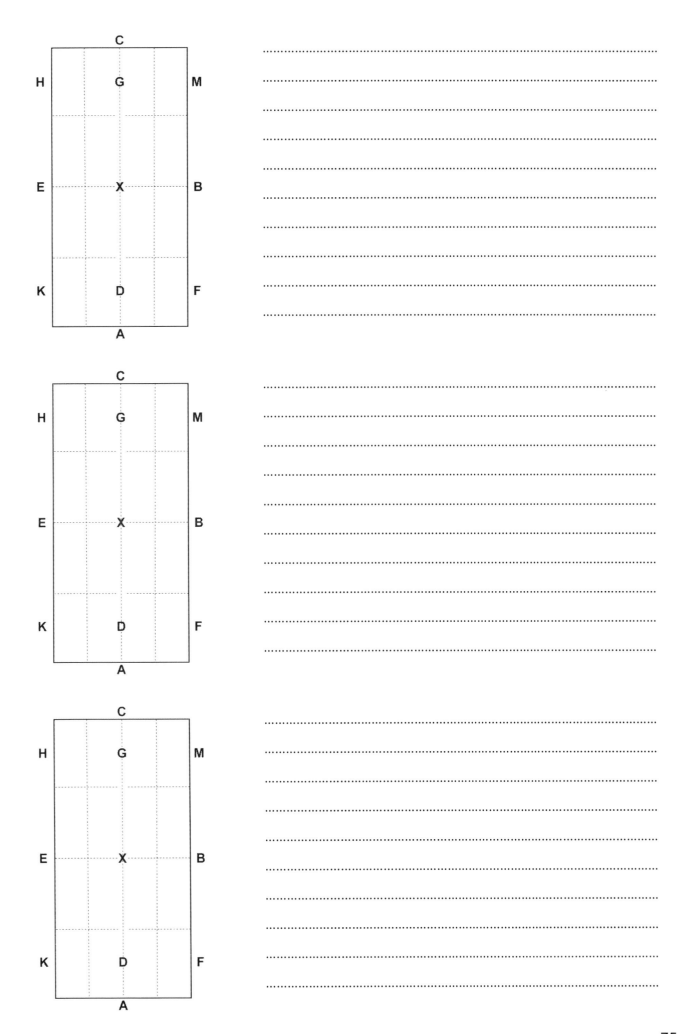

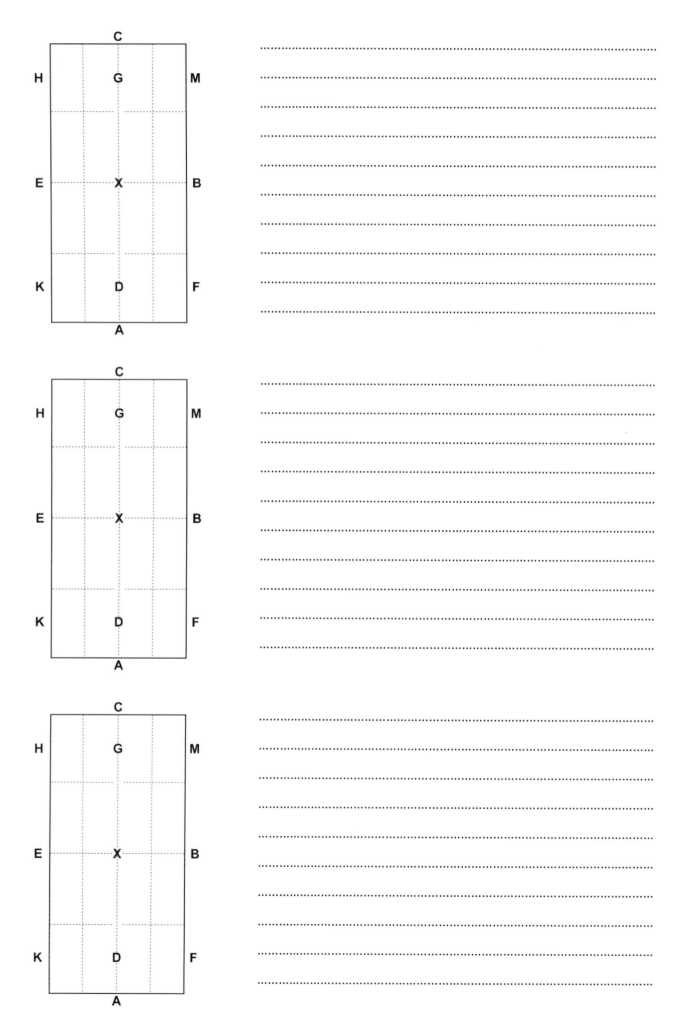

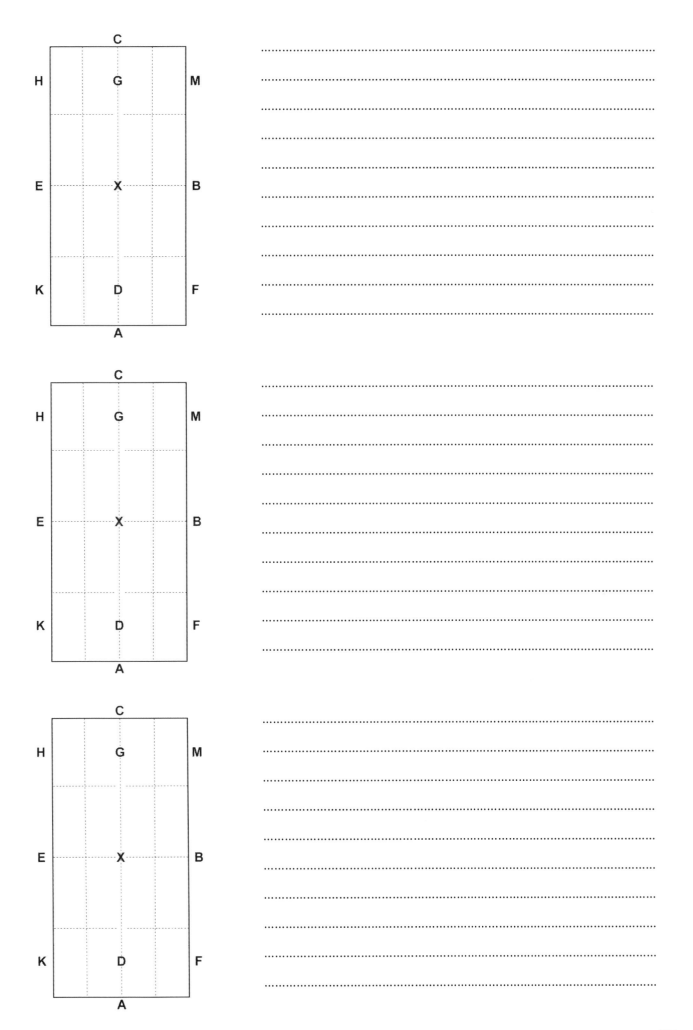

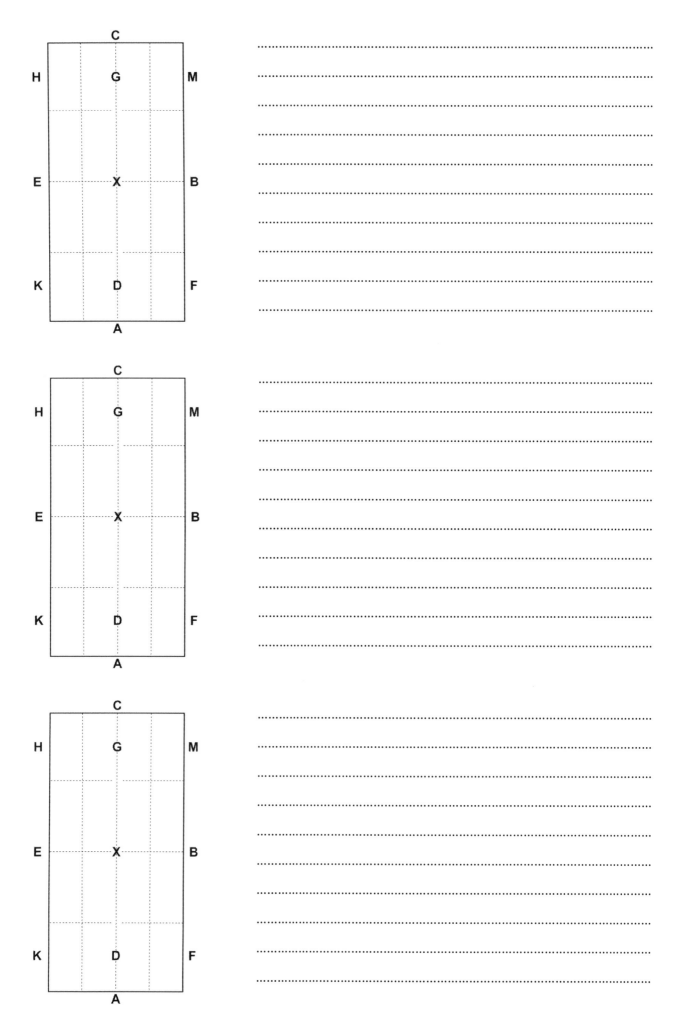

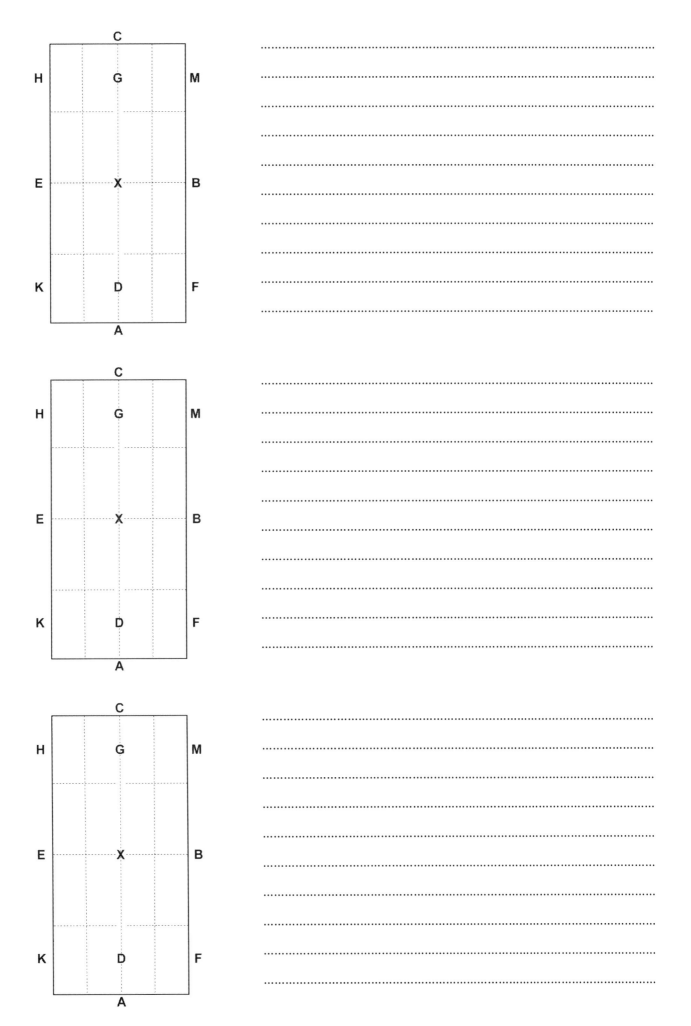

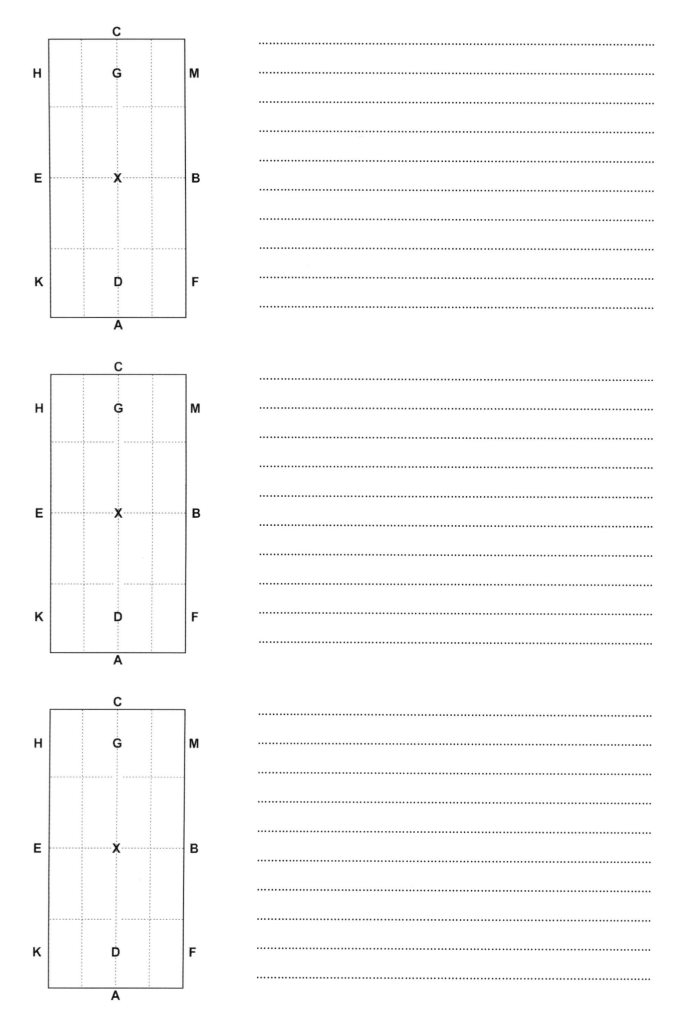

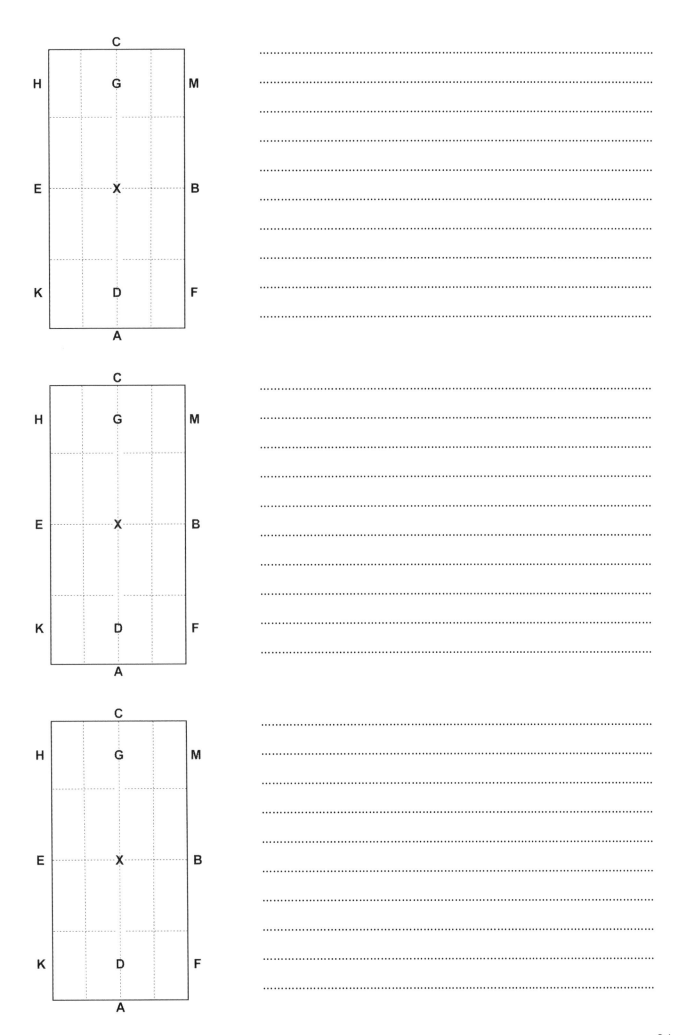

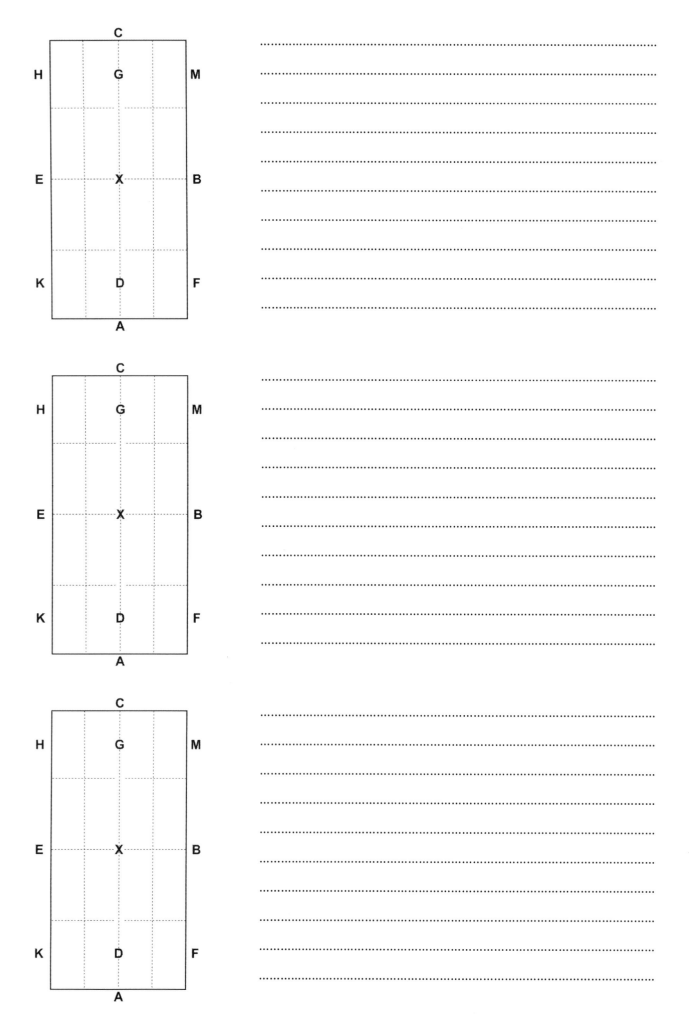

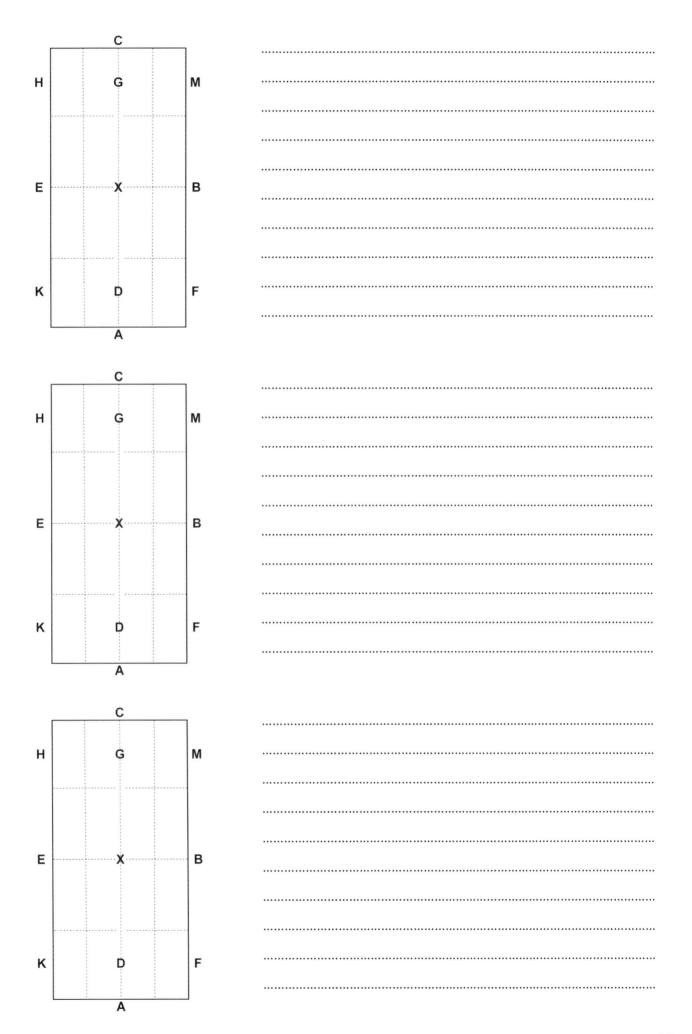

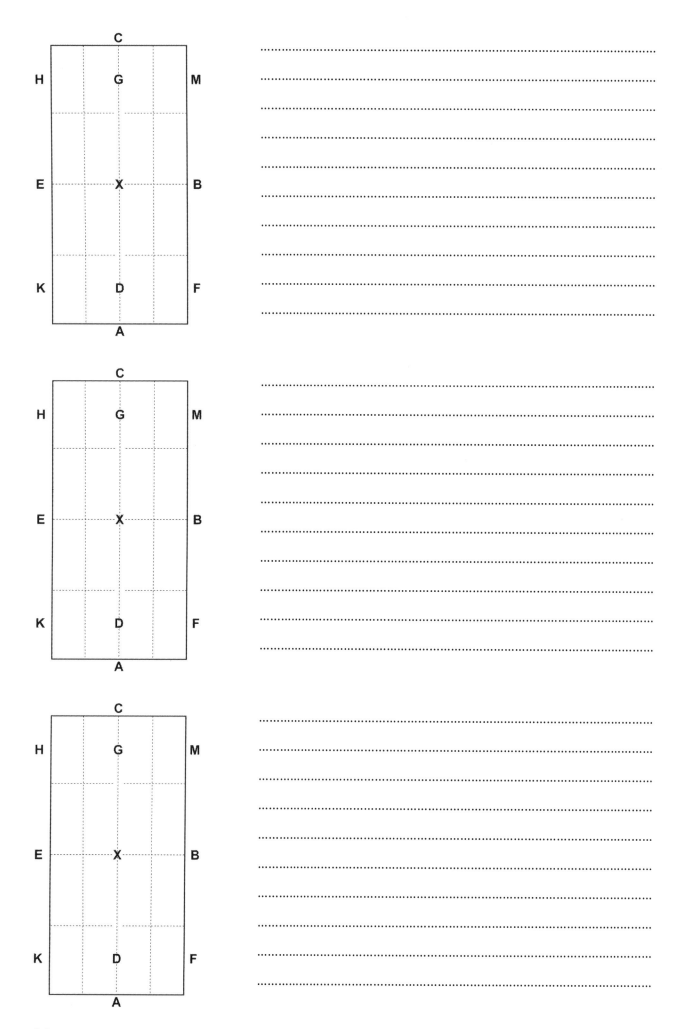

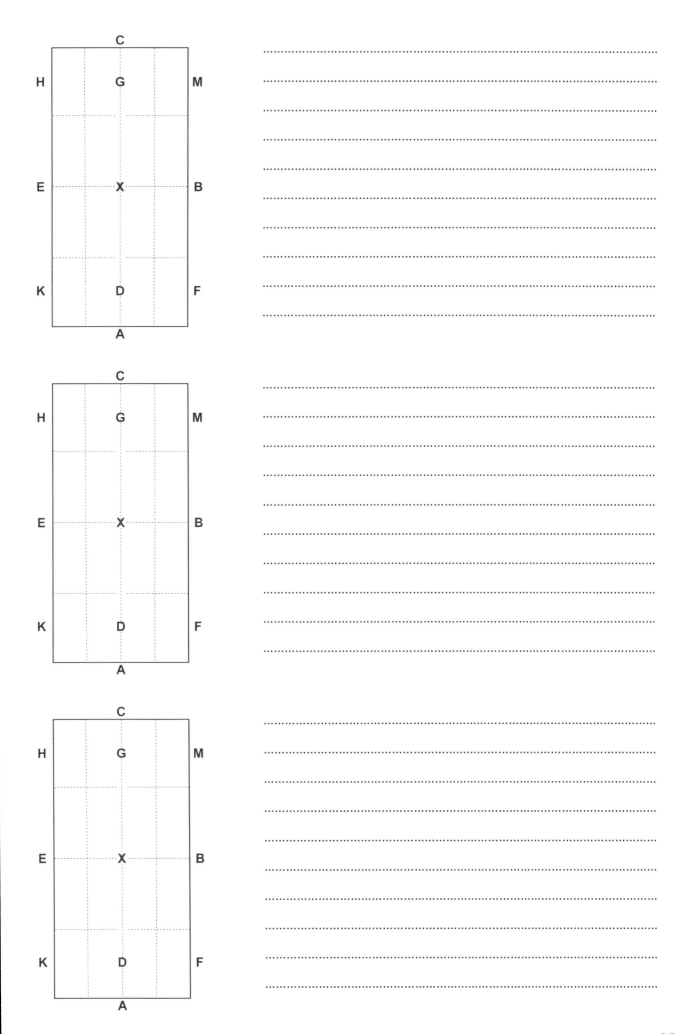

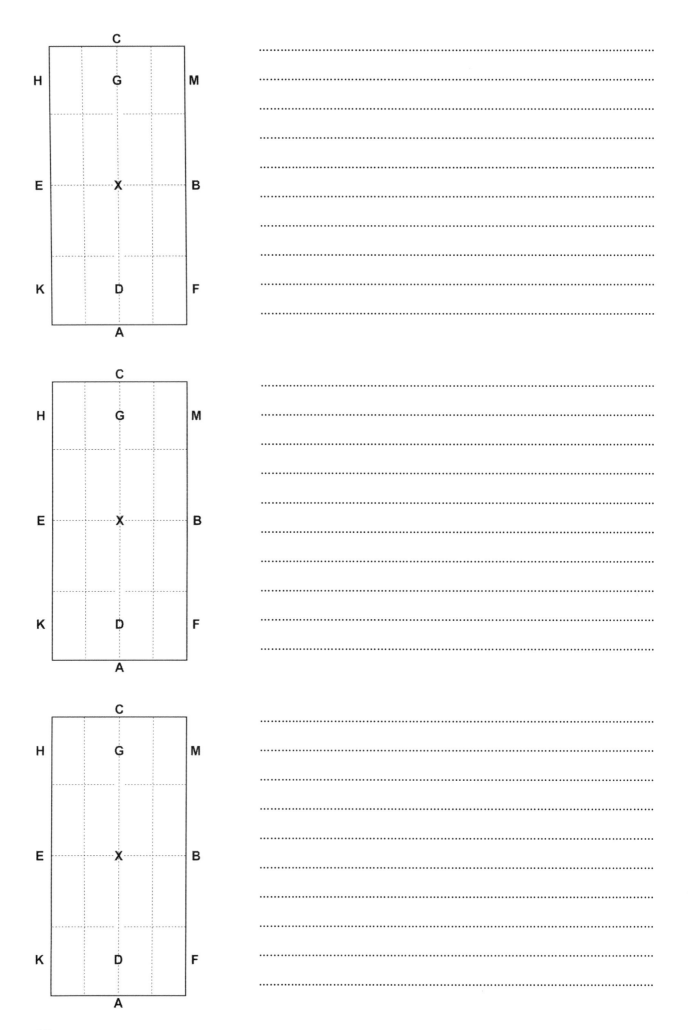

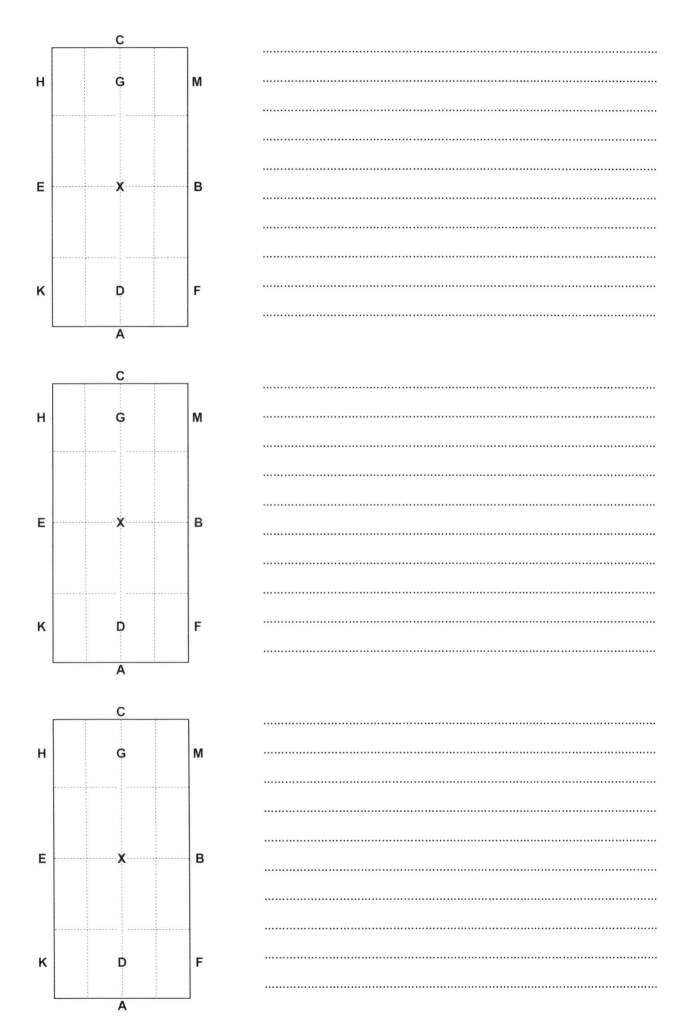

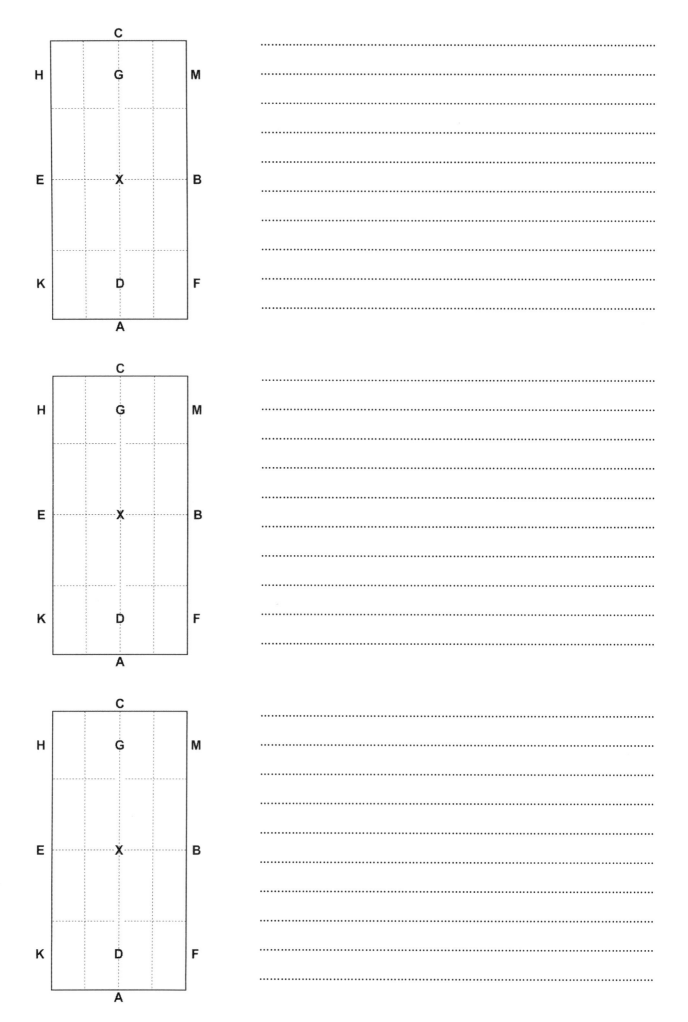

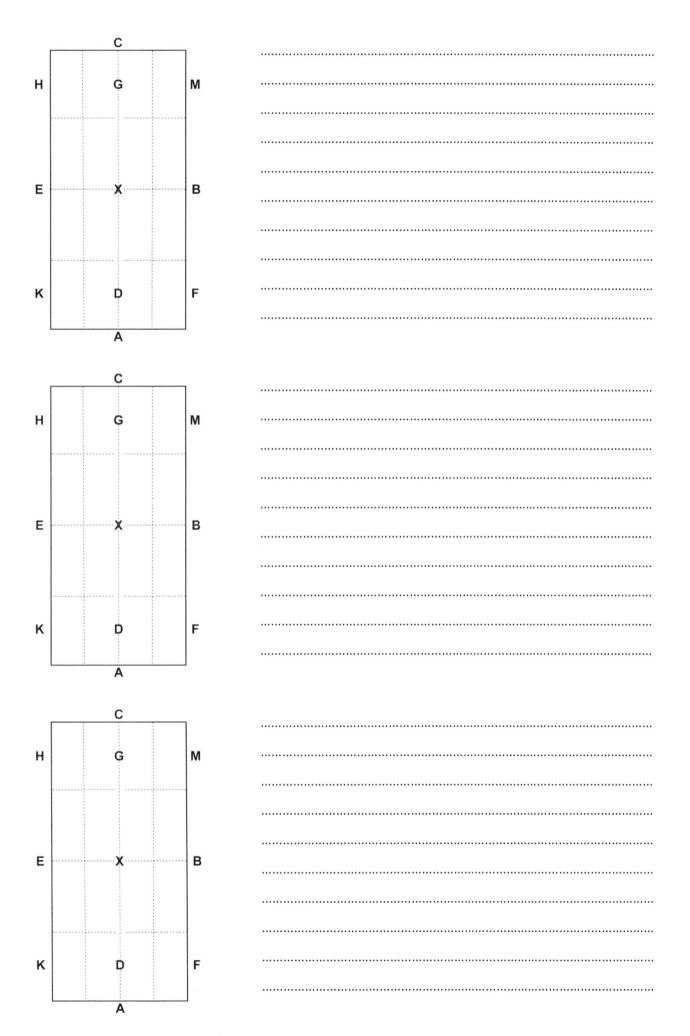

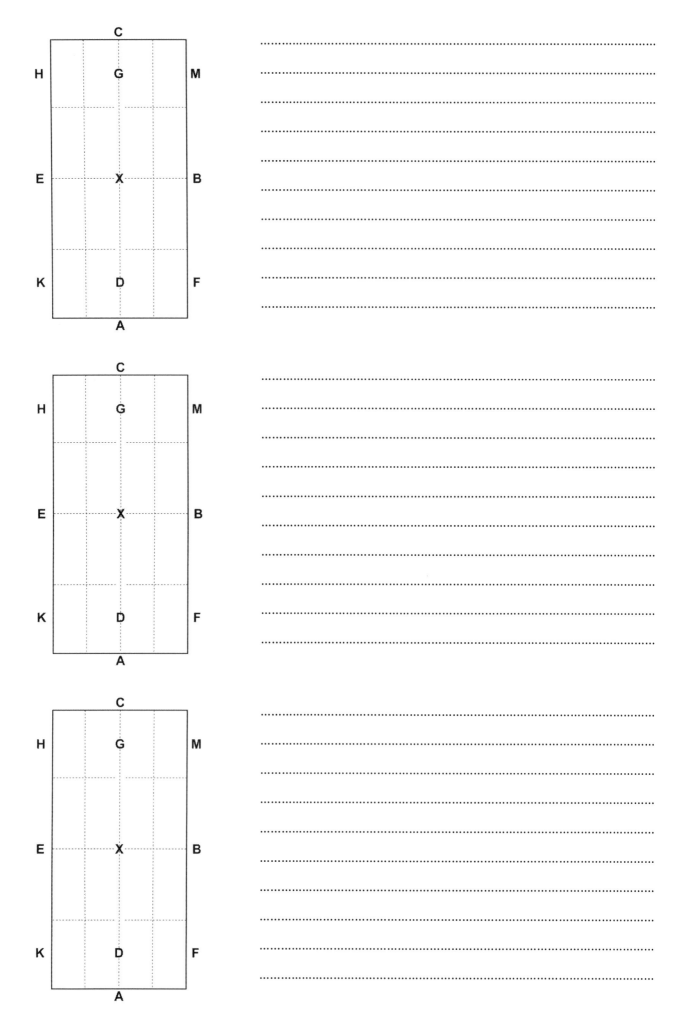

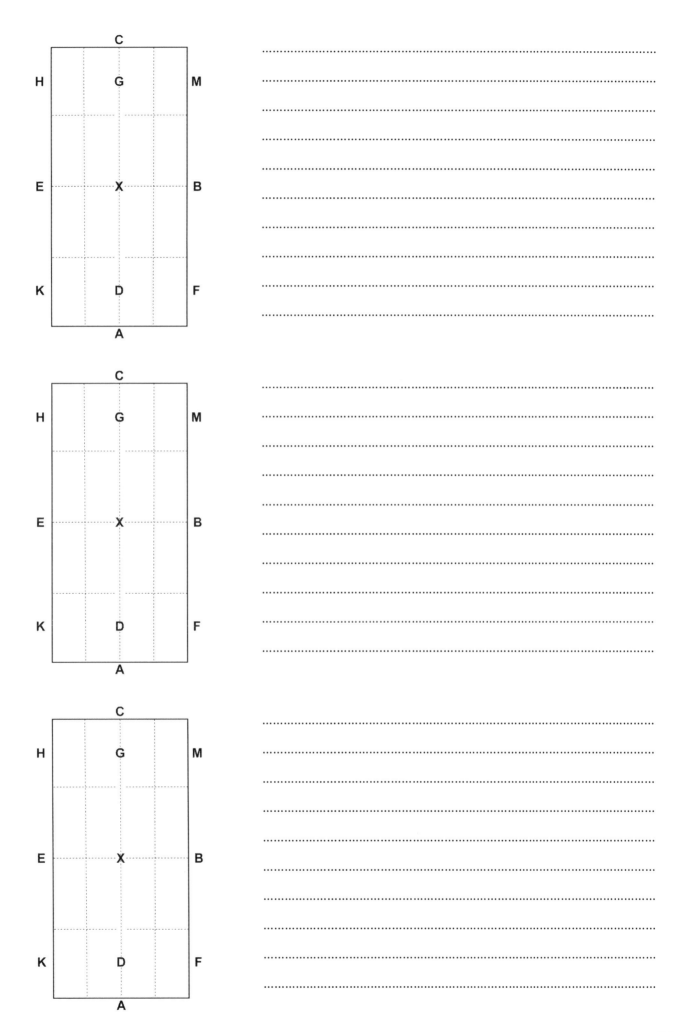

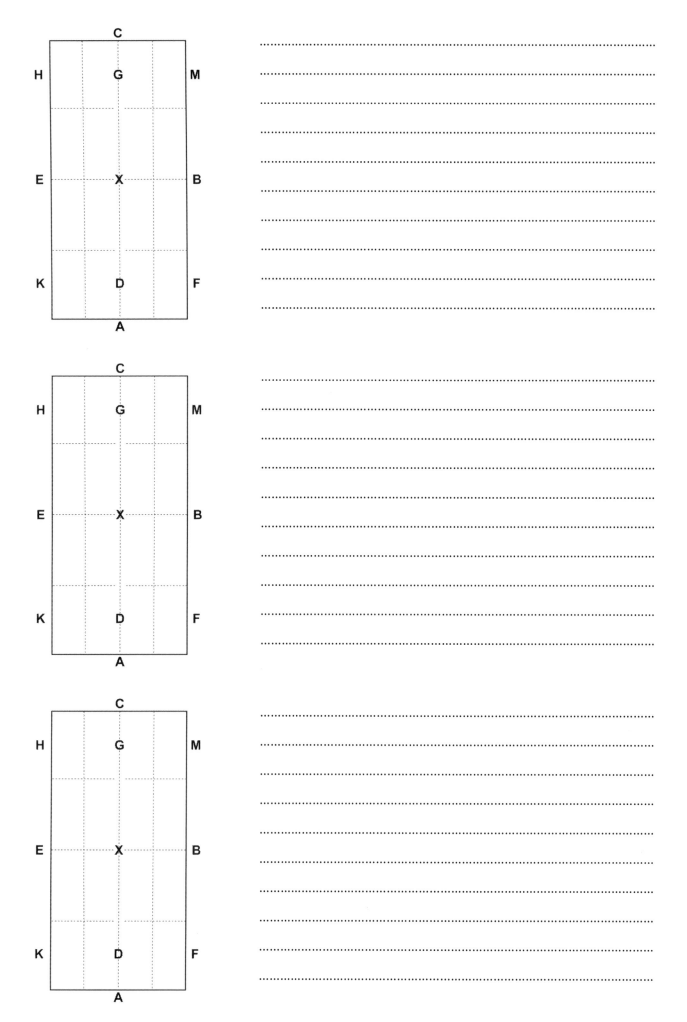

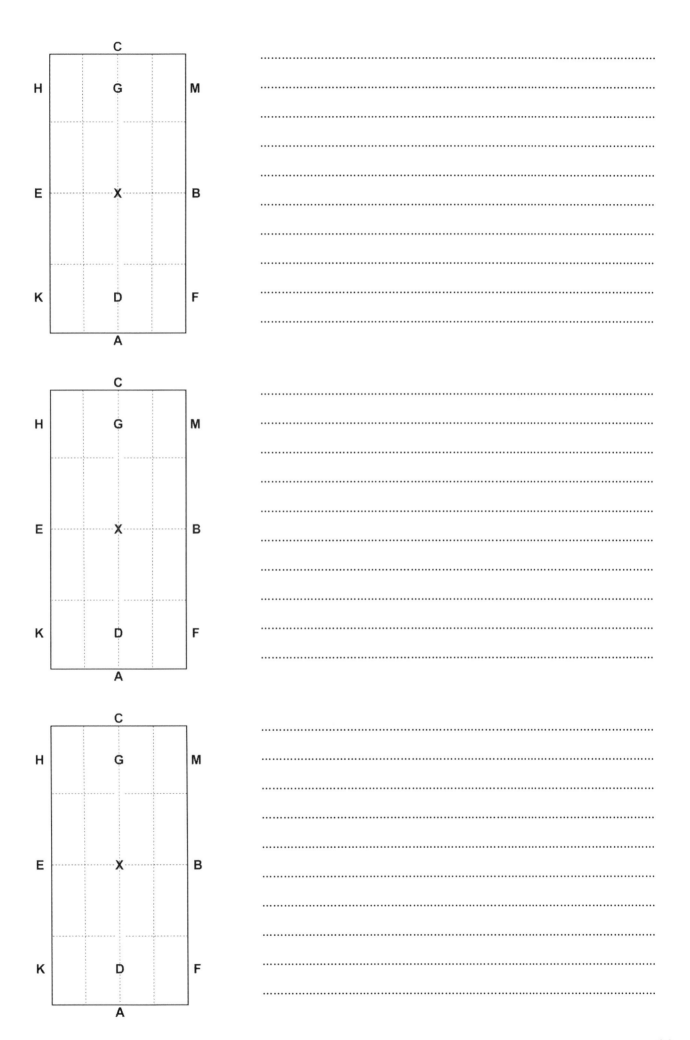

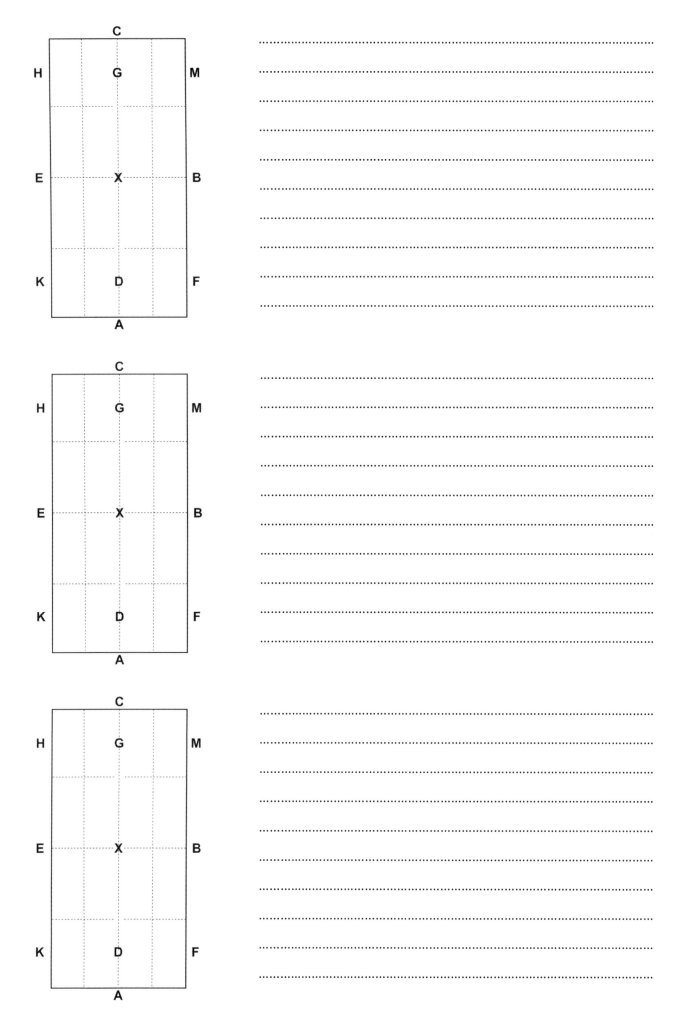

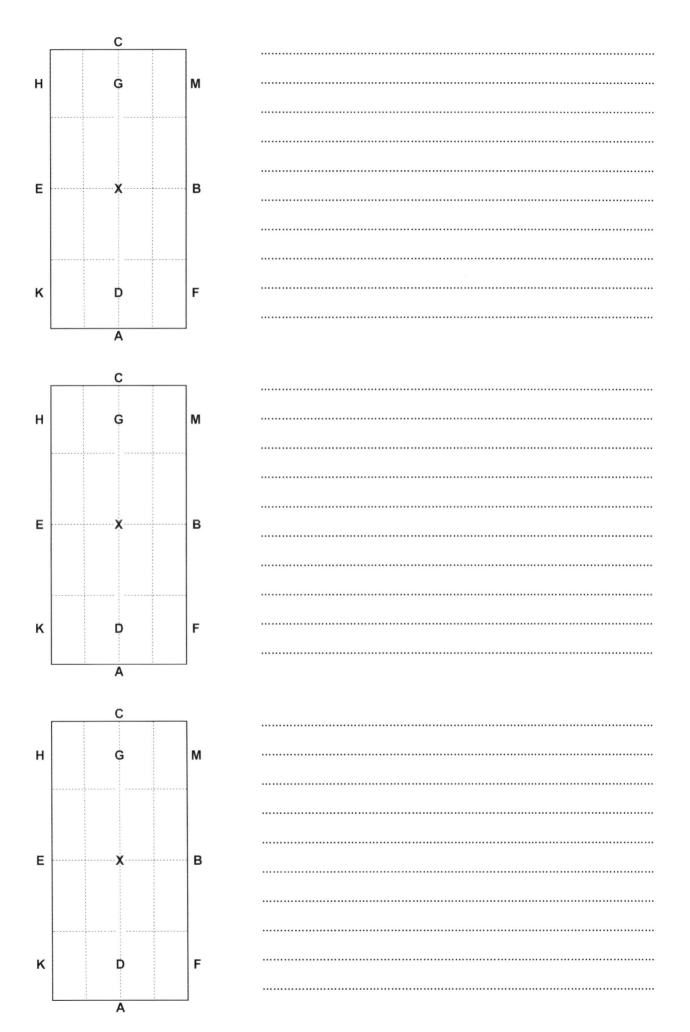

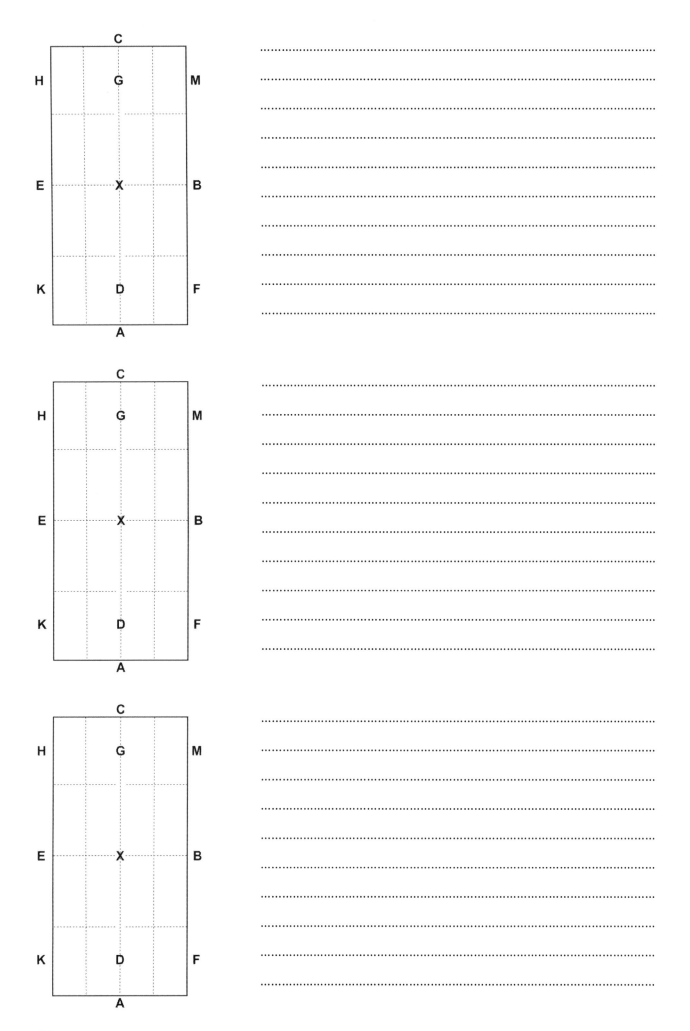

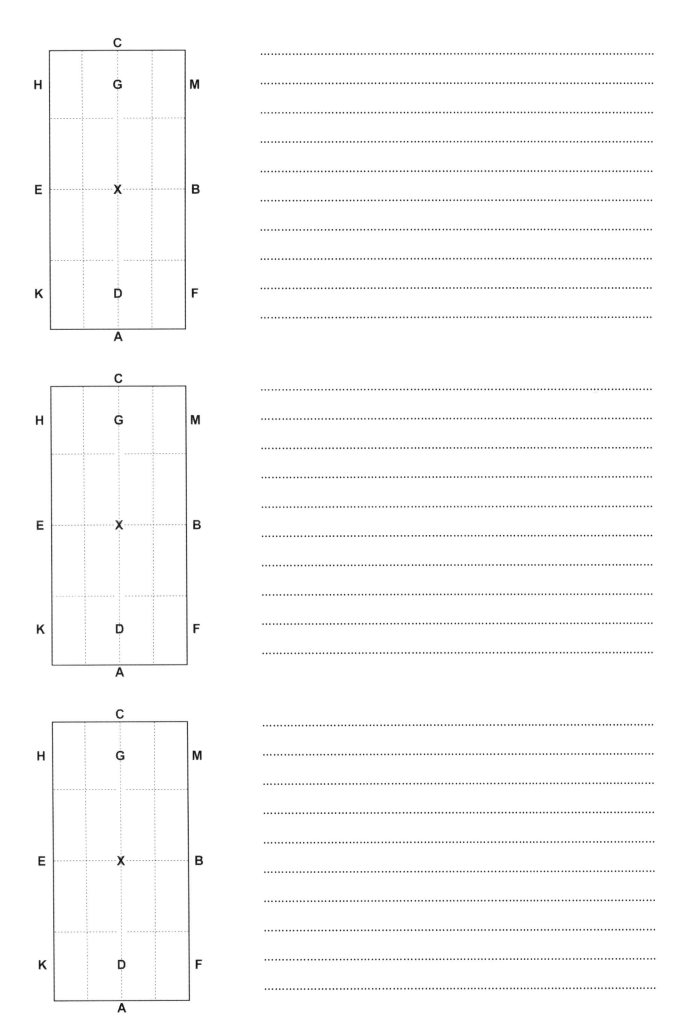

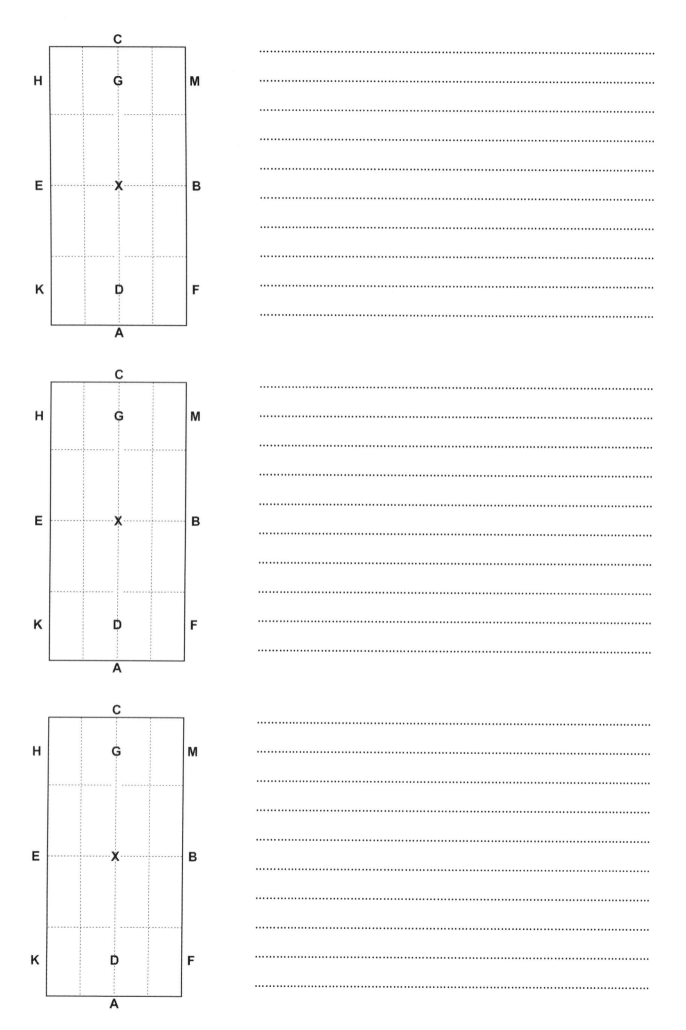

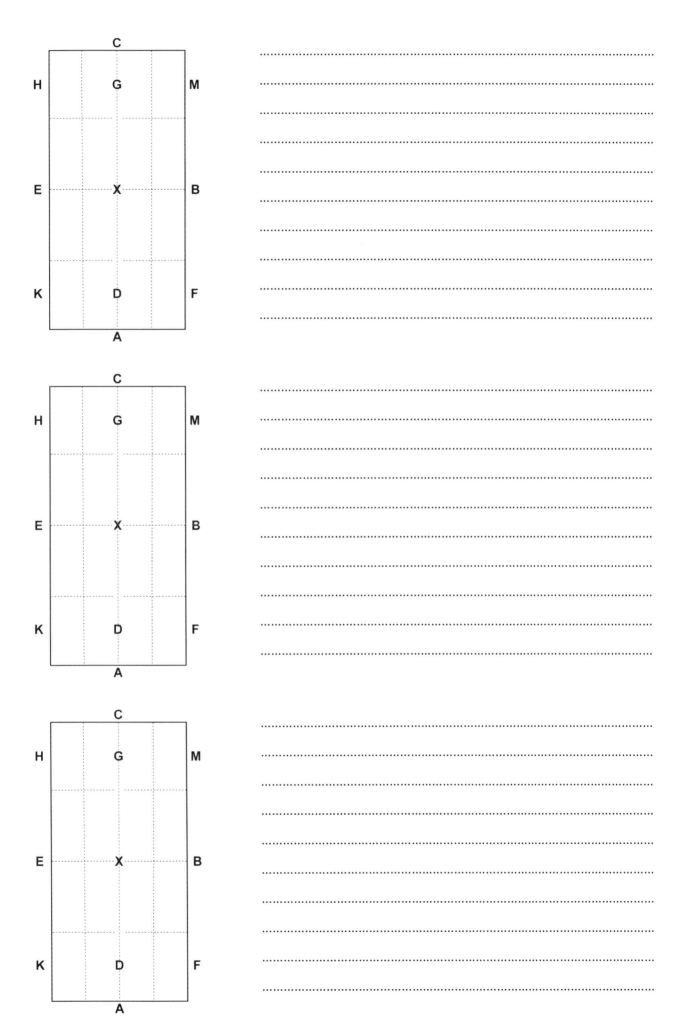

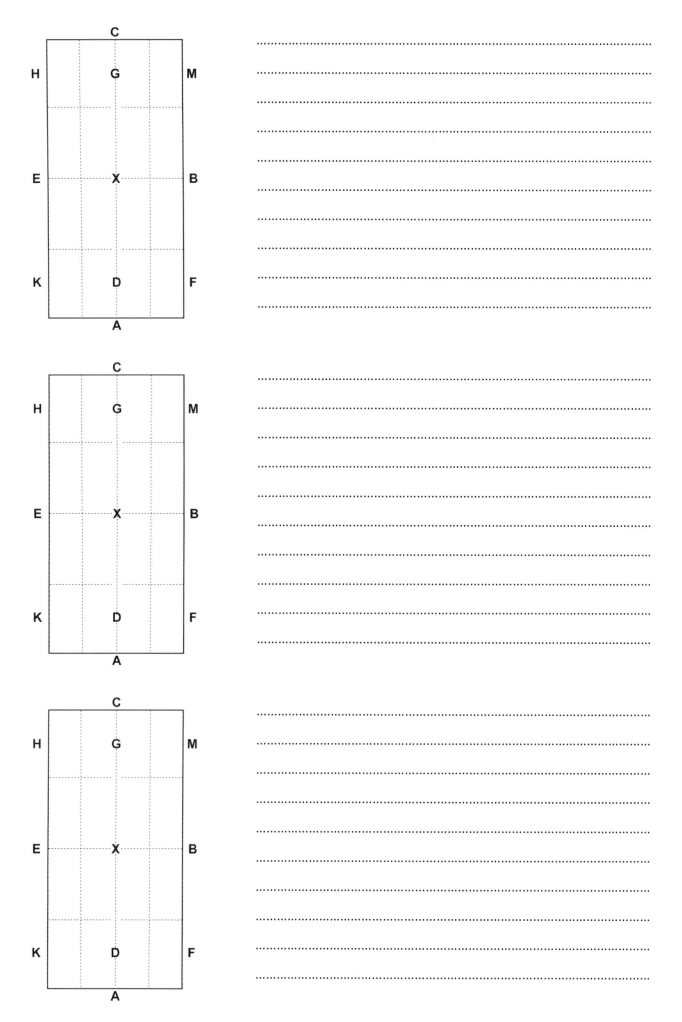

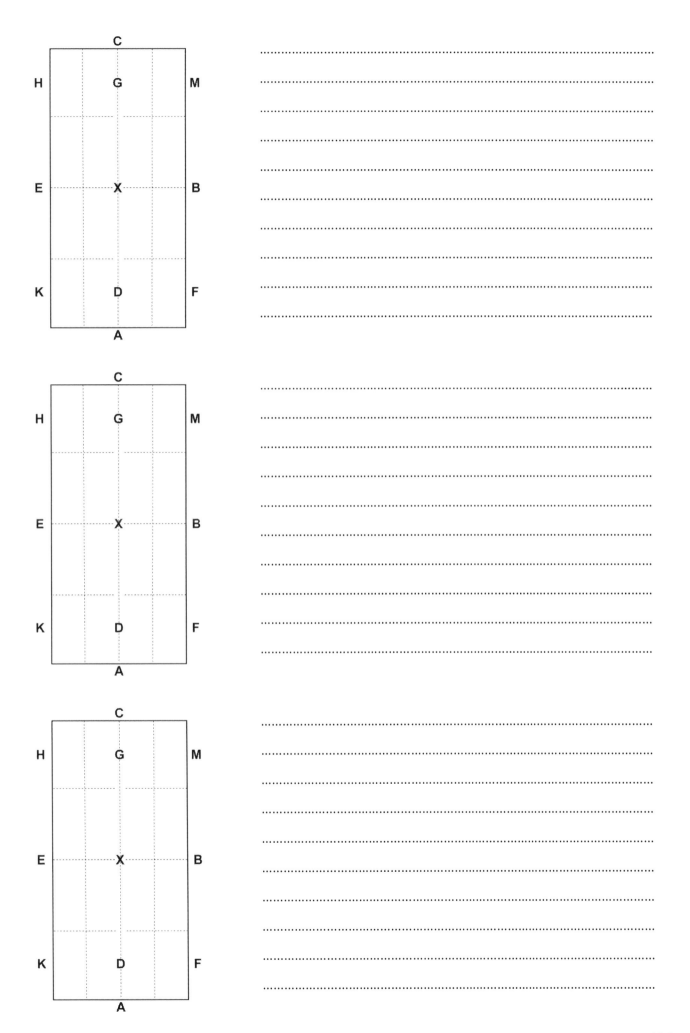

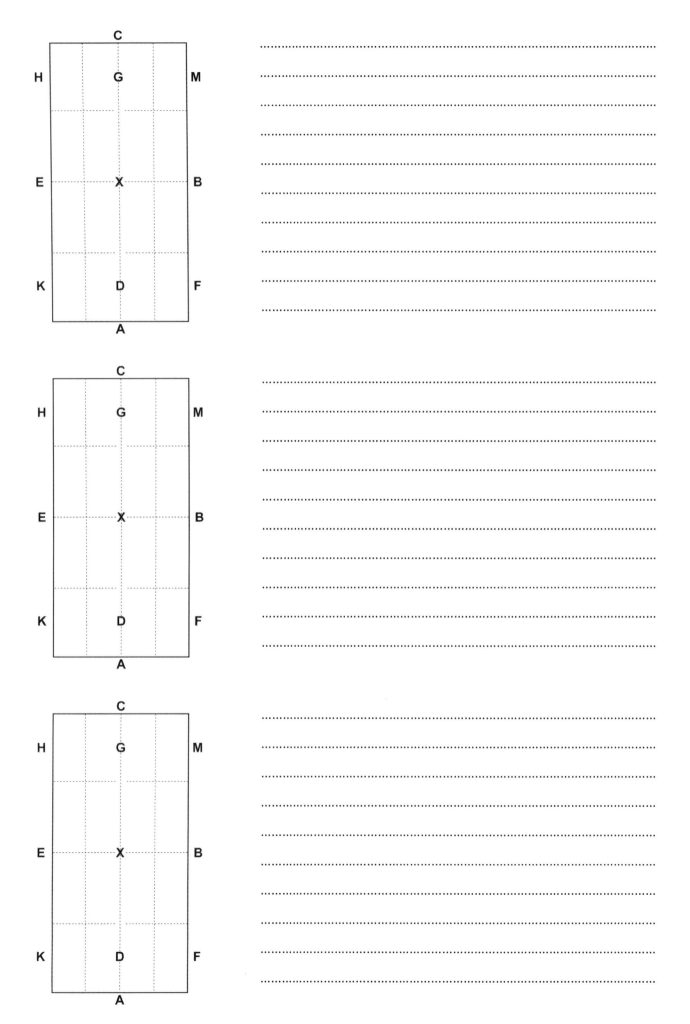

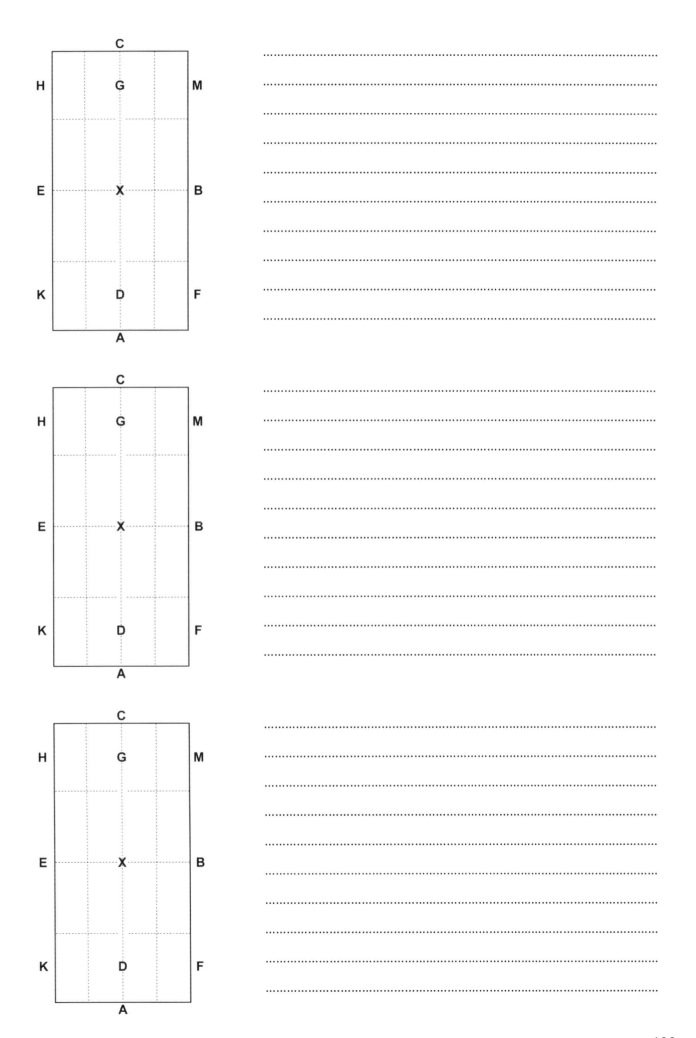

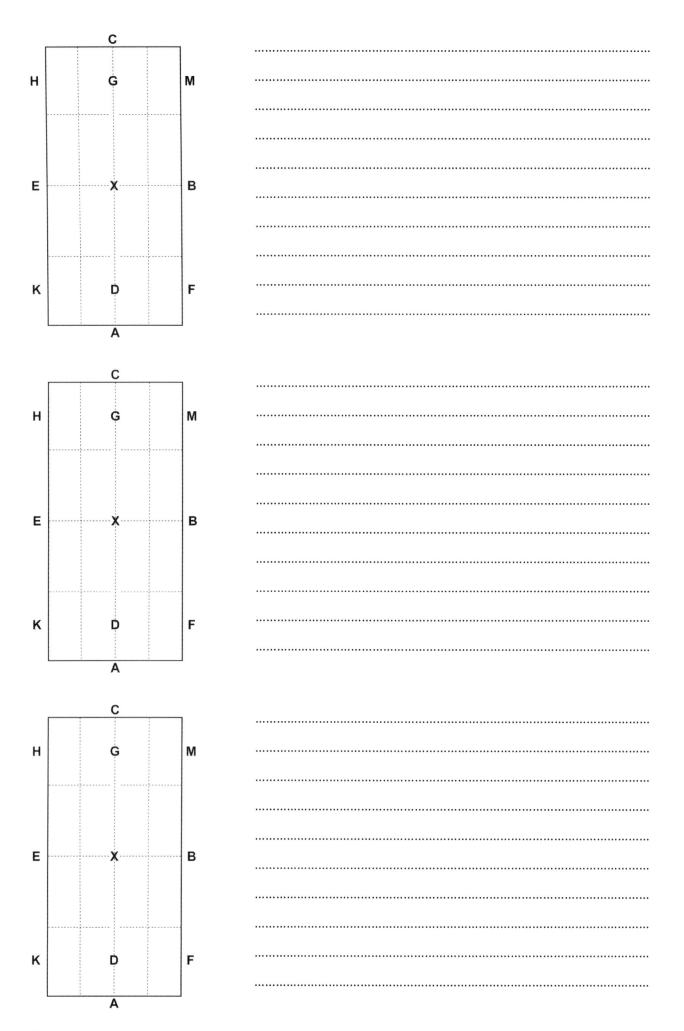

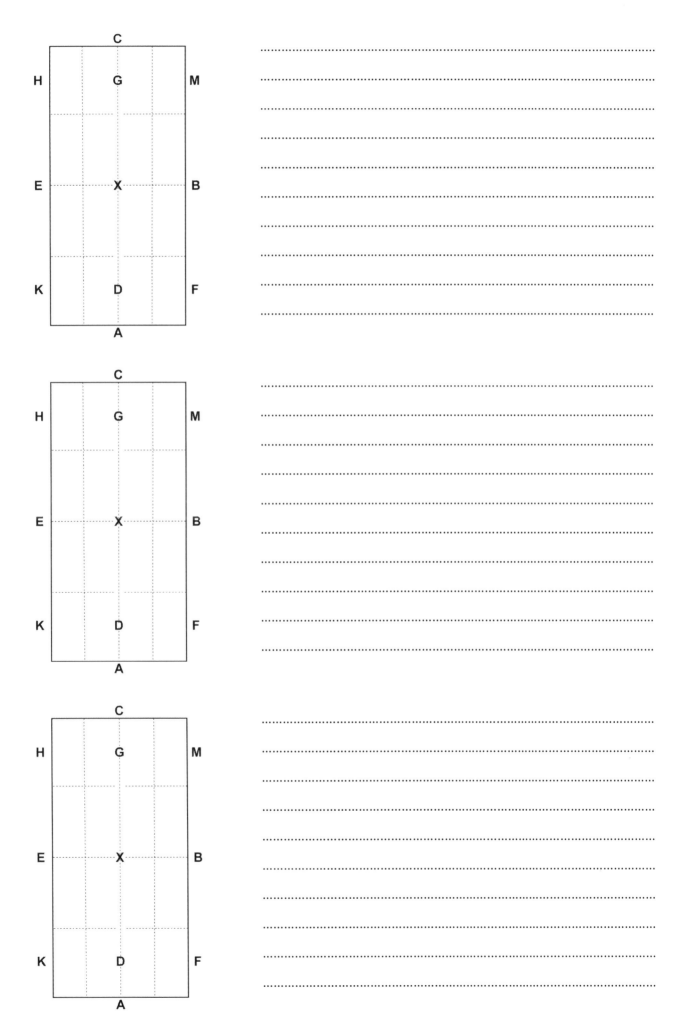

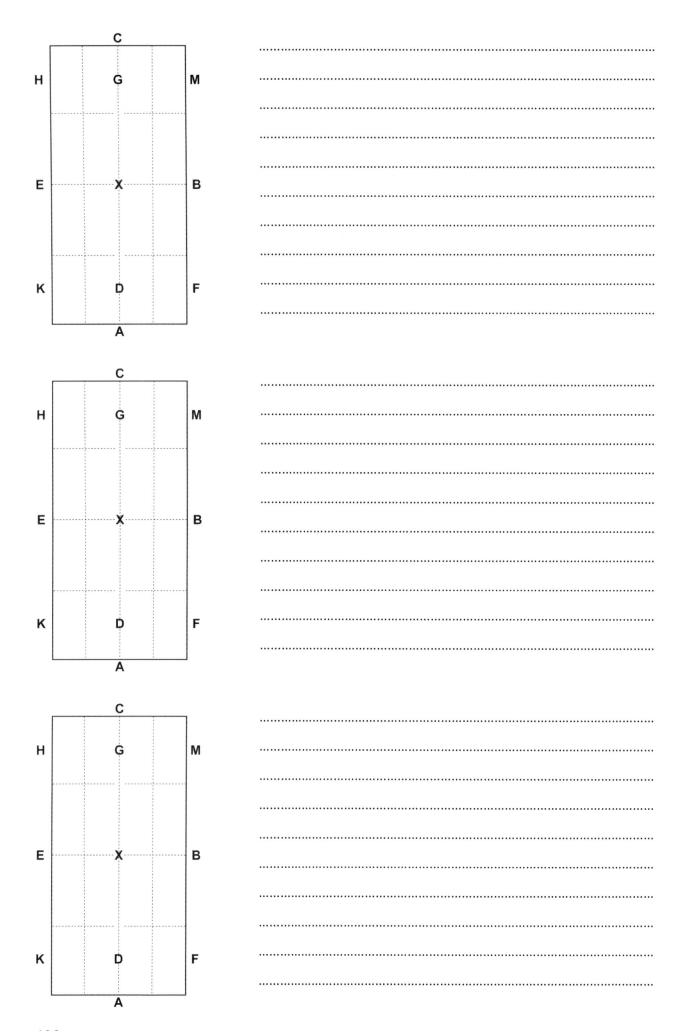

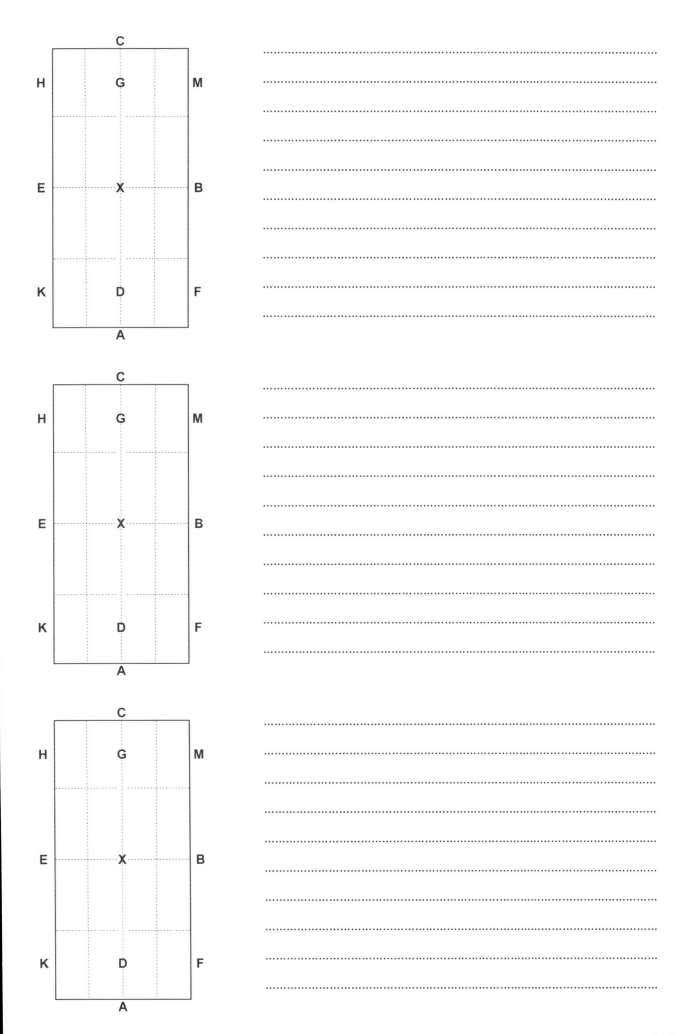

107

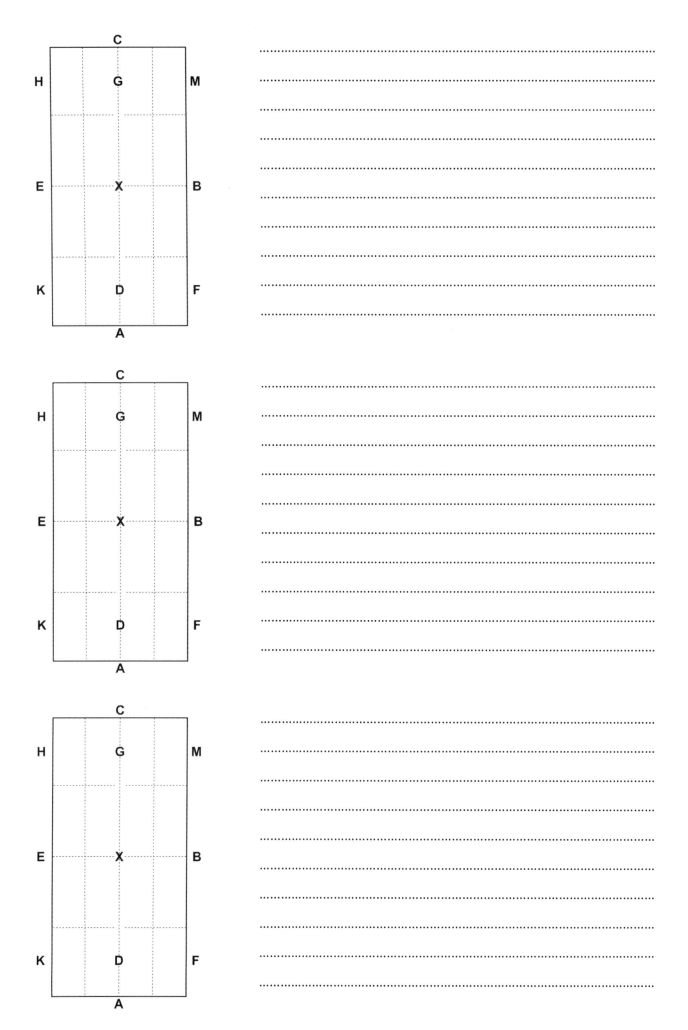

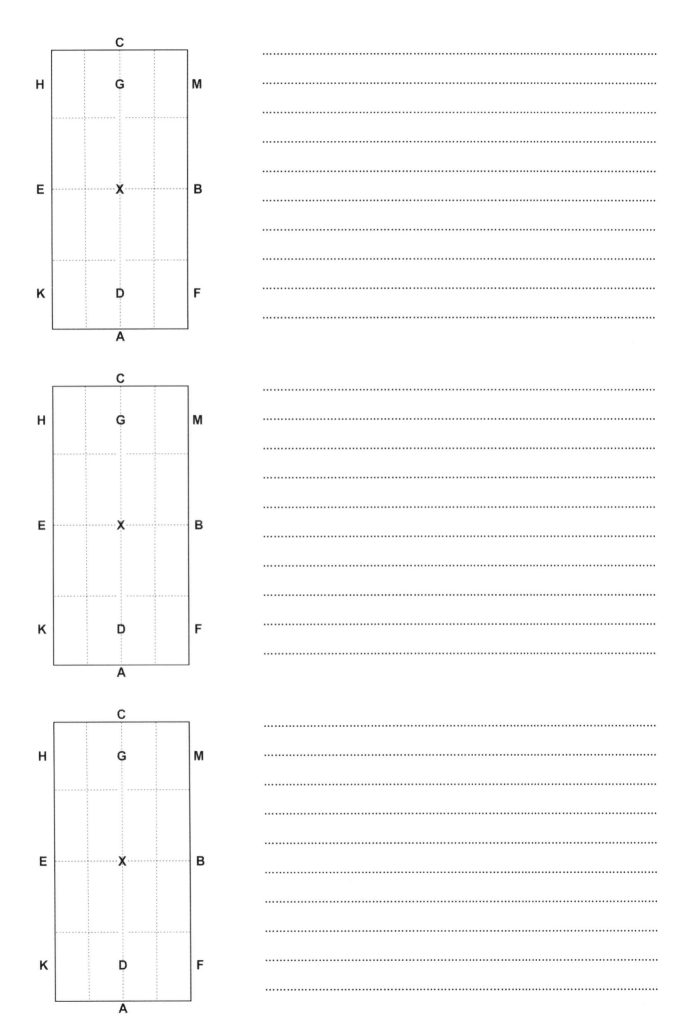

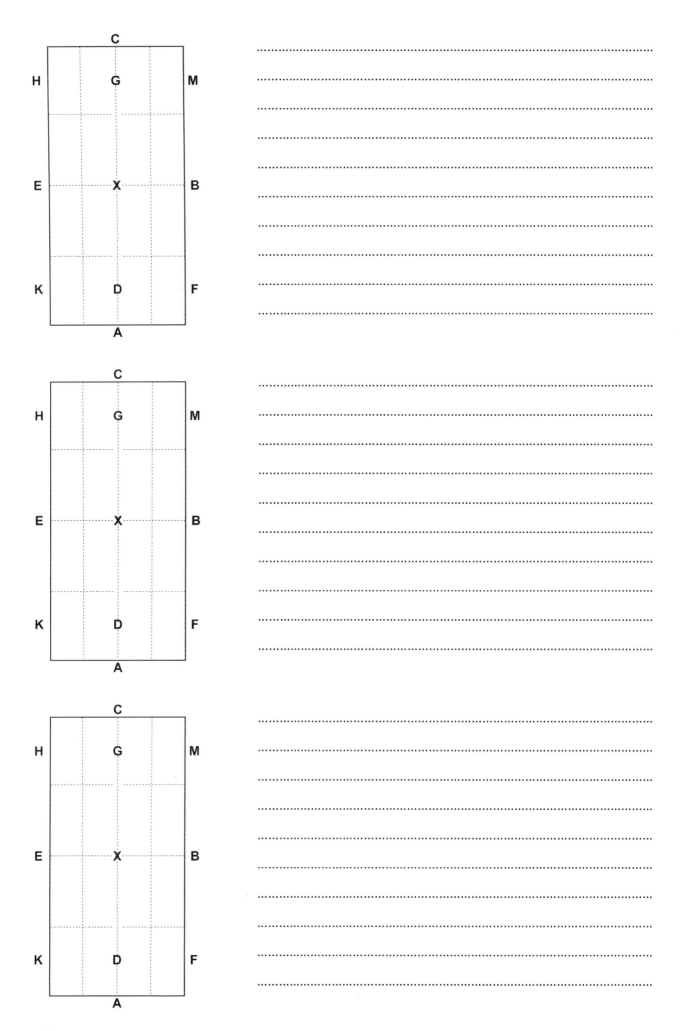

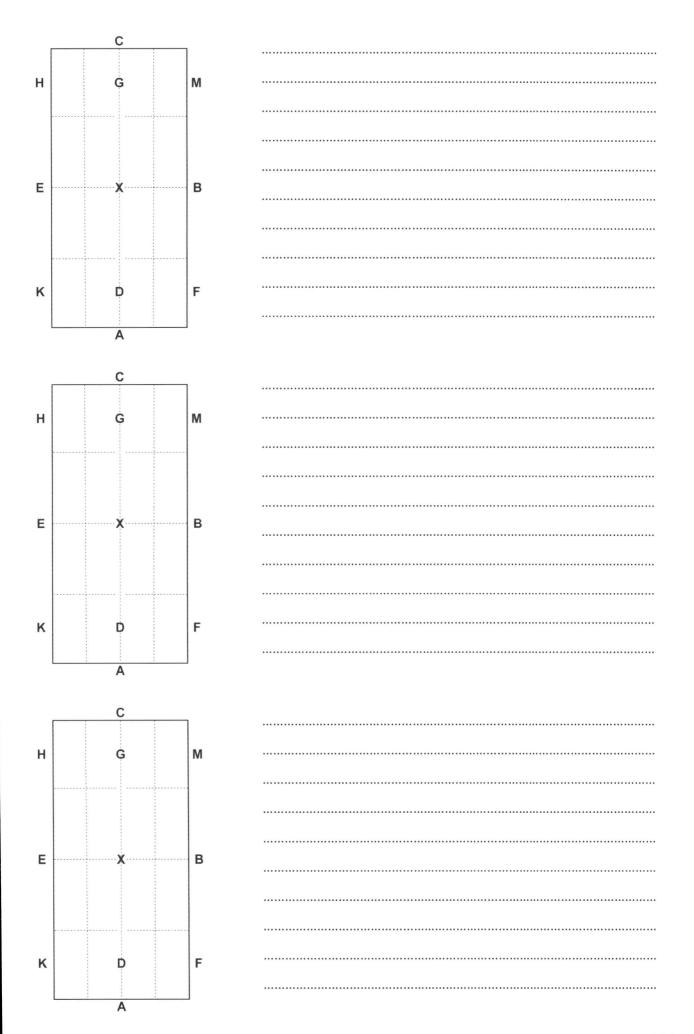

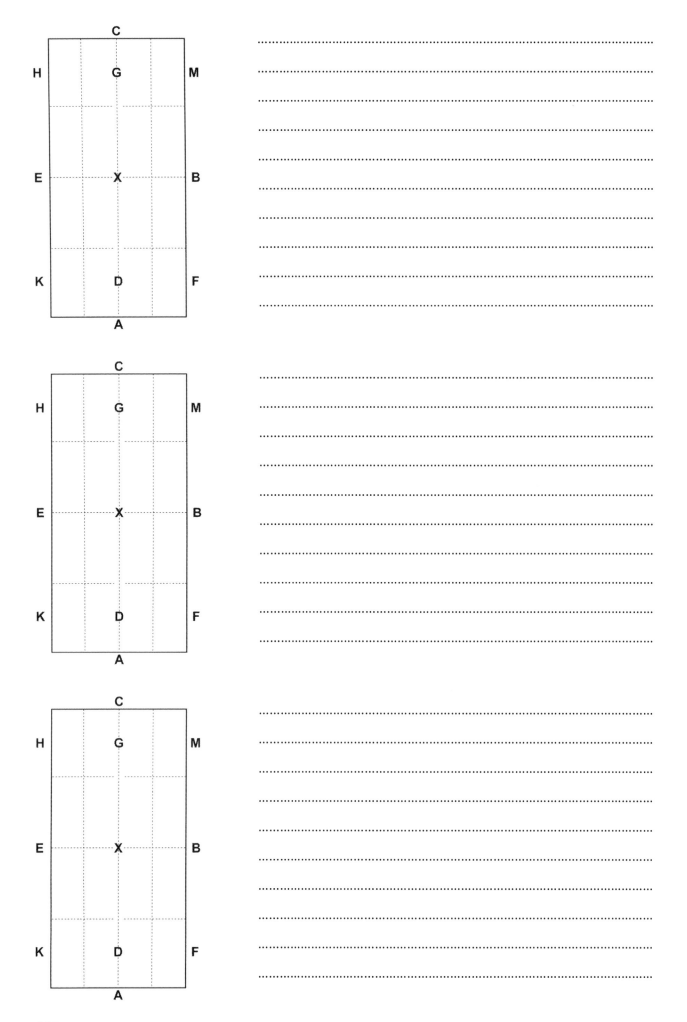

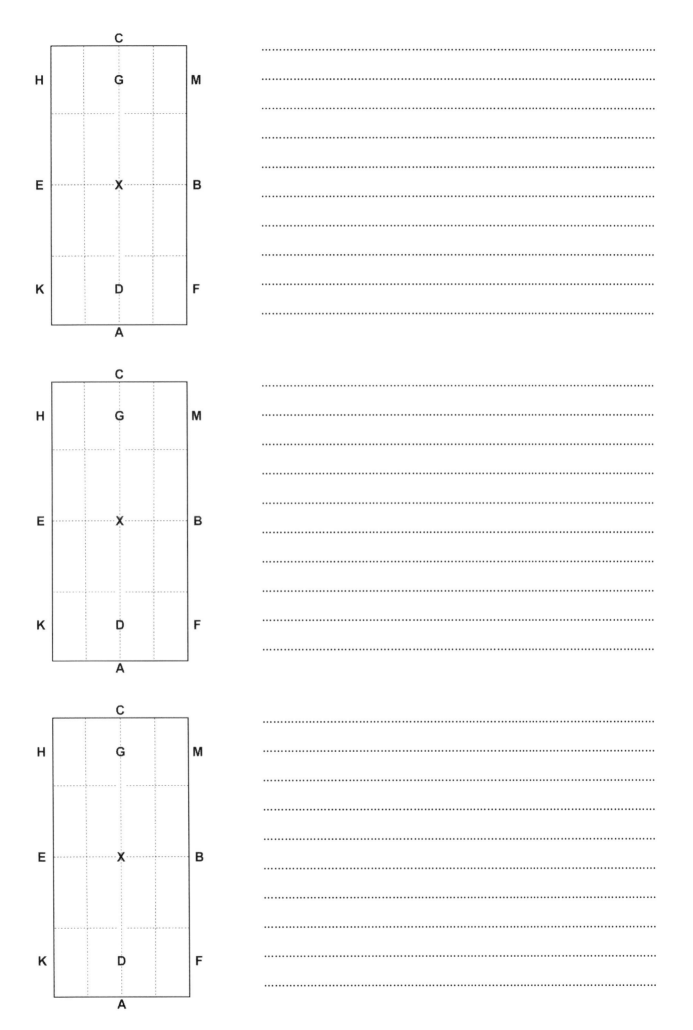

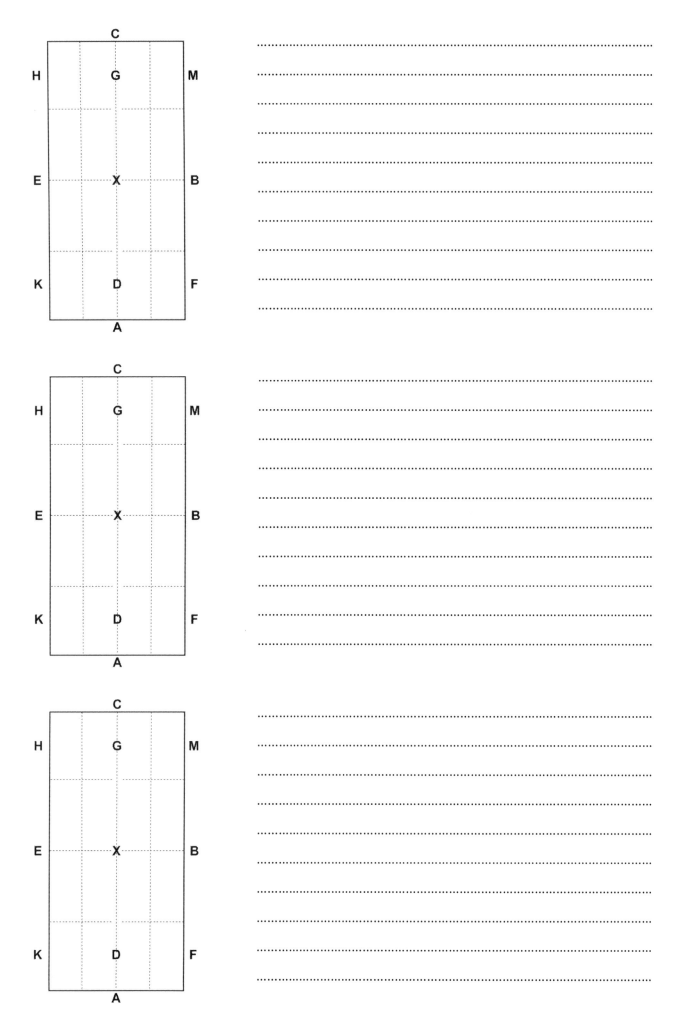

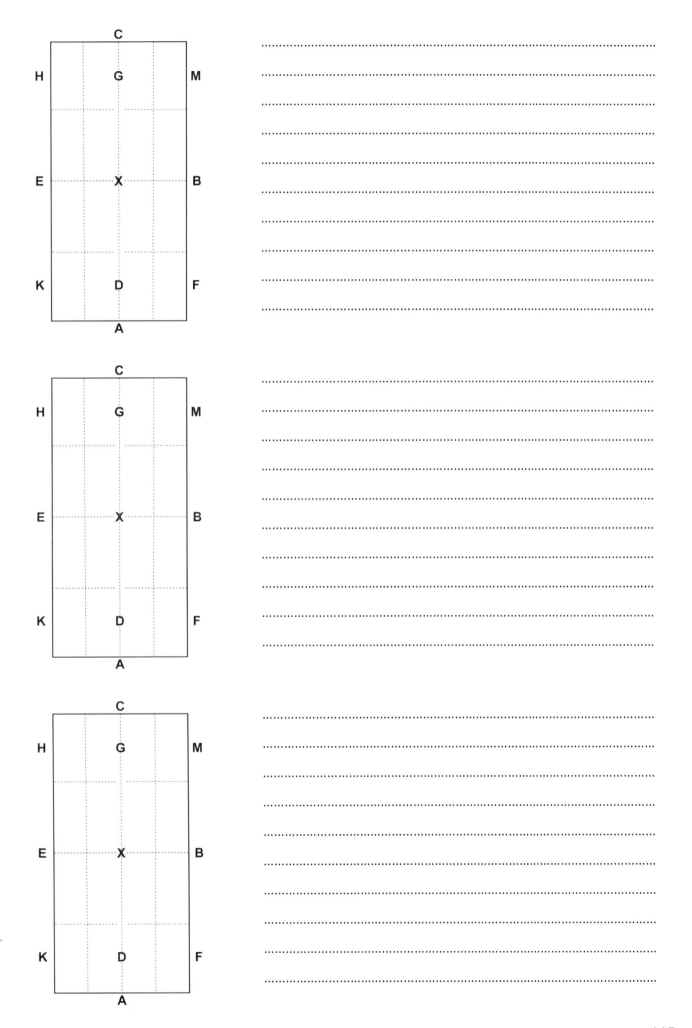

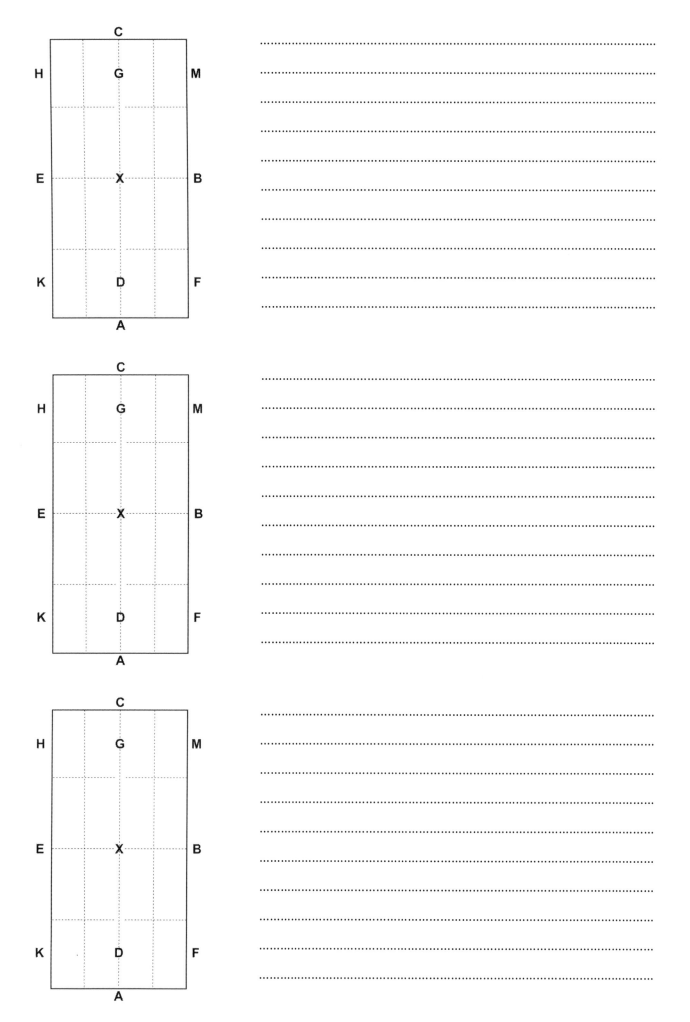

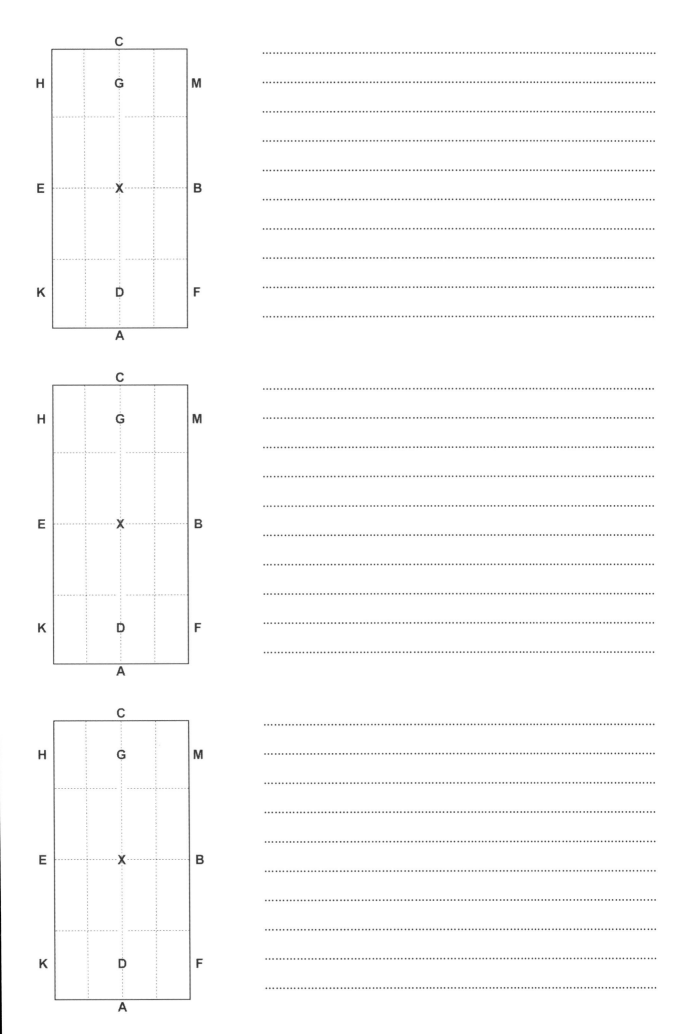

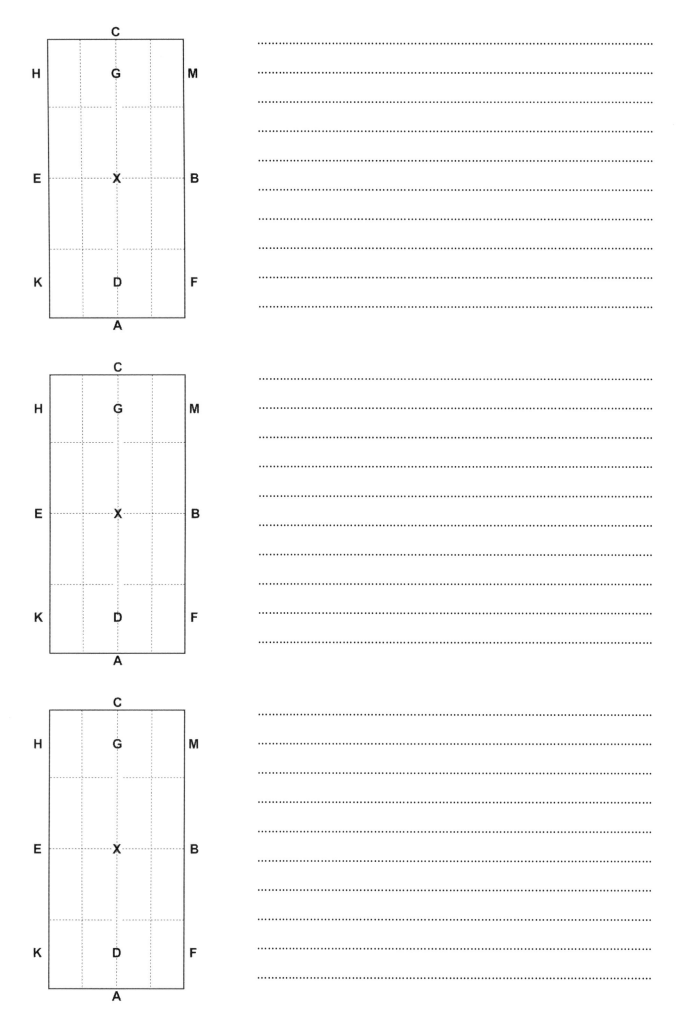

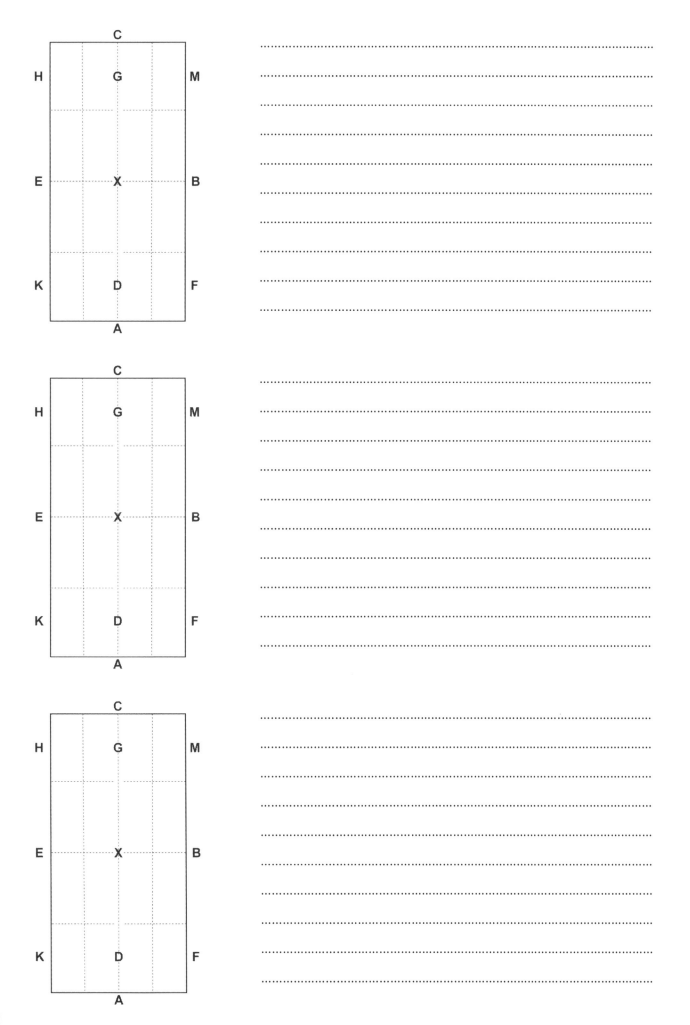

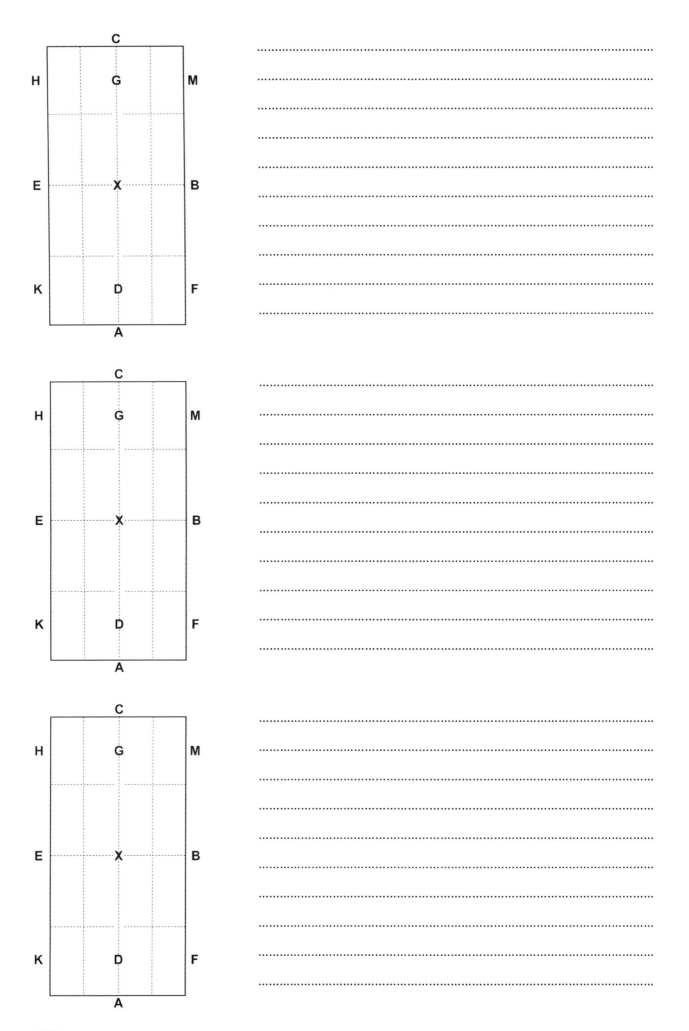

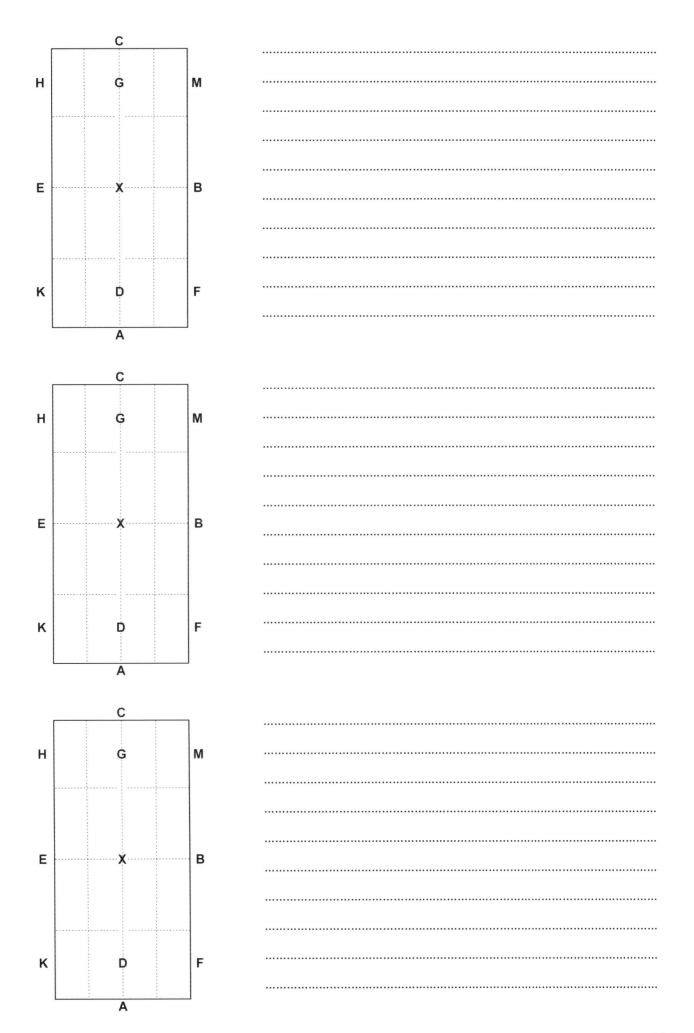

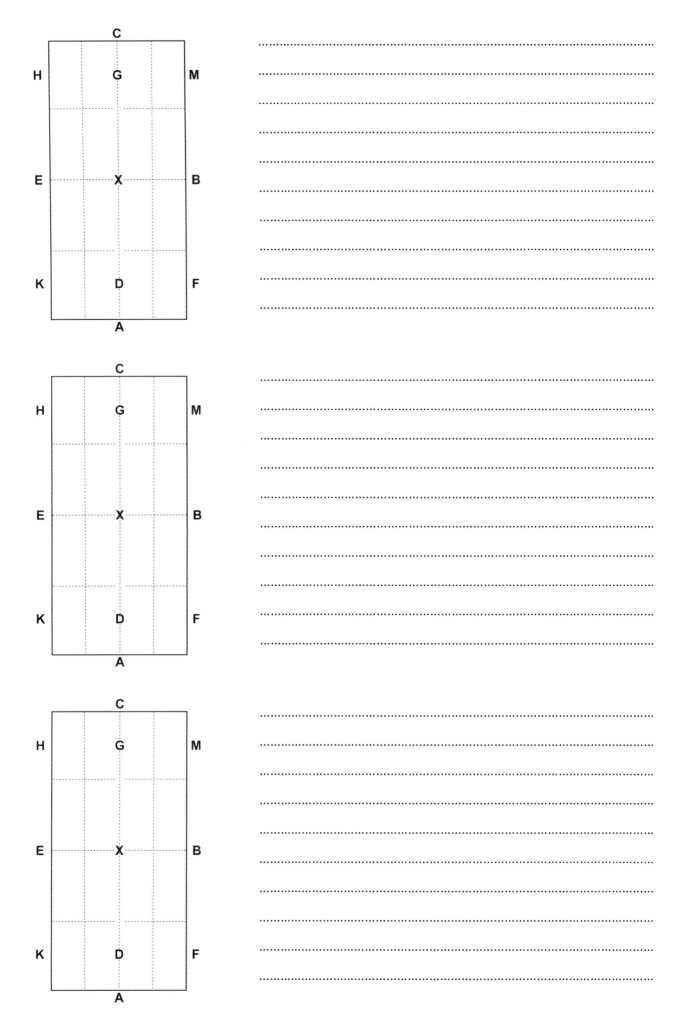

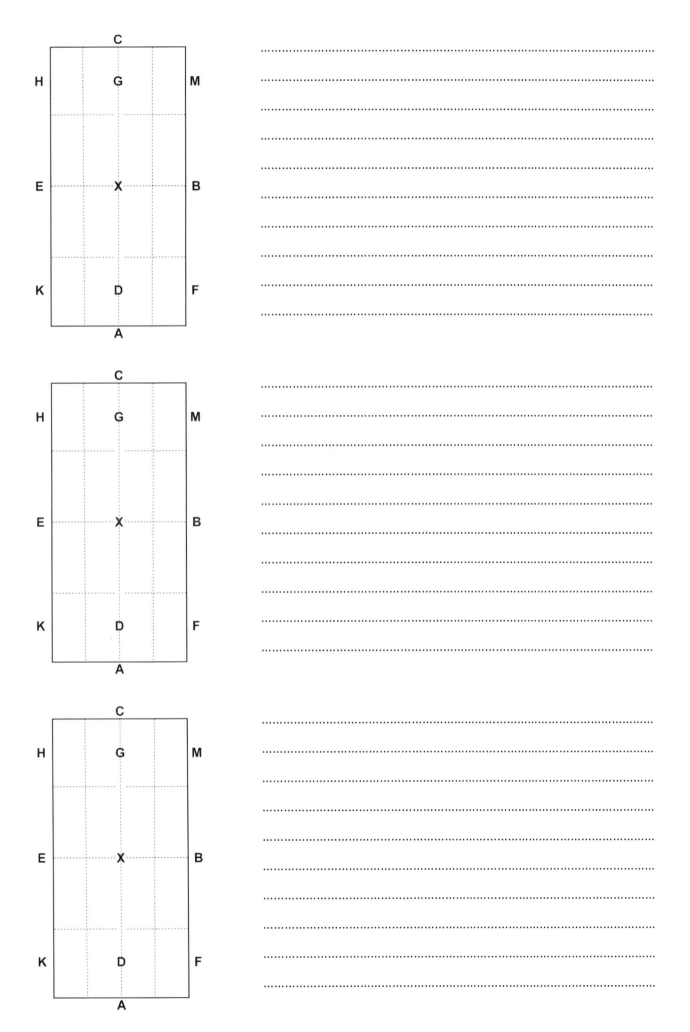

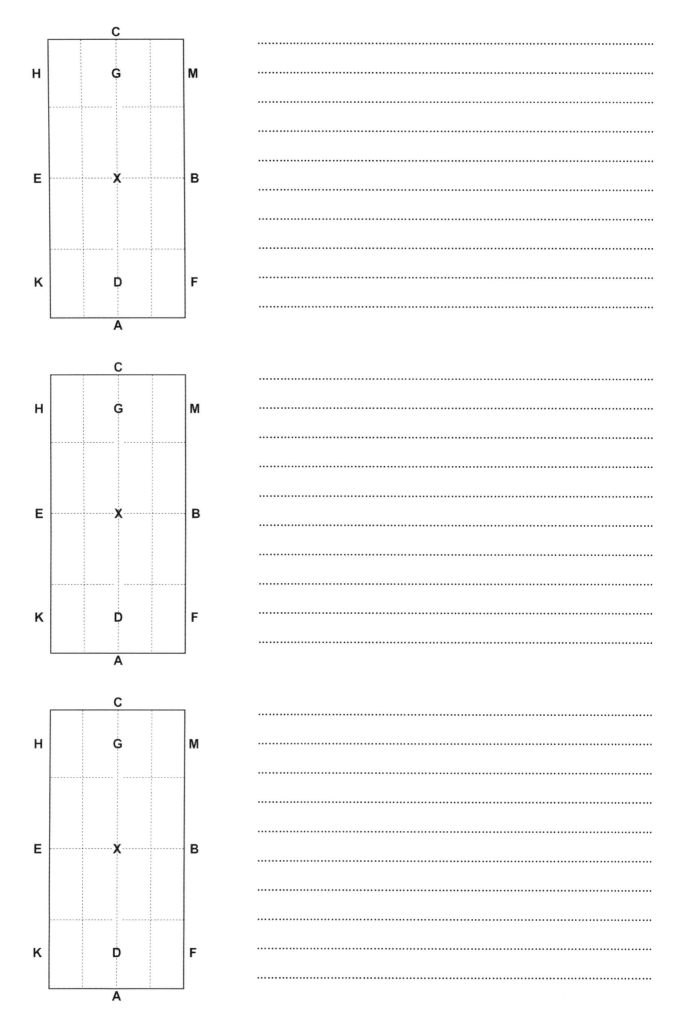

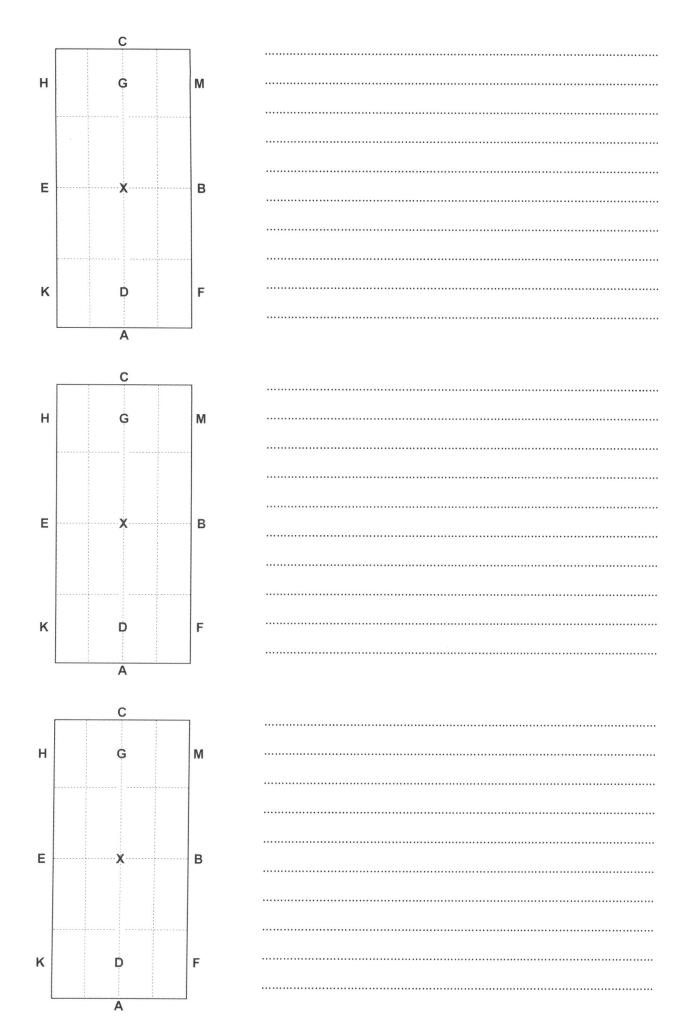

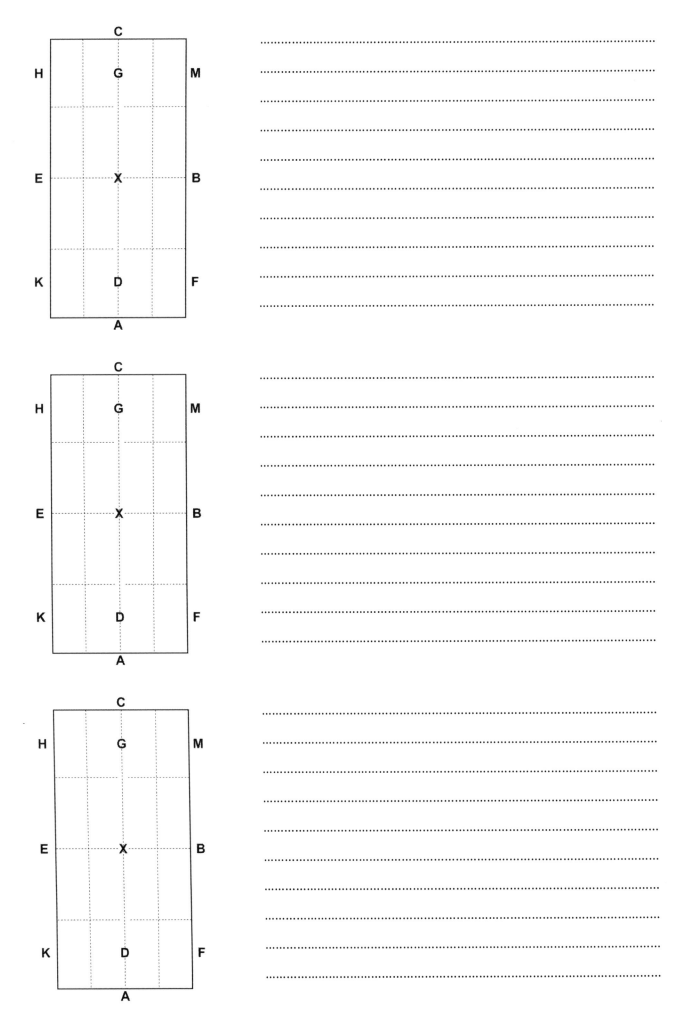

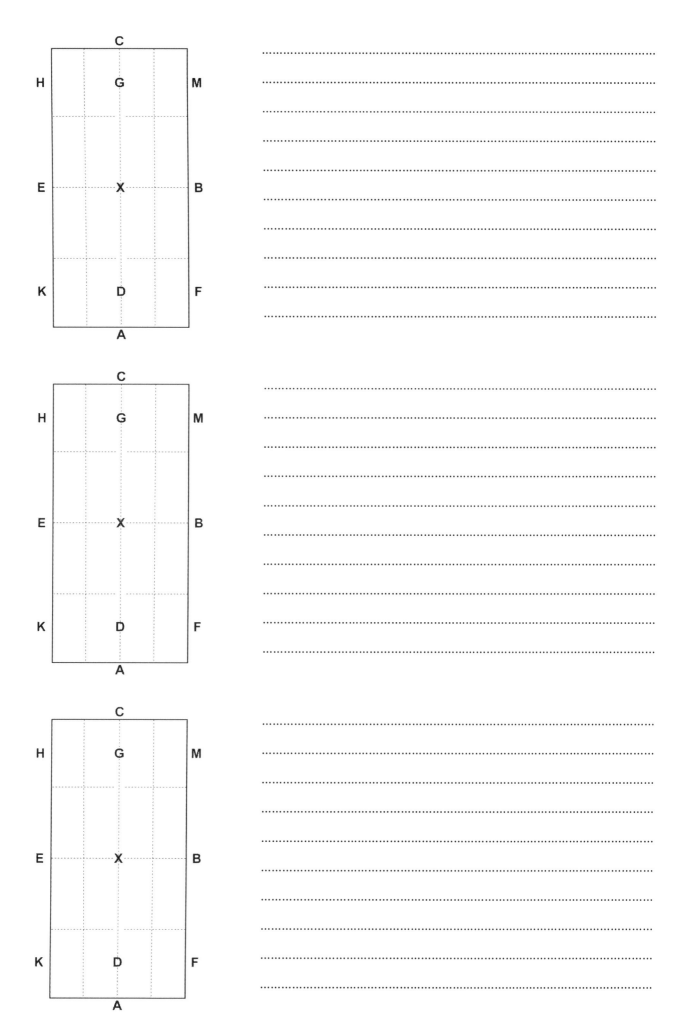

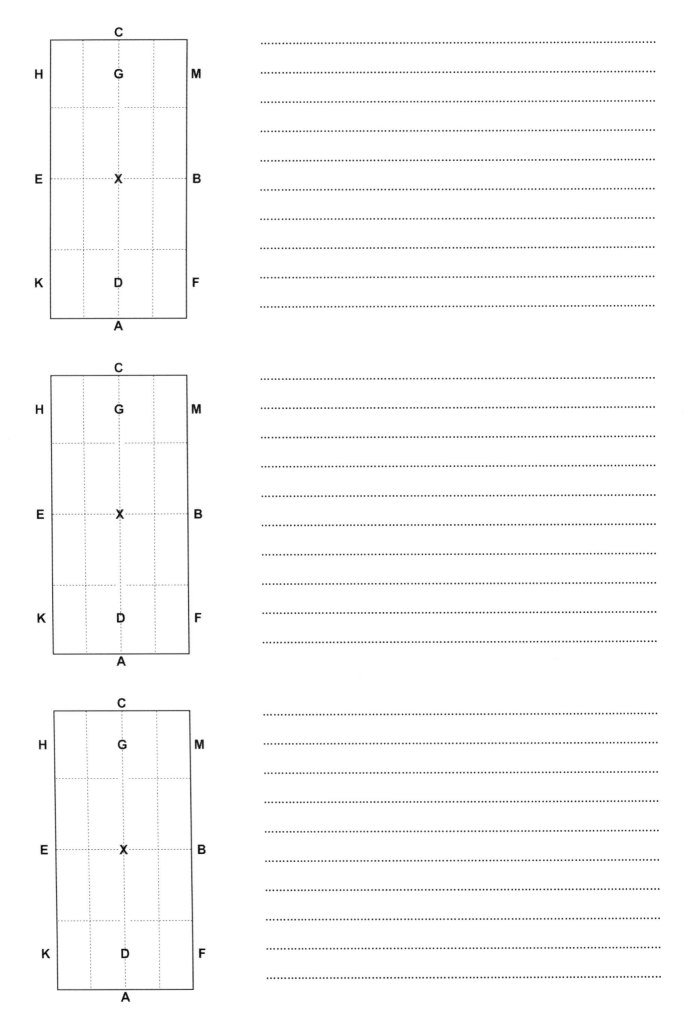

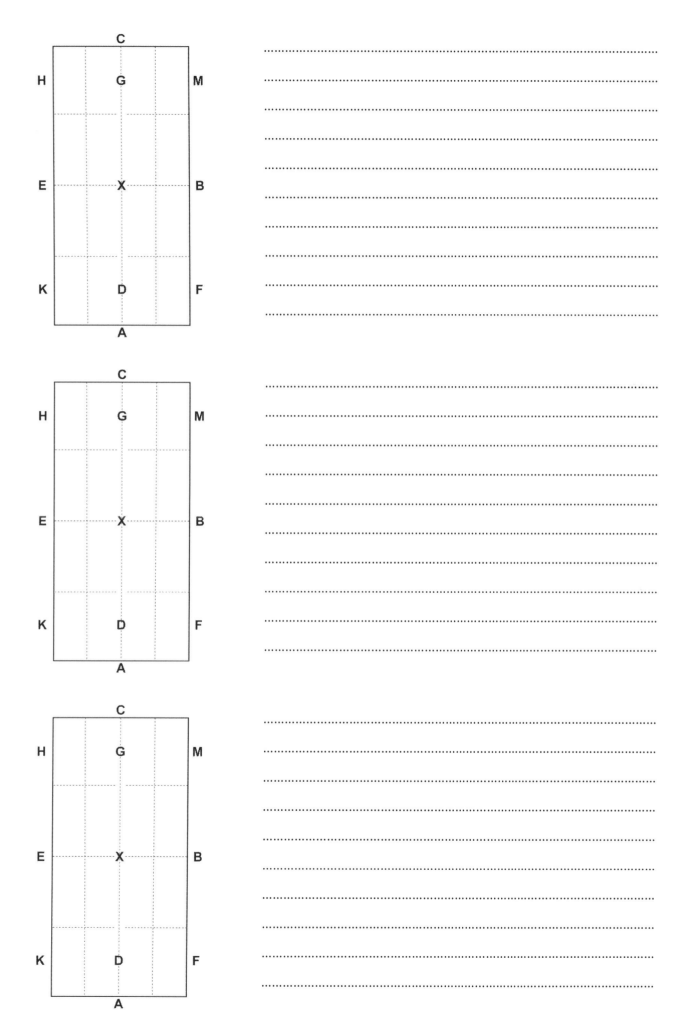

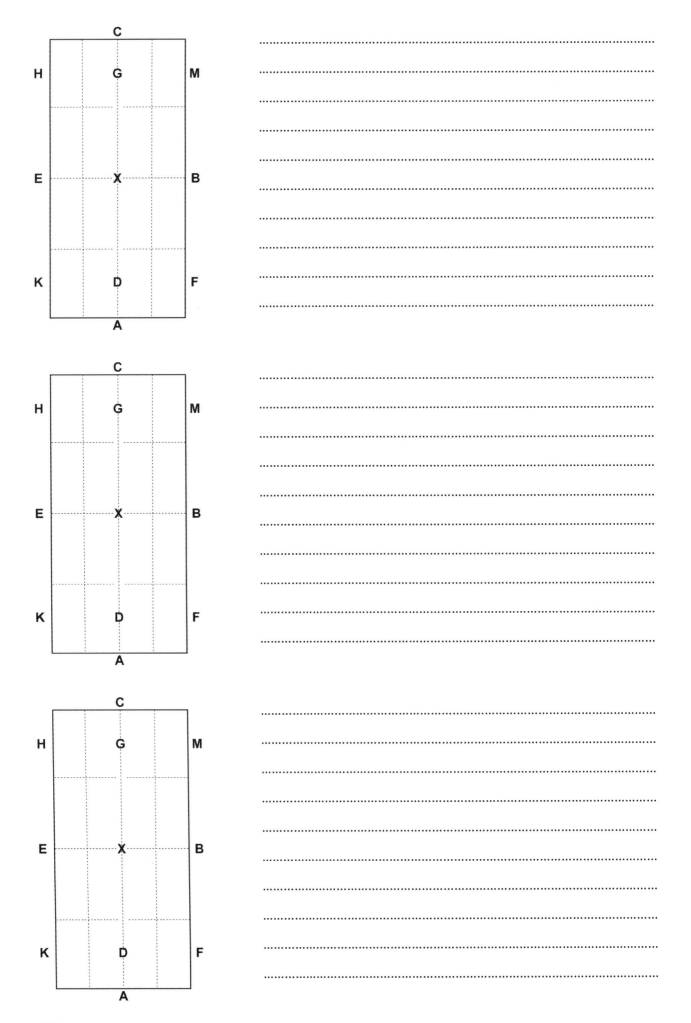

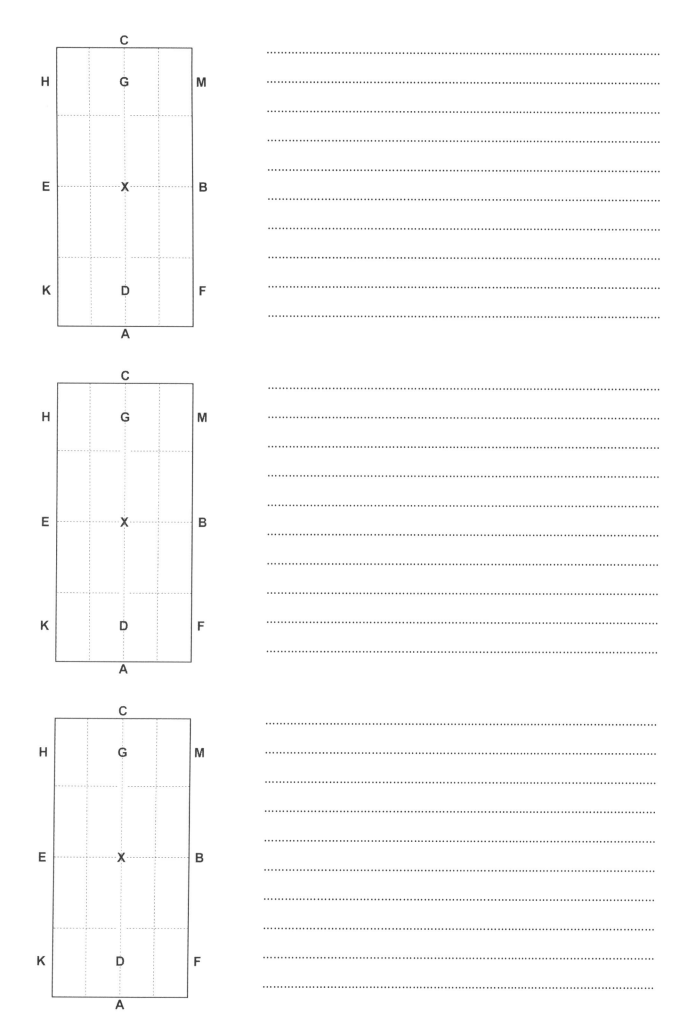

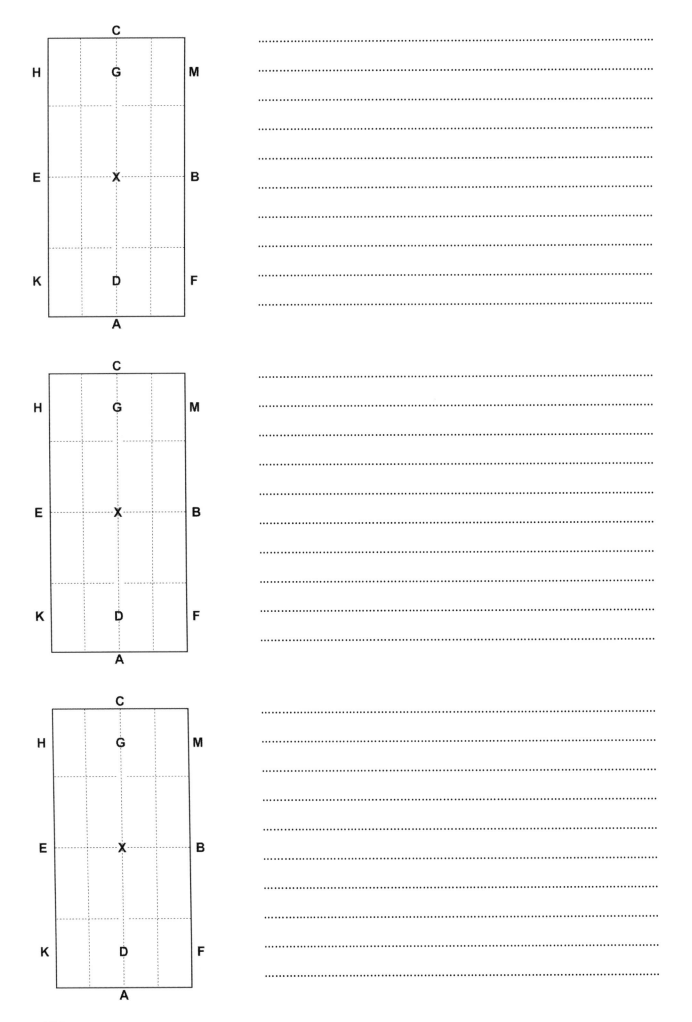

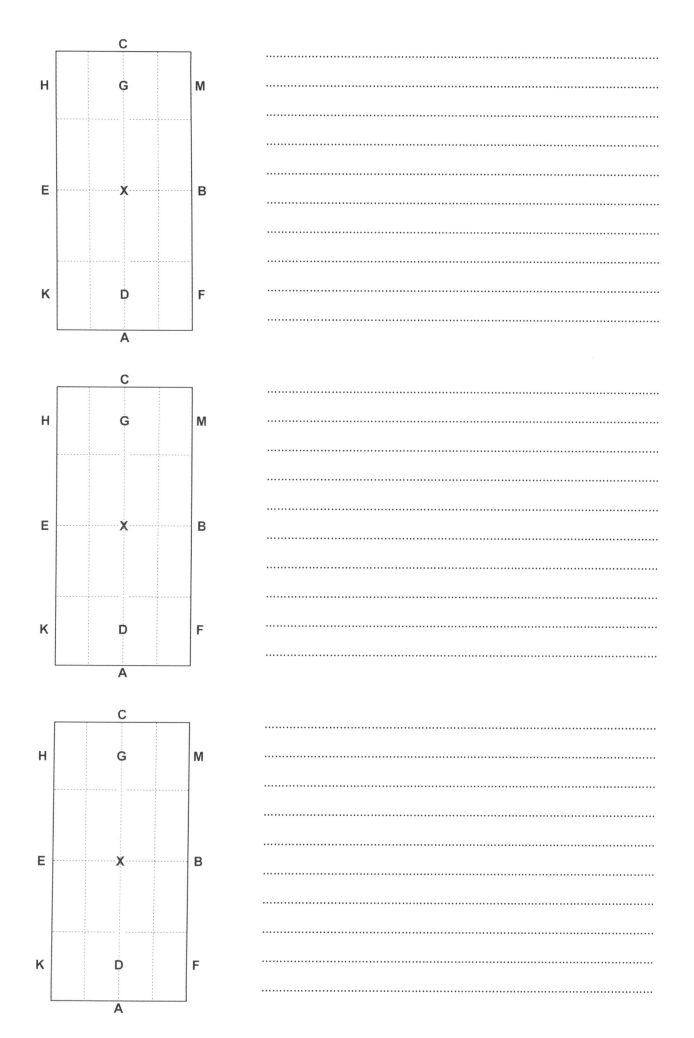

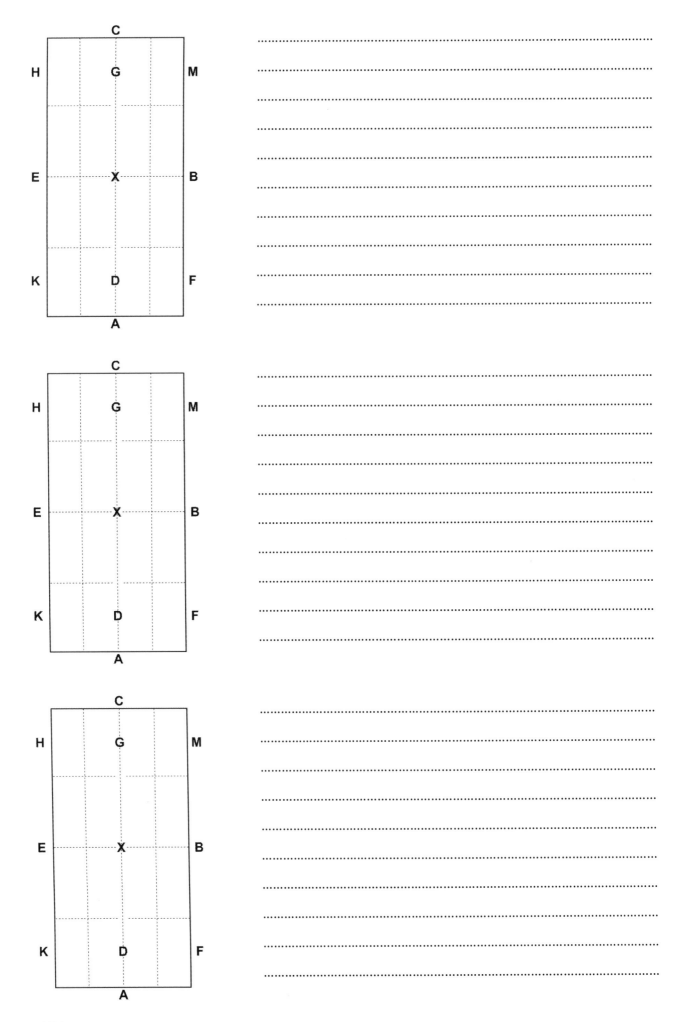

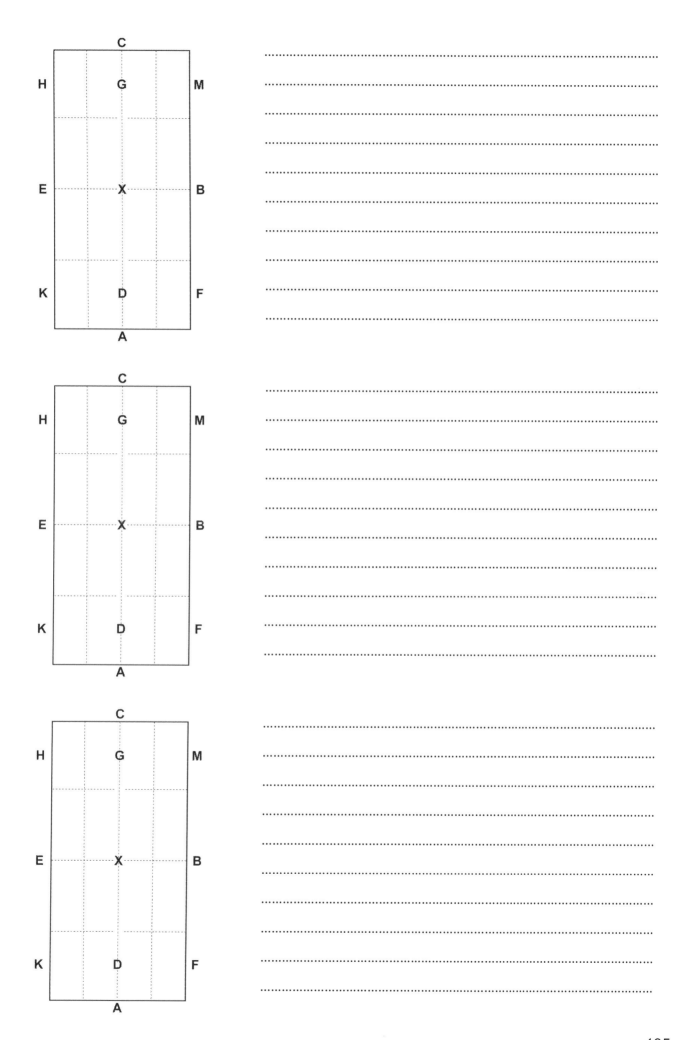

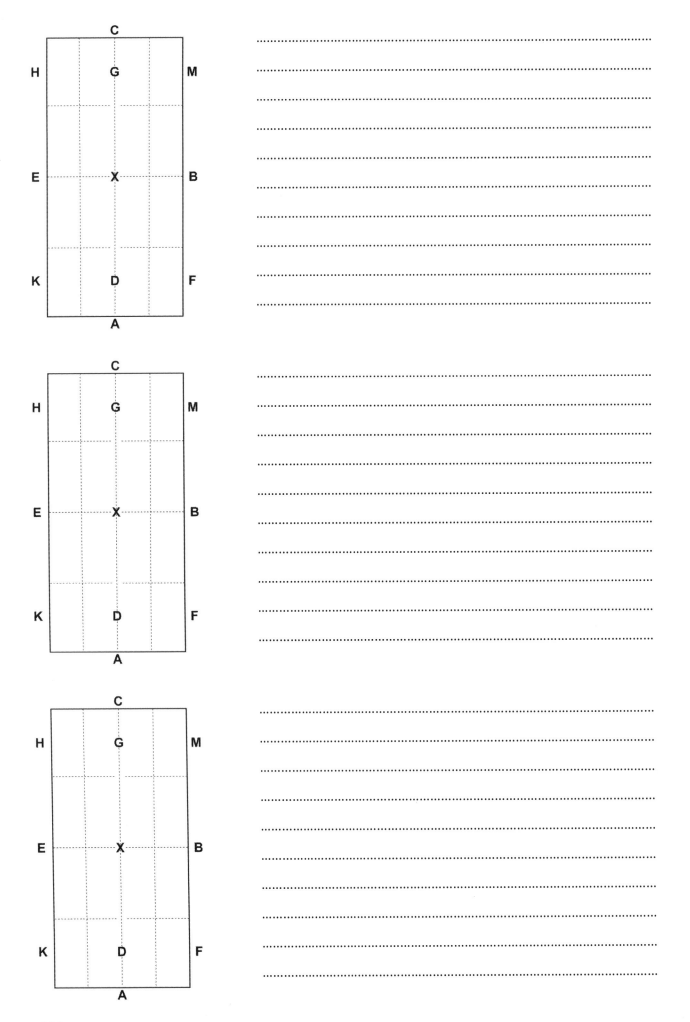

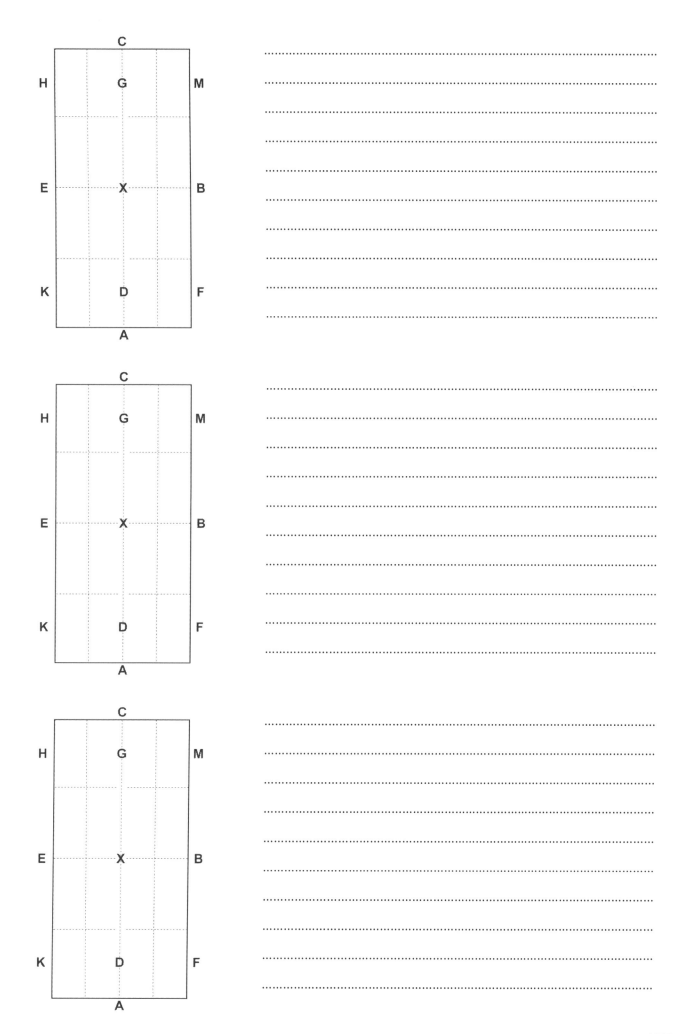

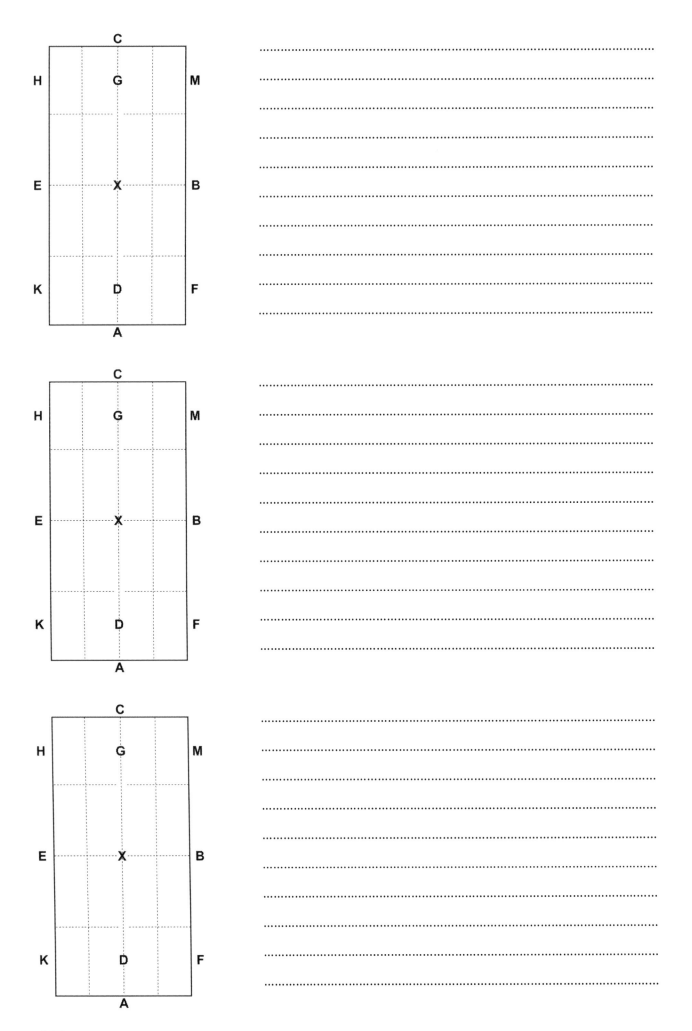

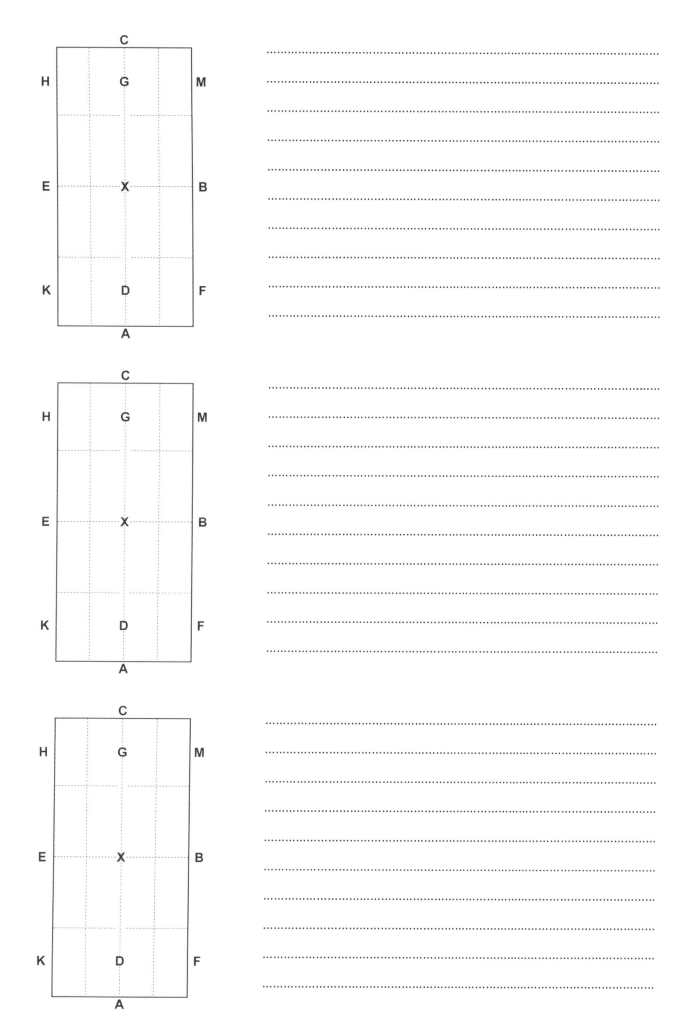

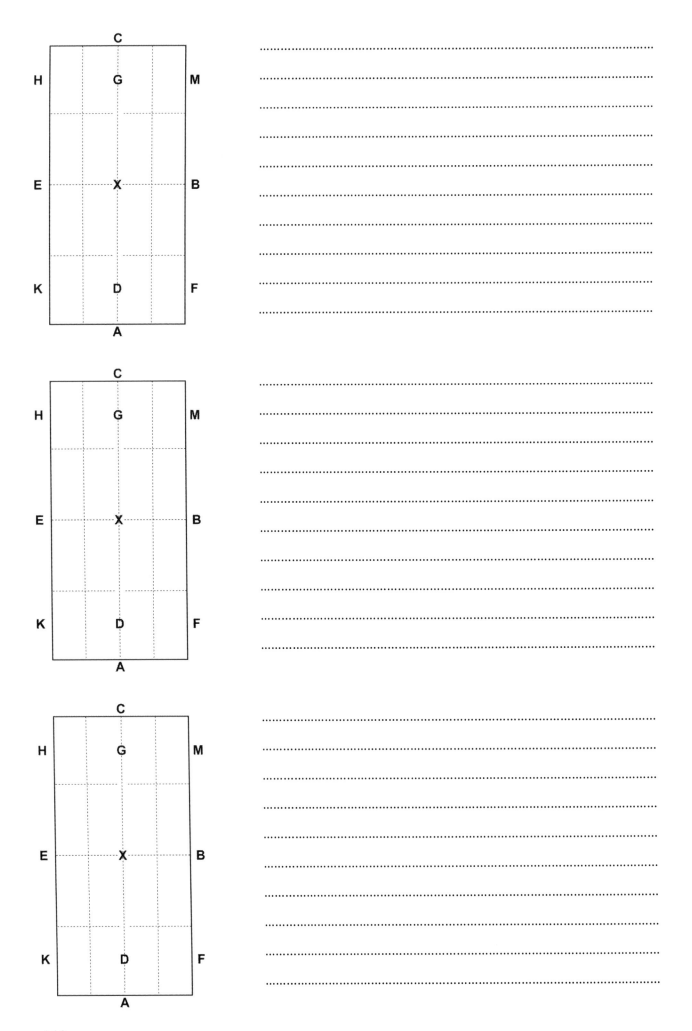

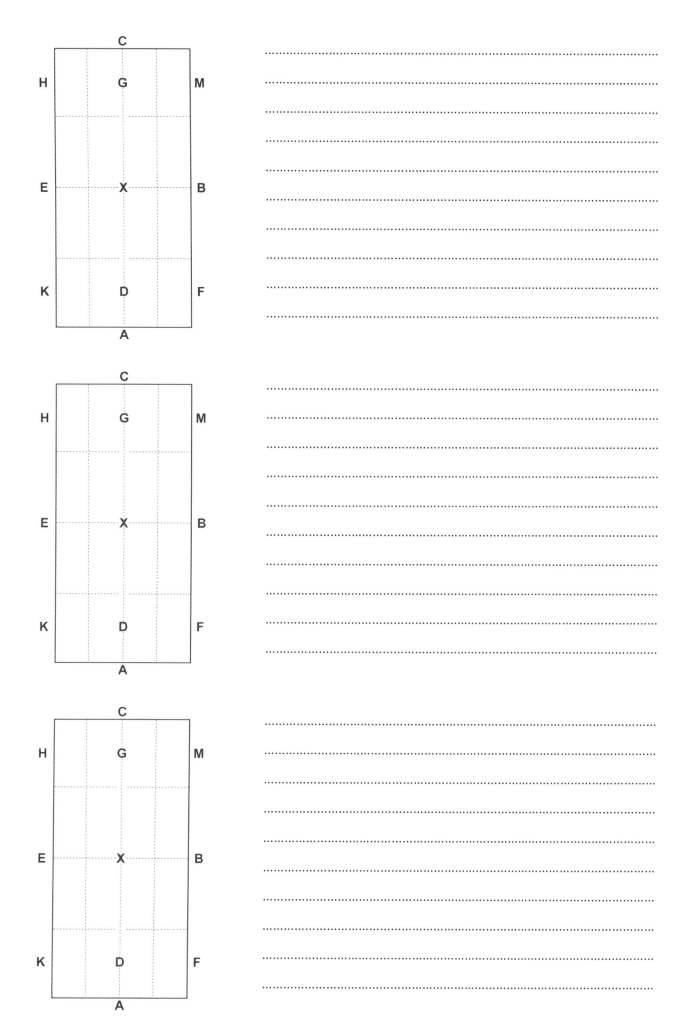

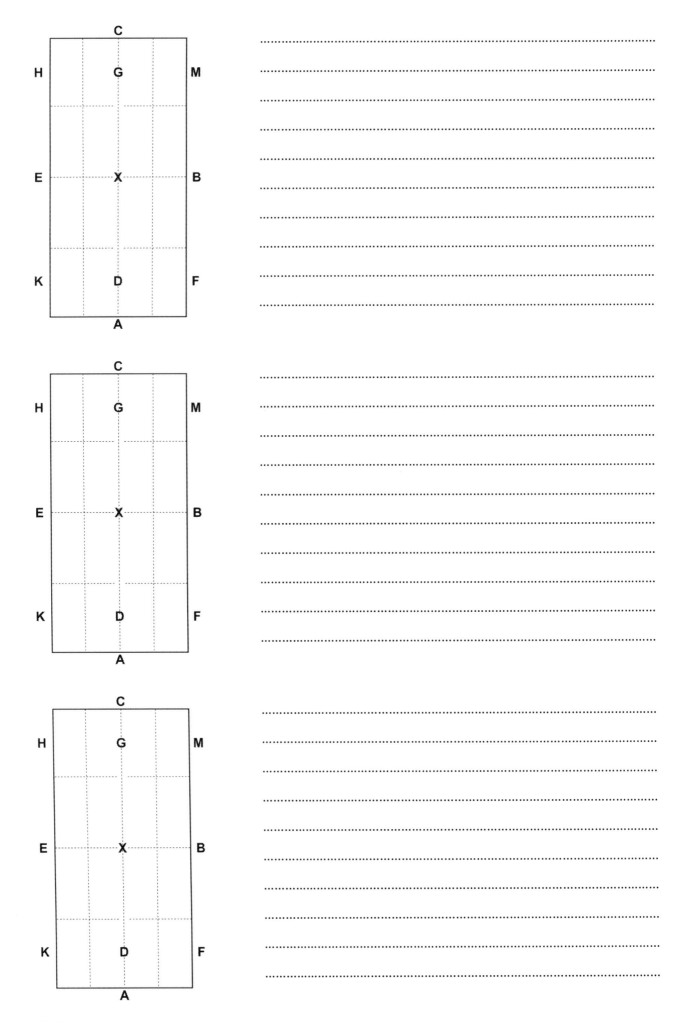

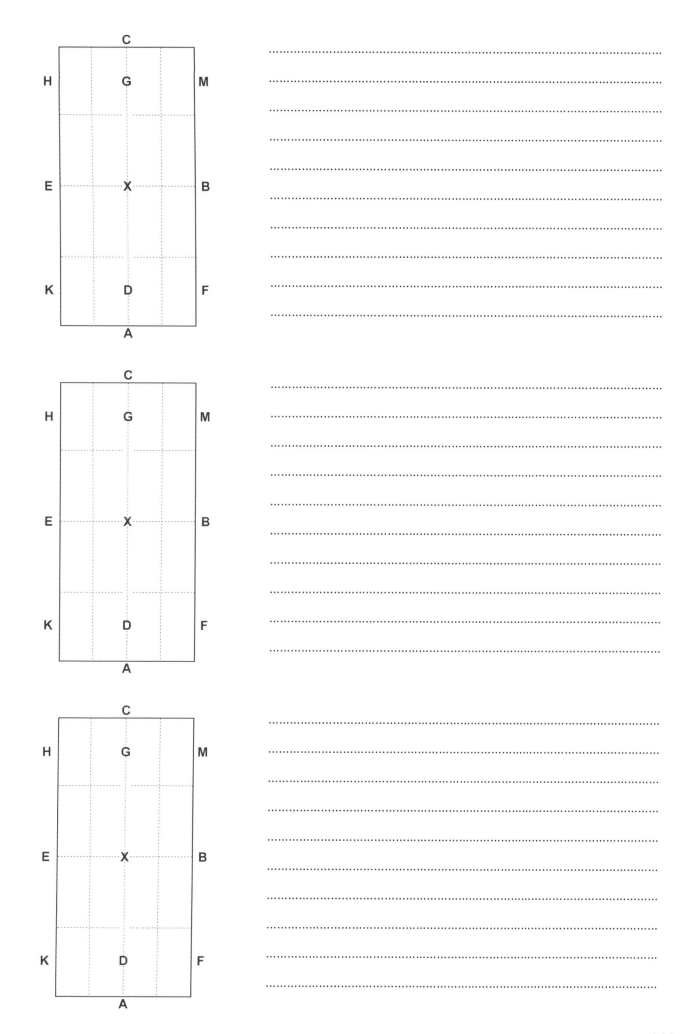

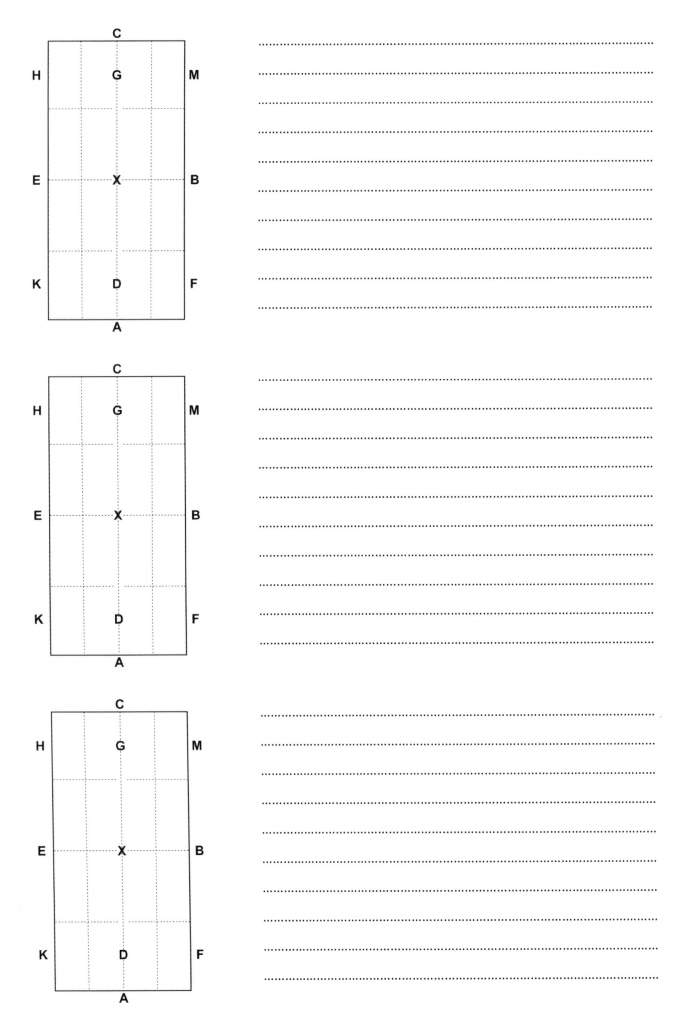

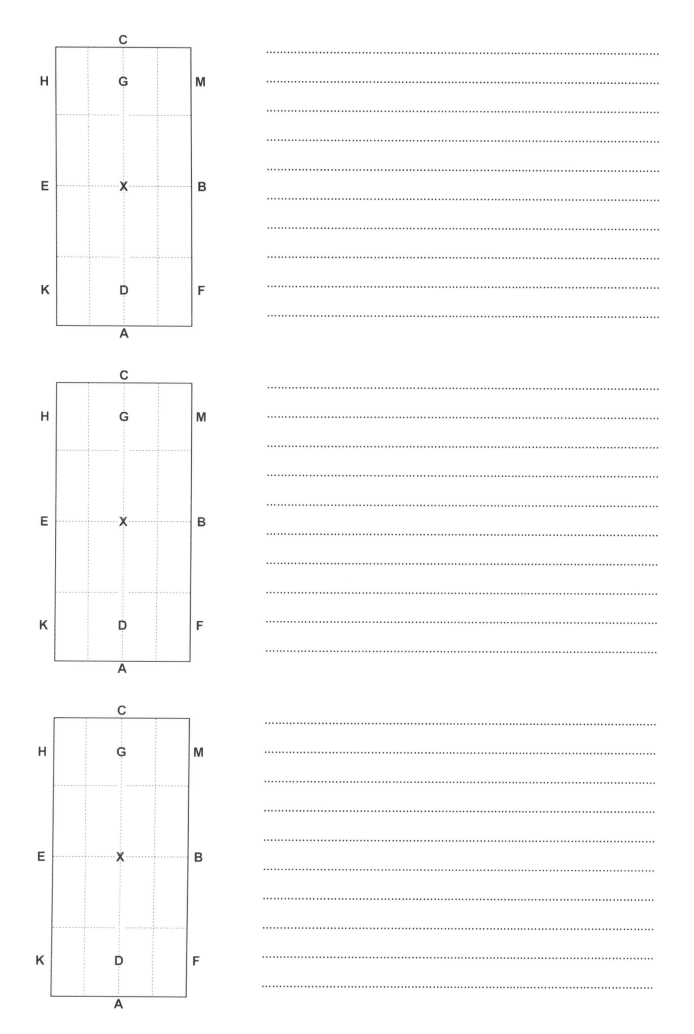

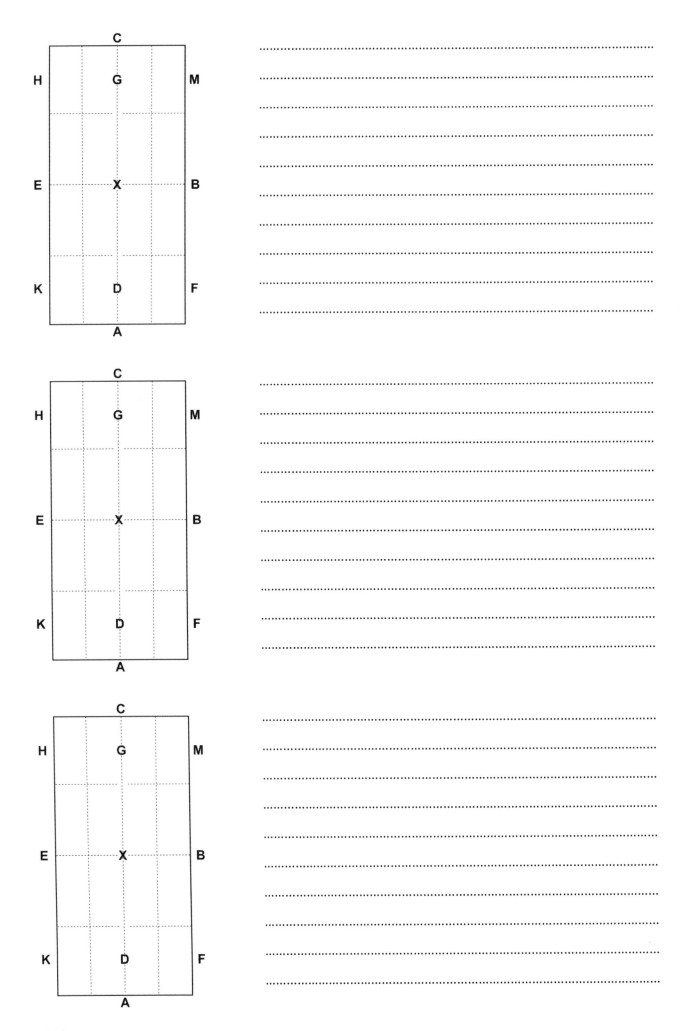

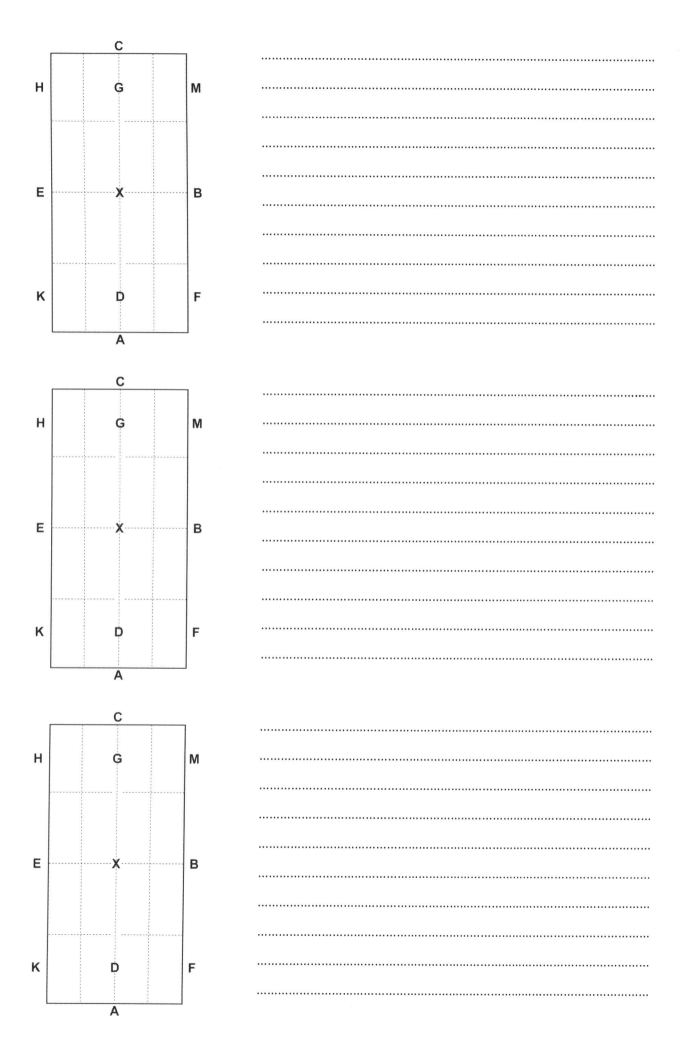

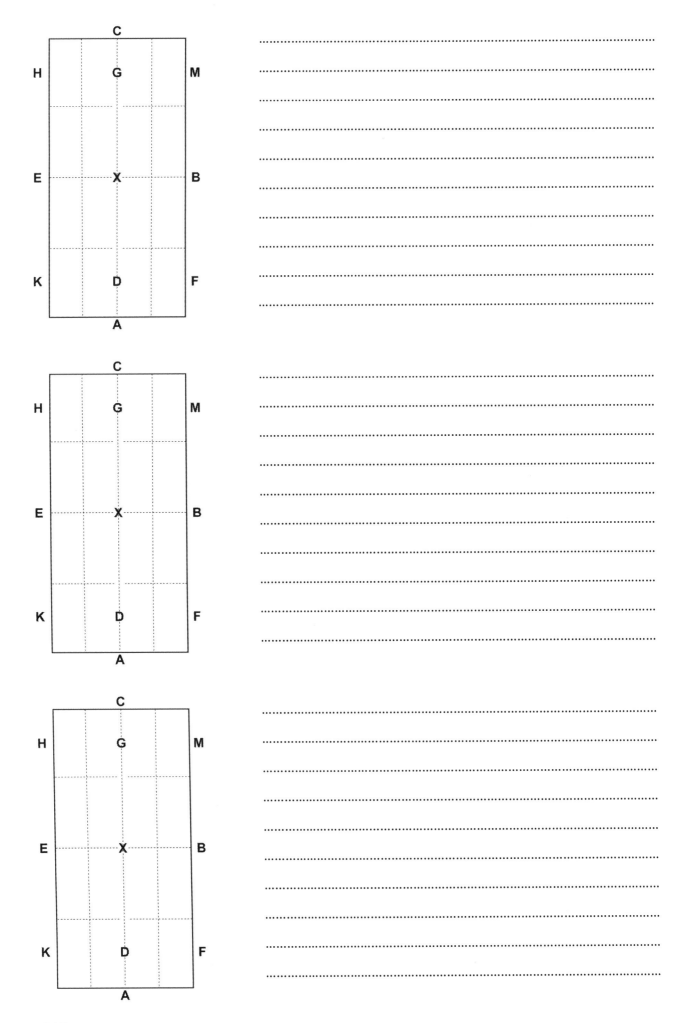

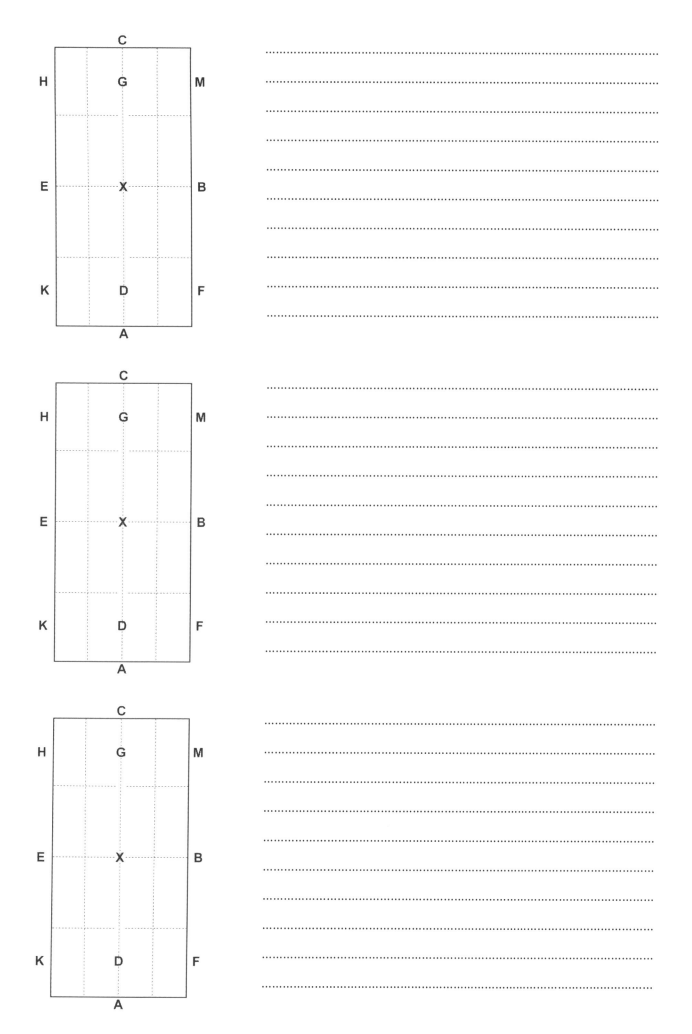

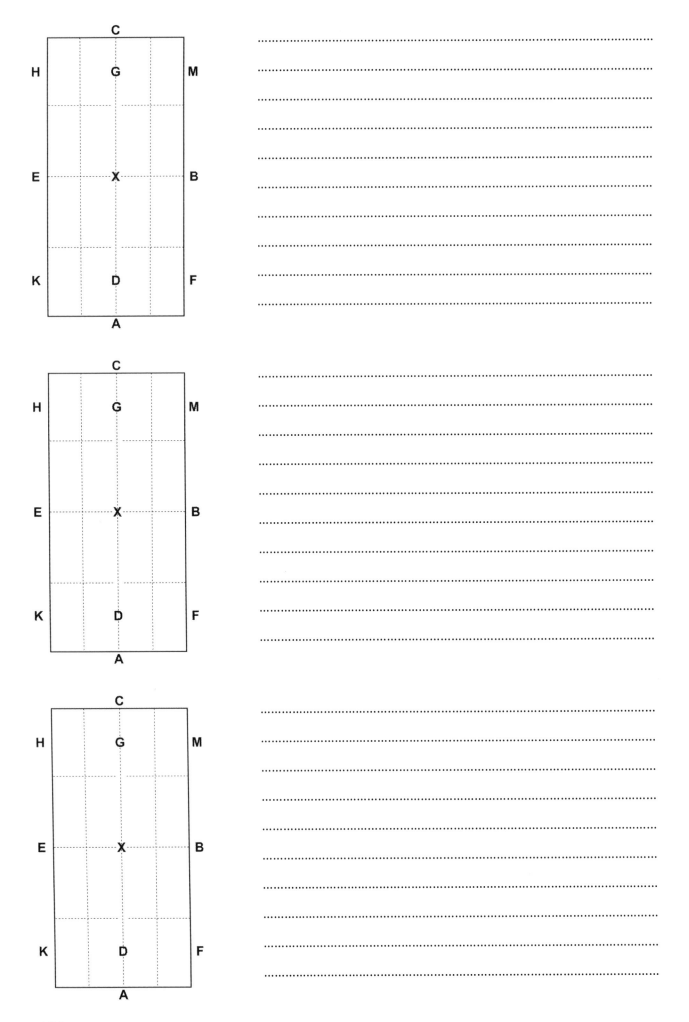

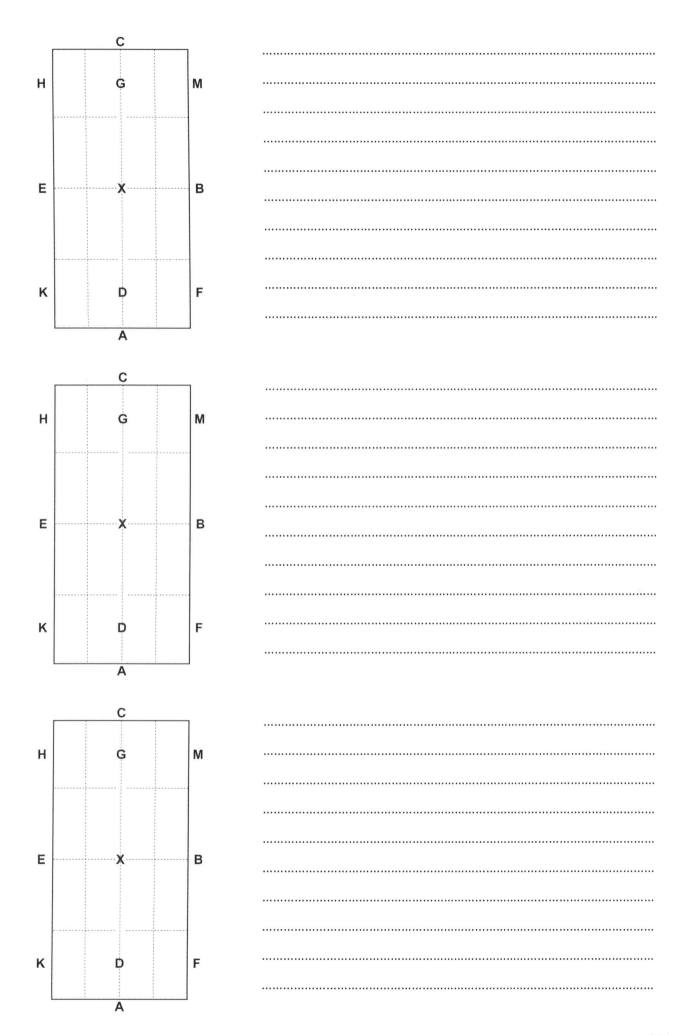

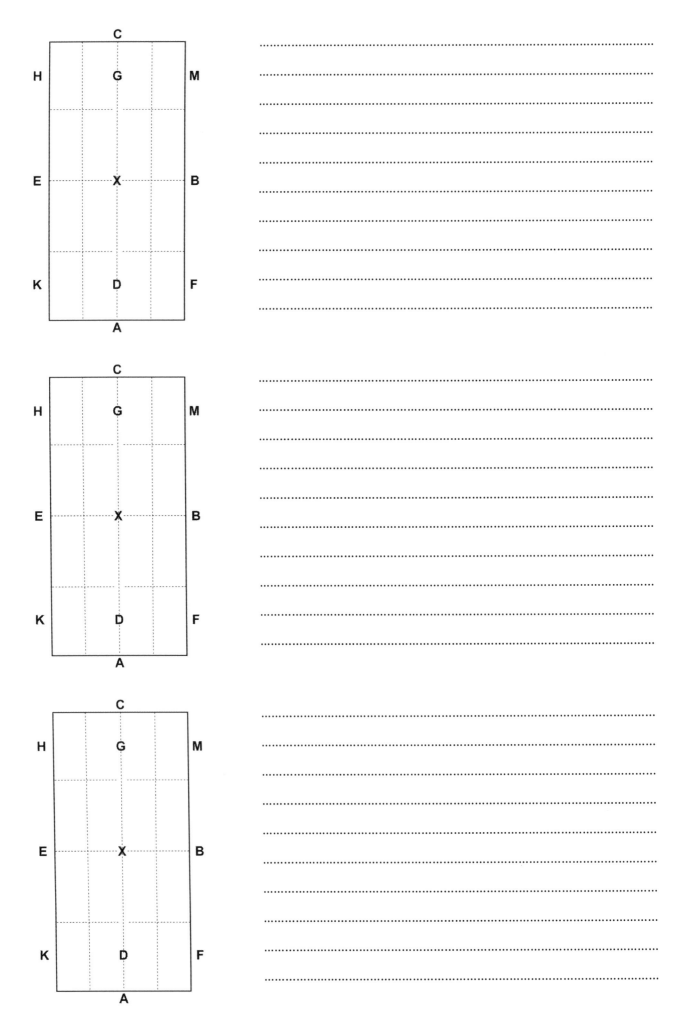

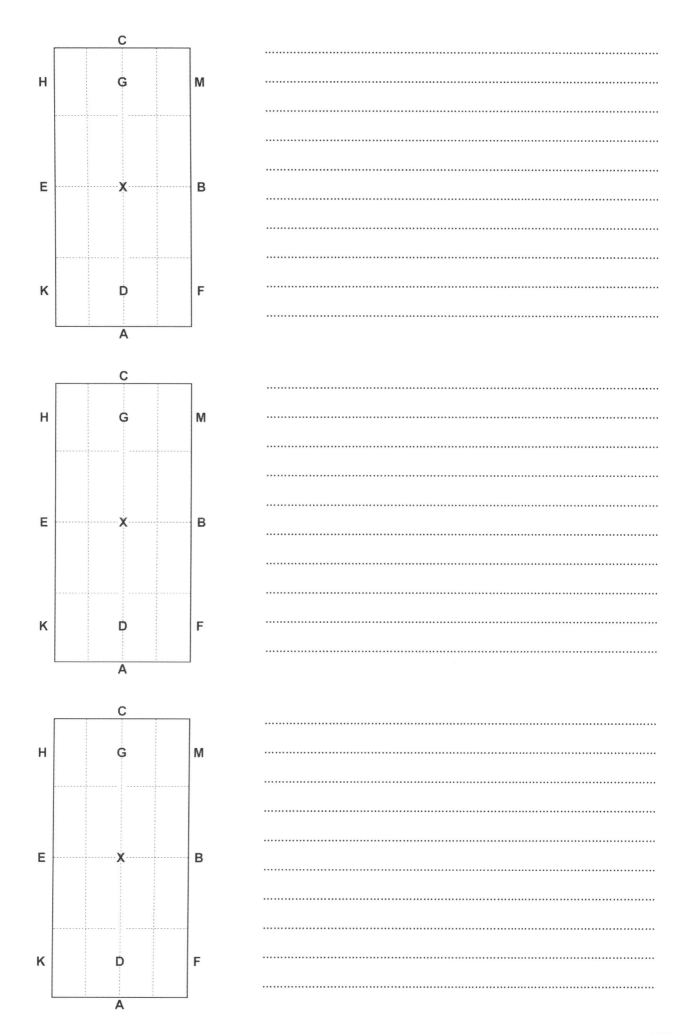

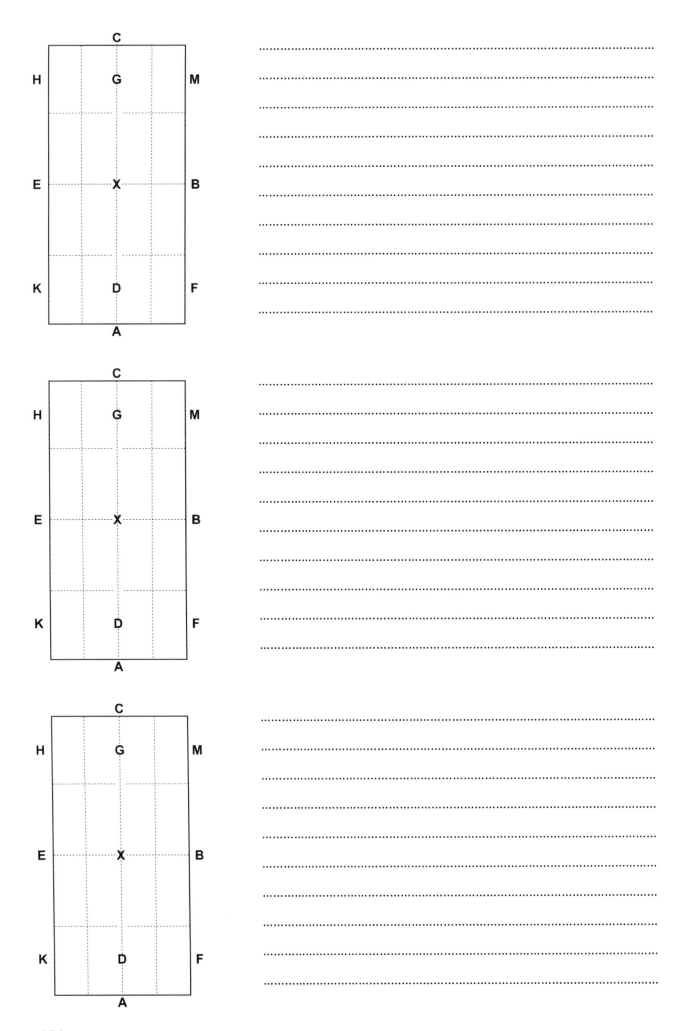

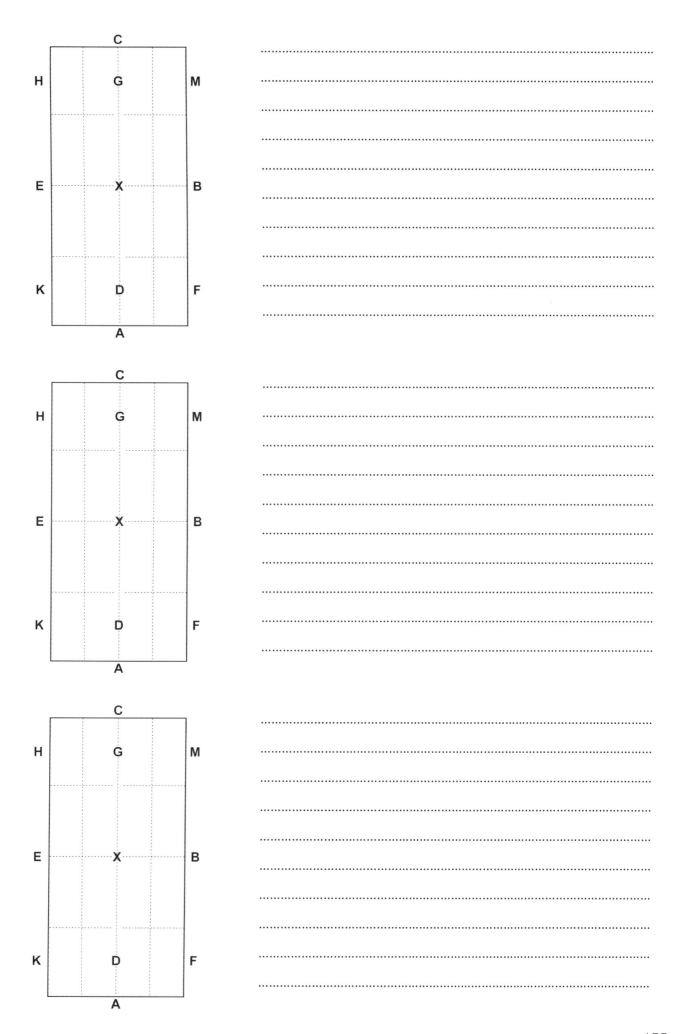

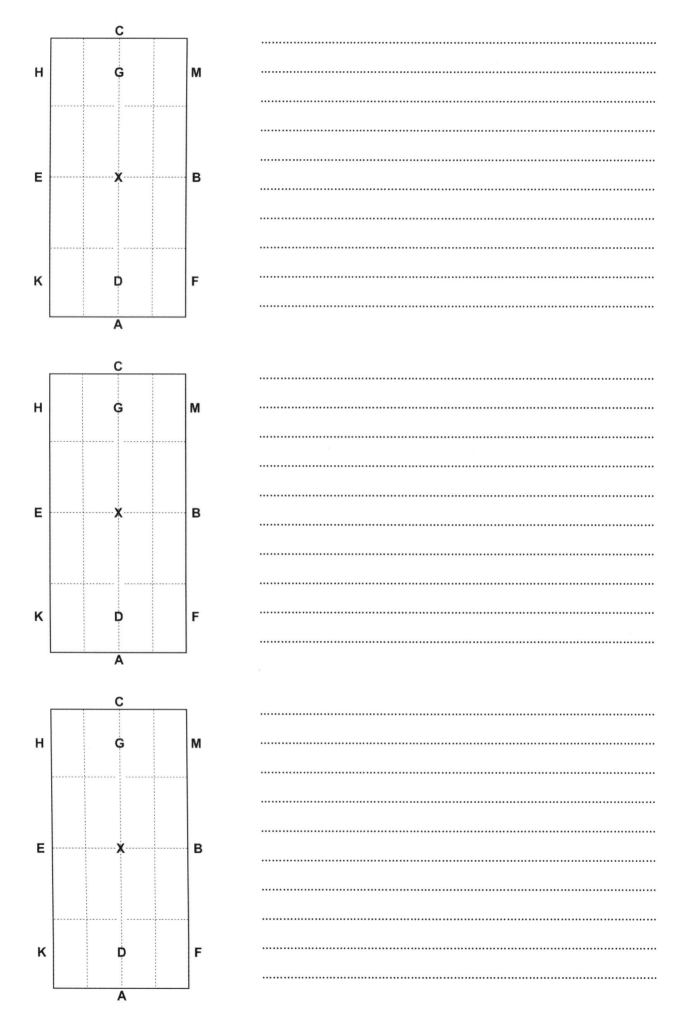

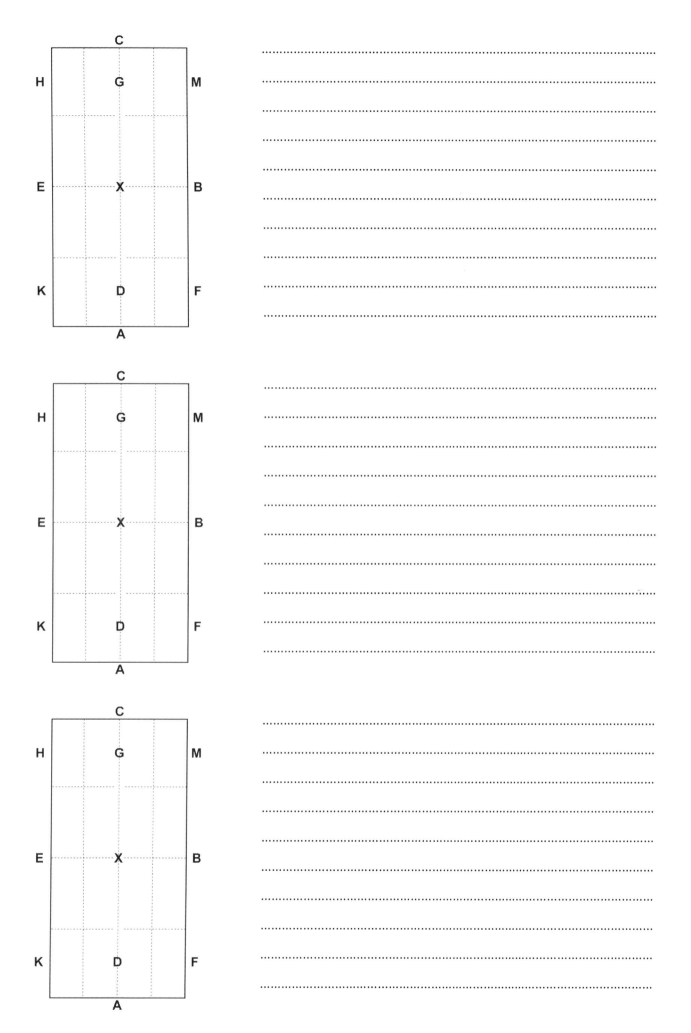

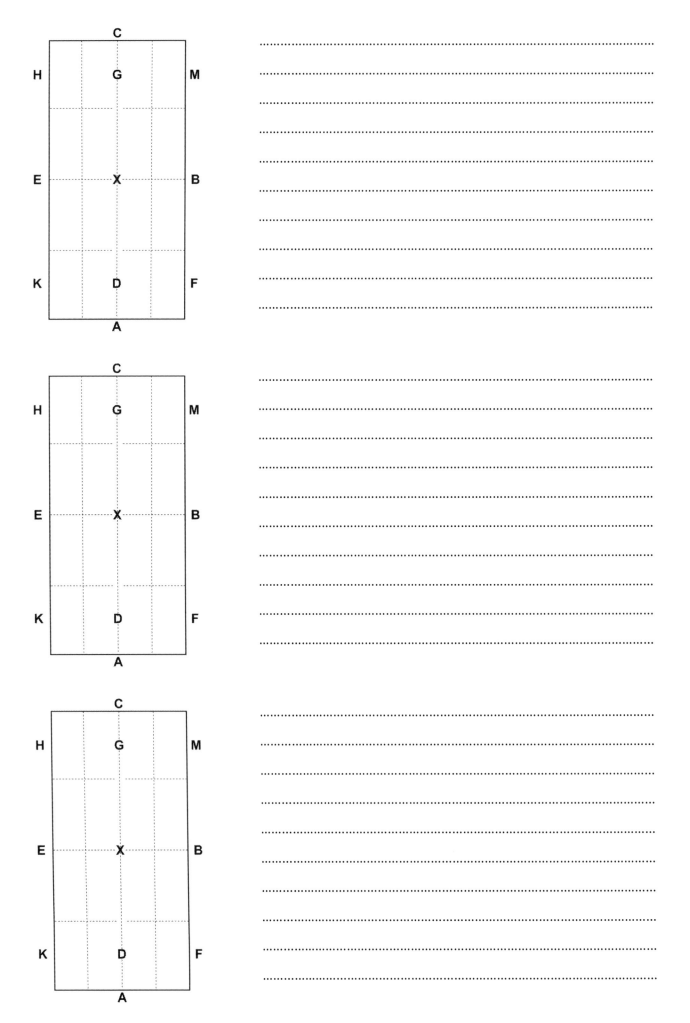

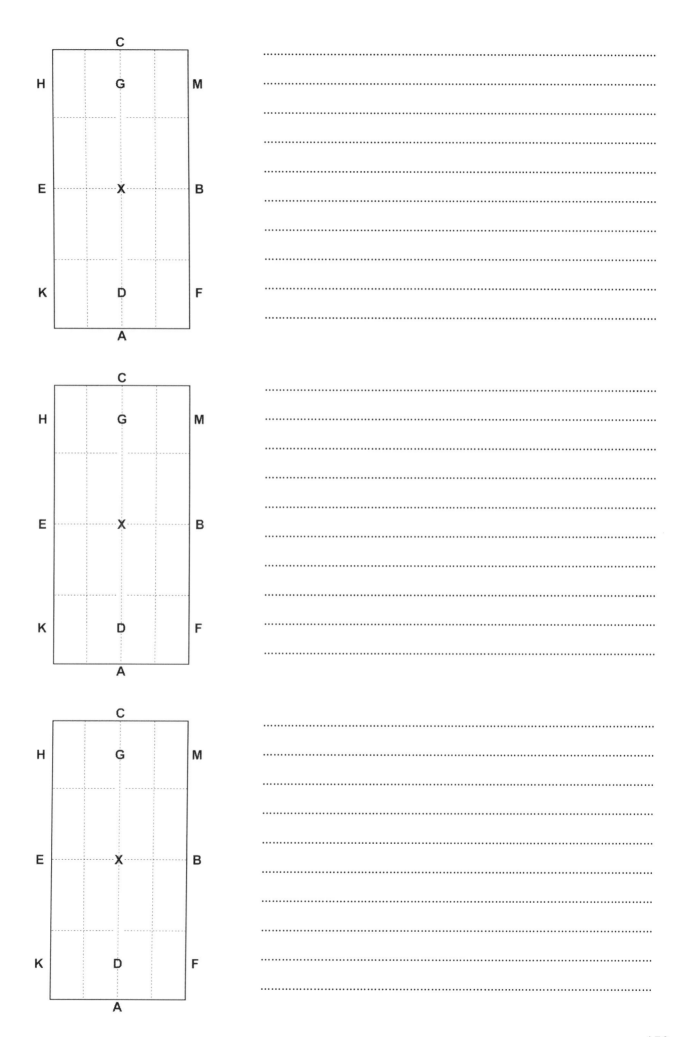

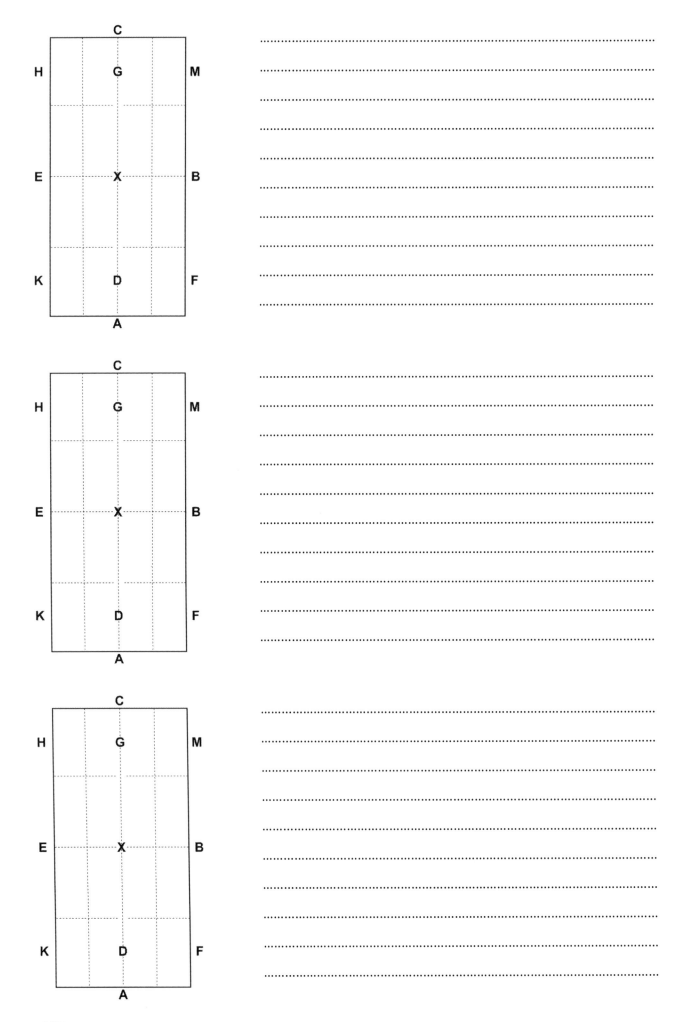

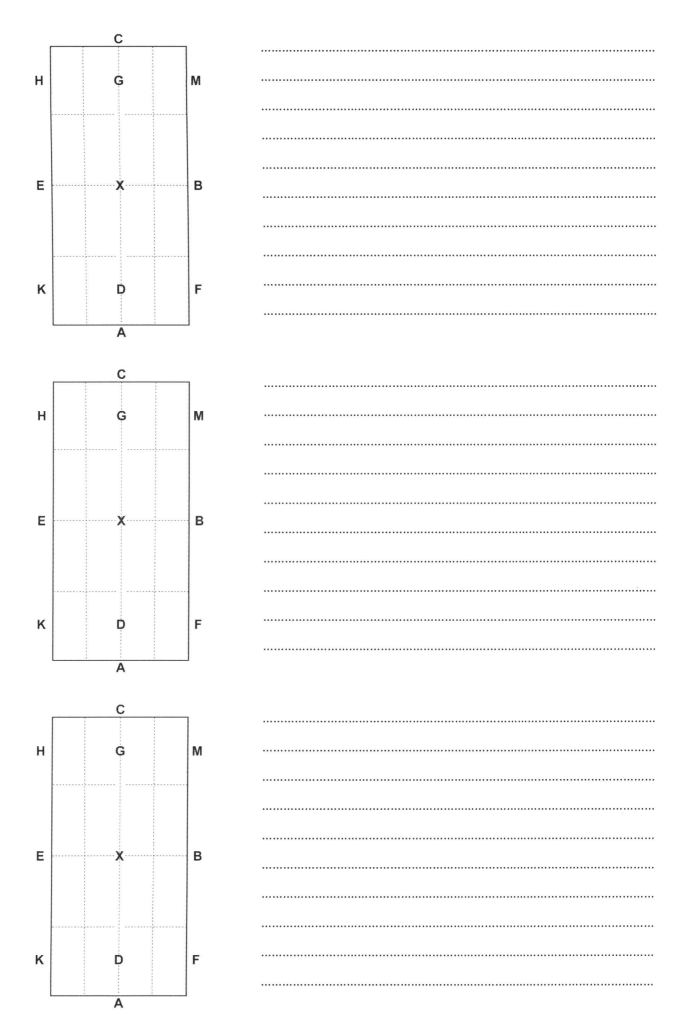

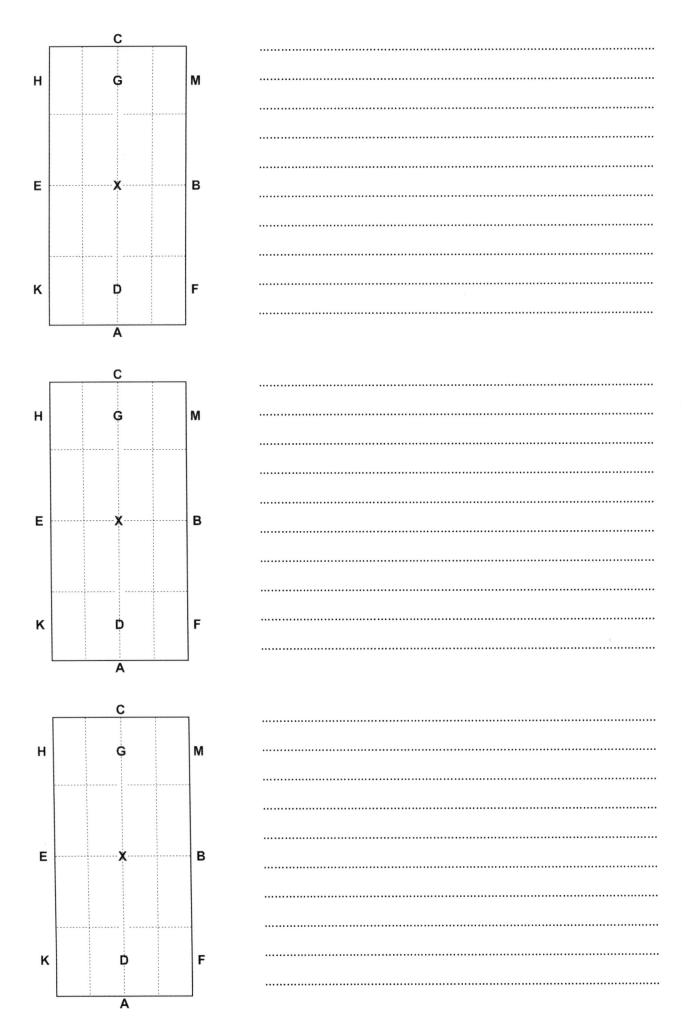

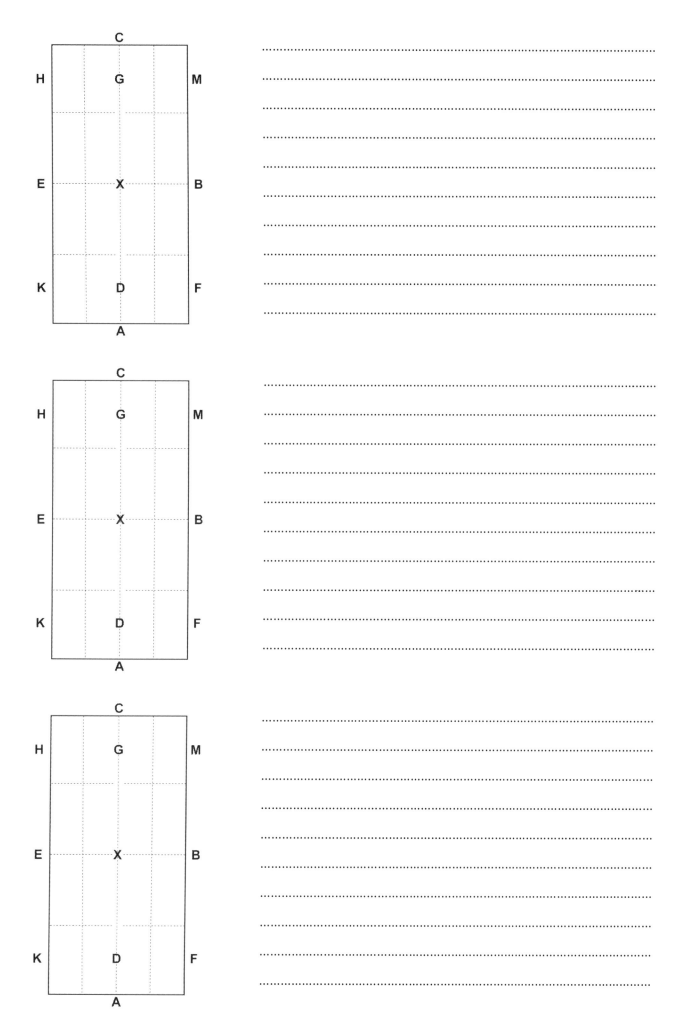

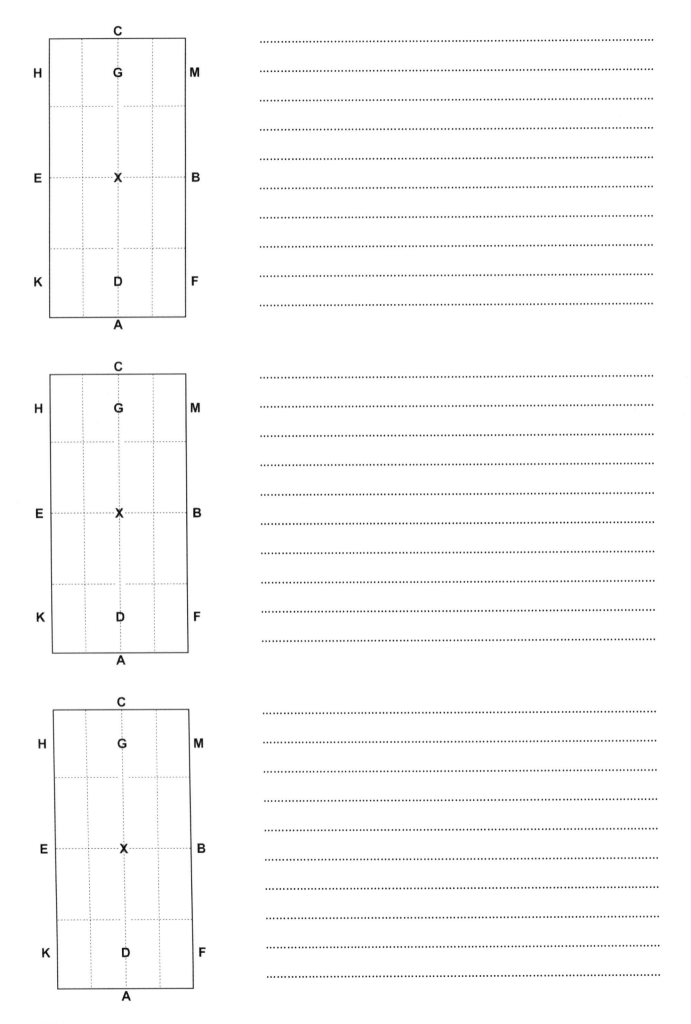

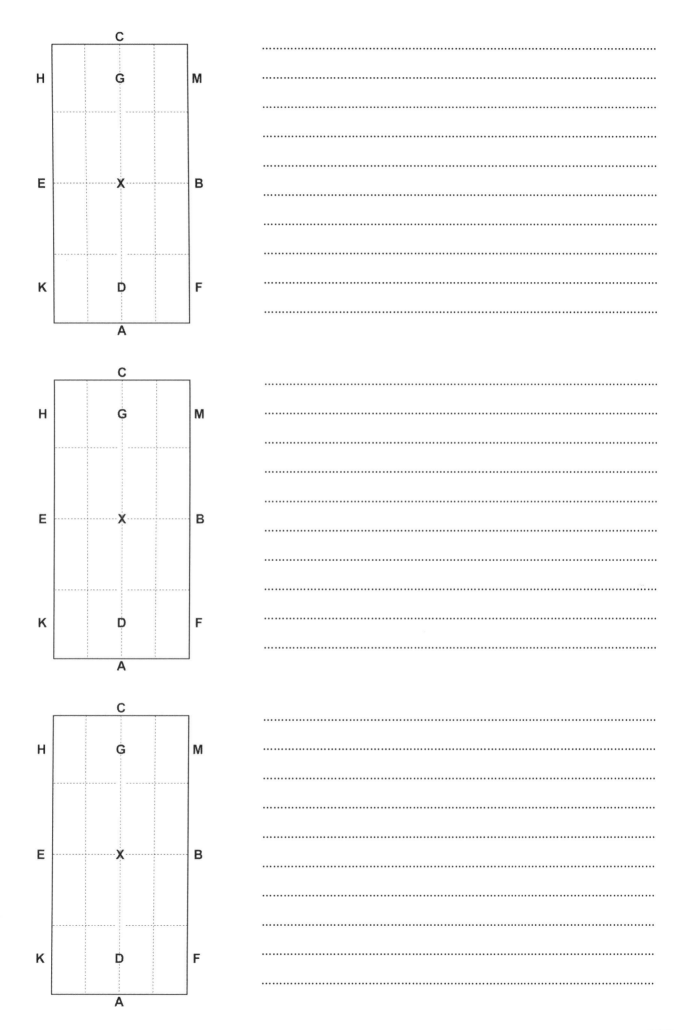

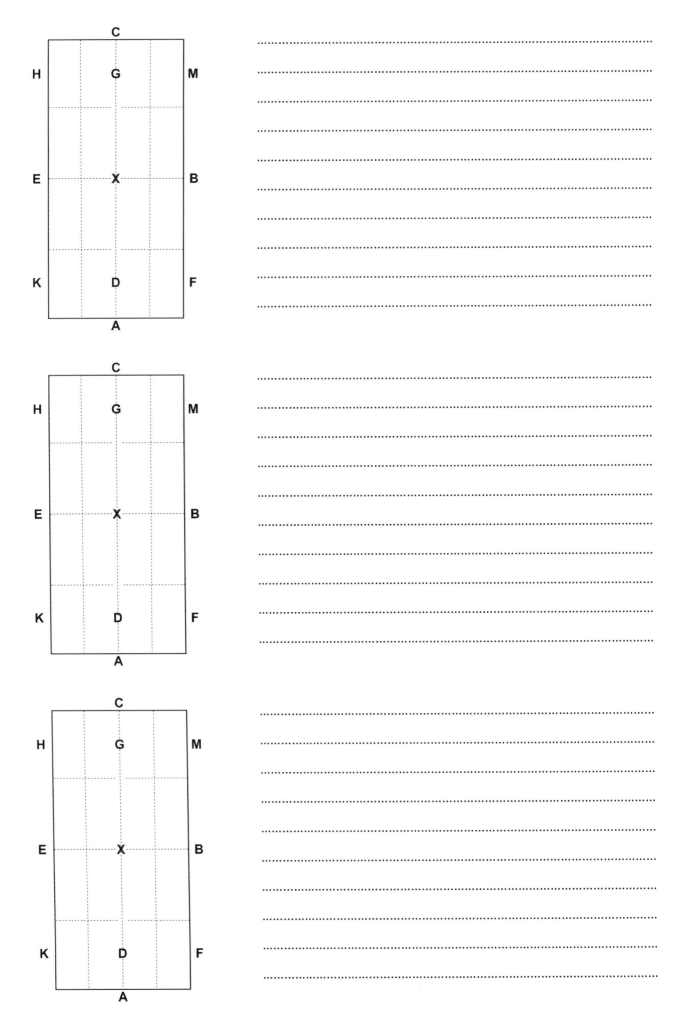

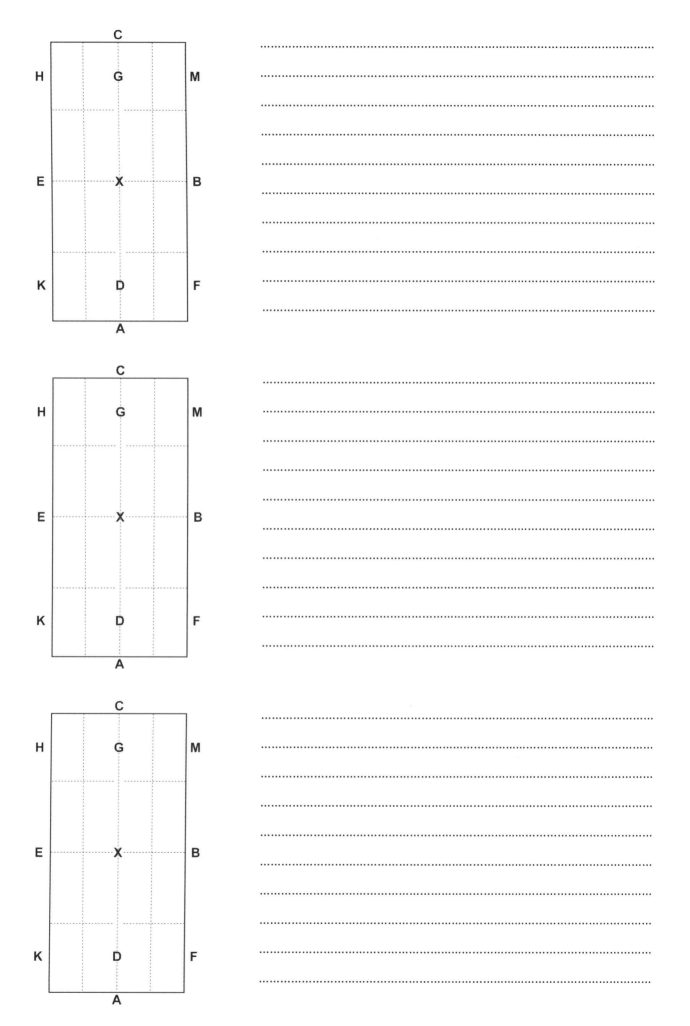

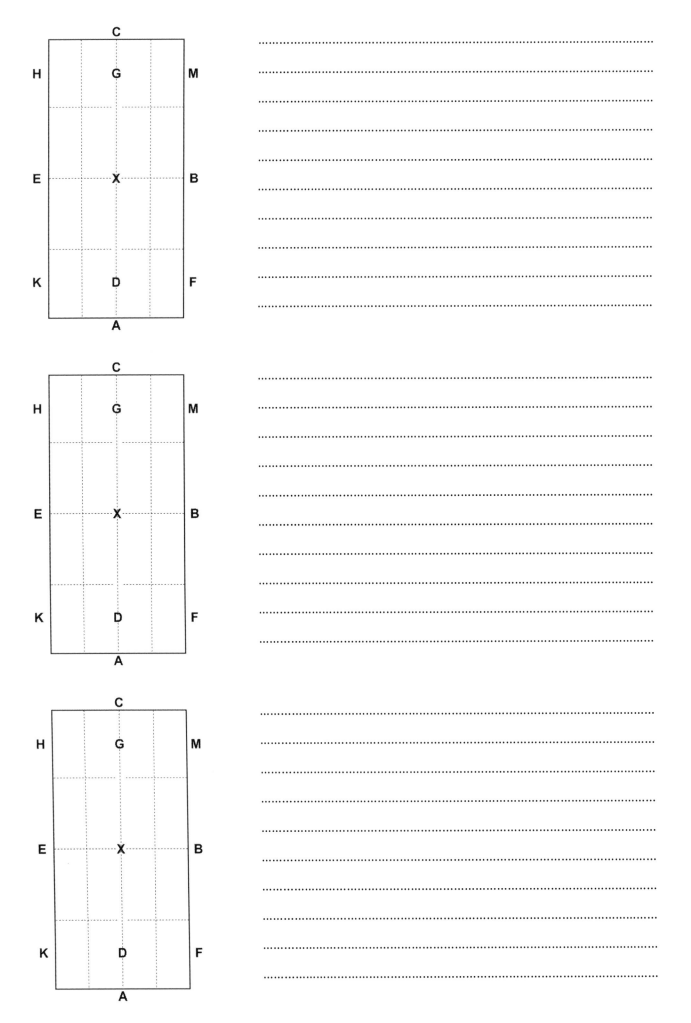

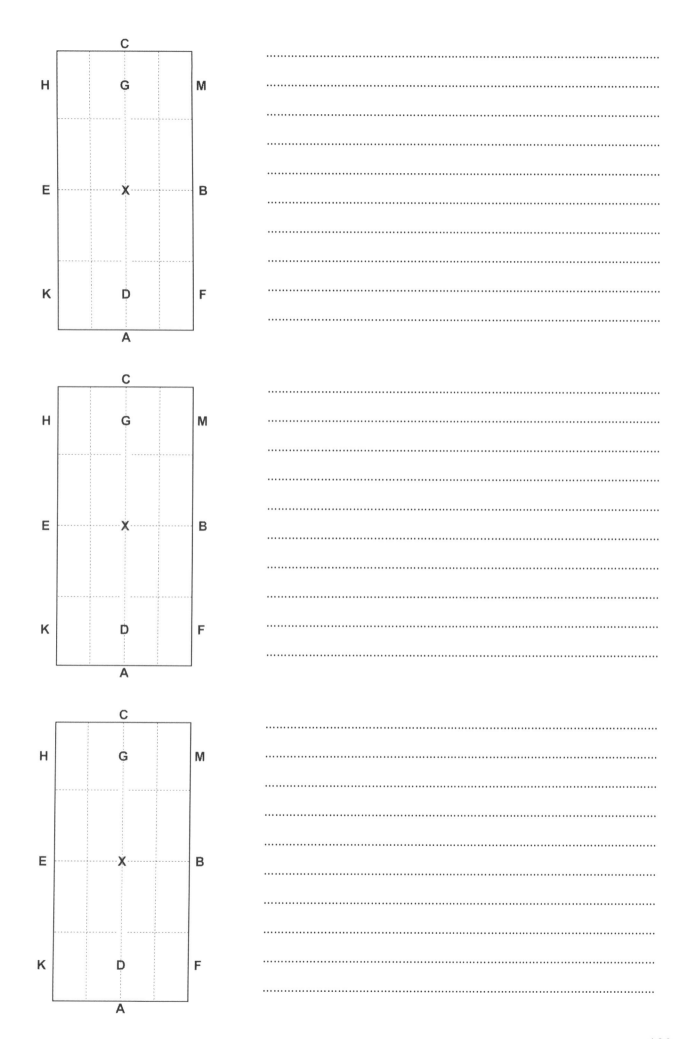

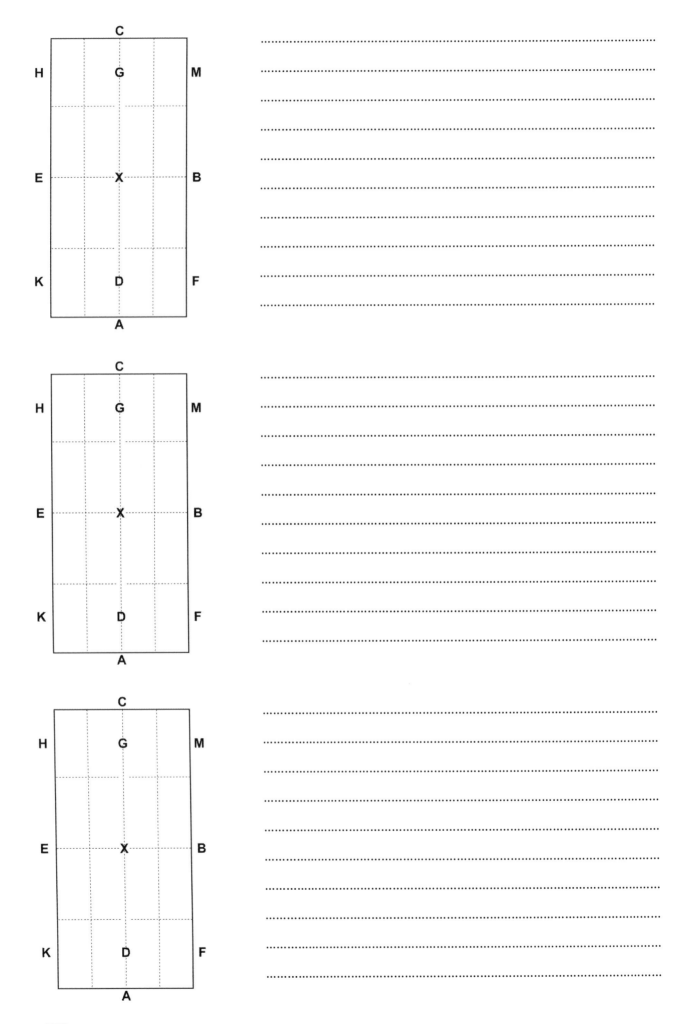

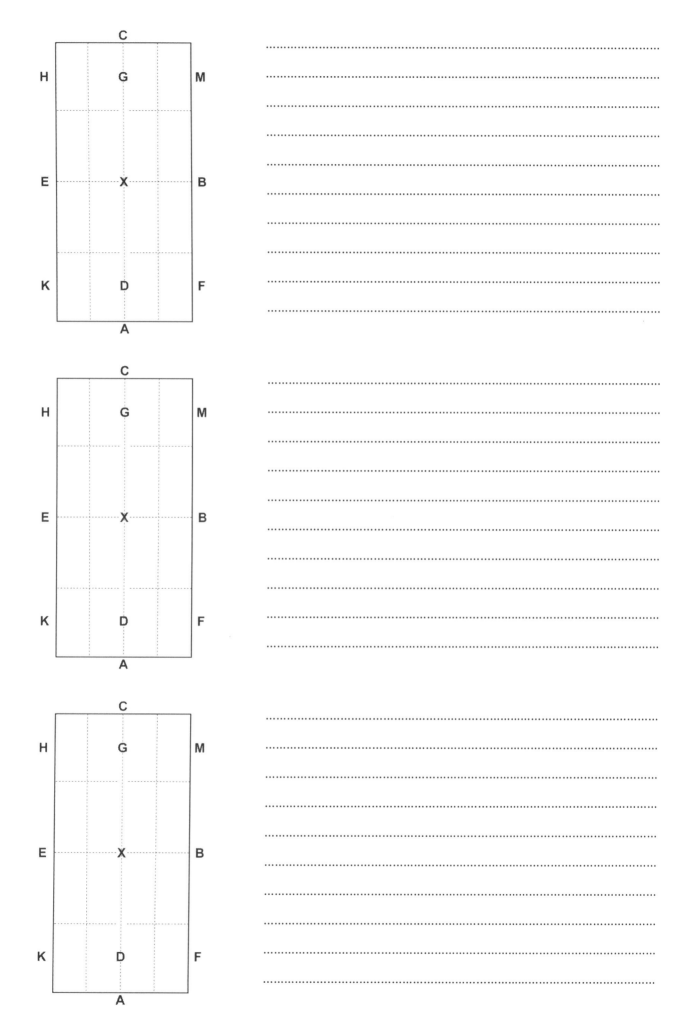

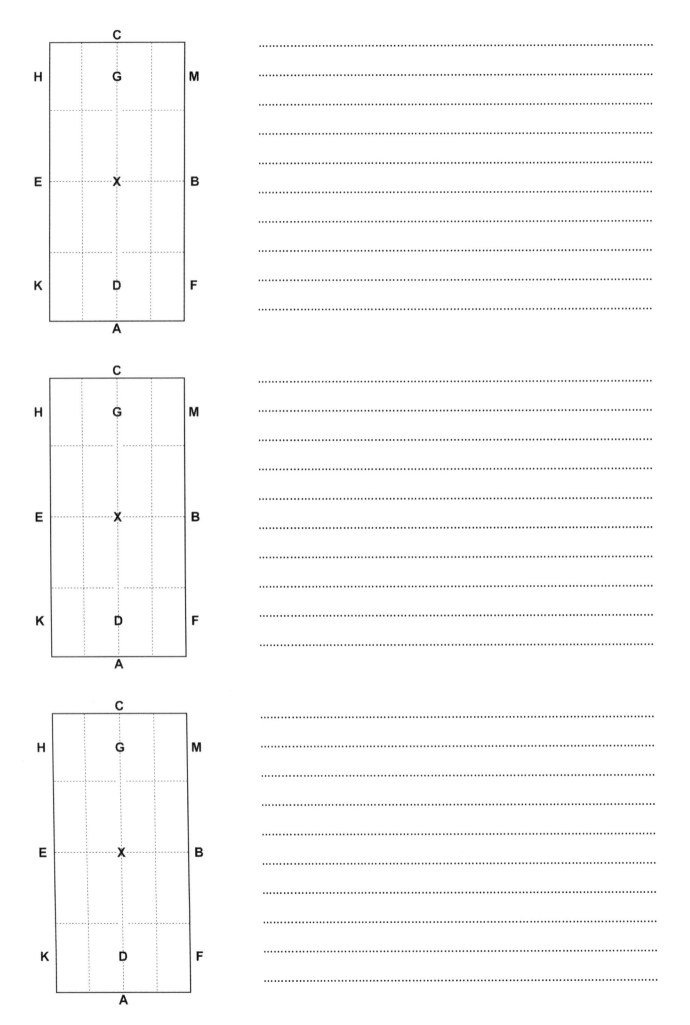

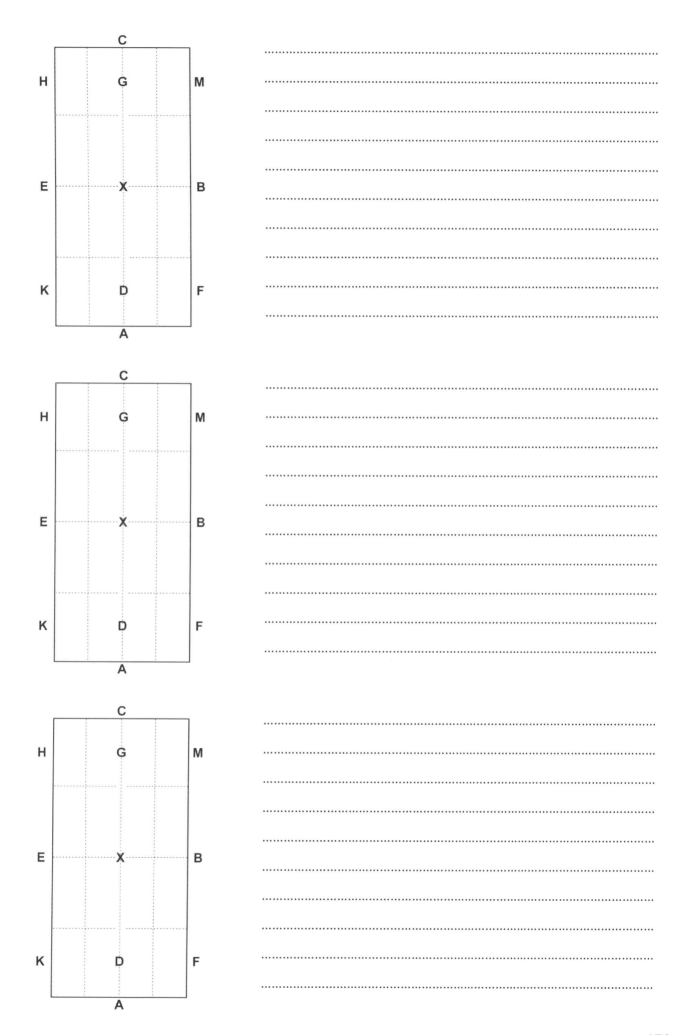

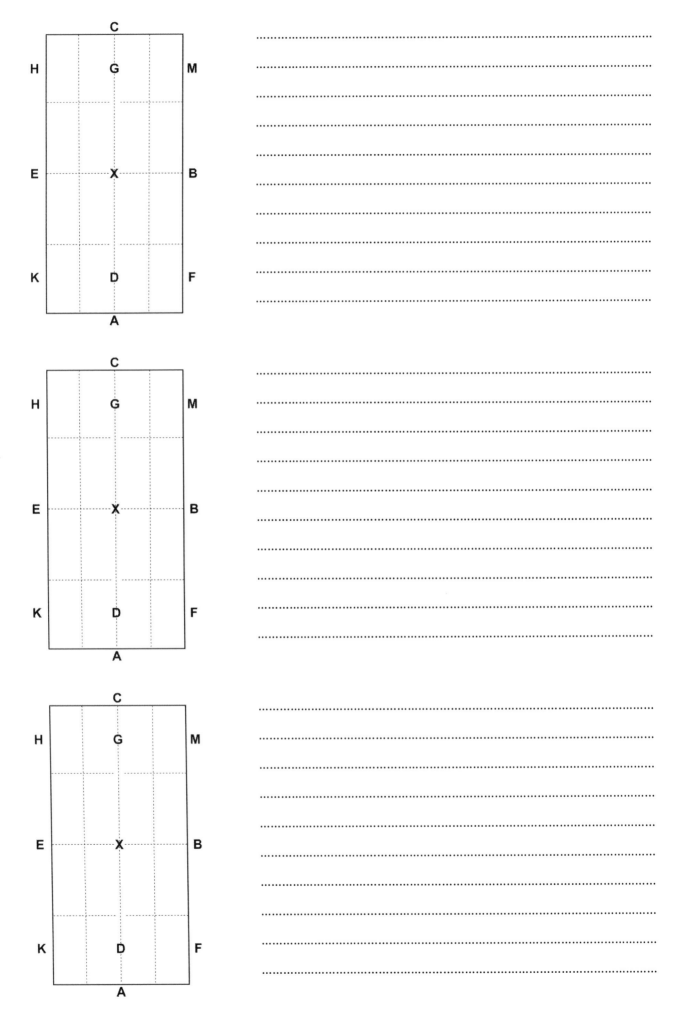

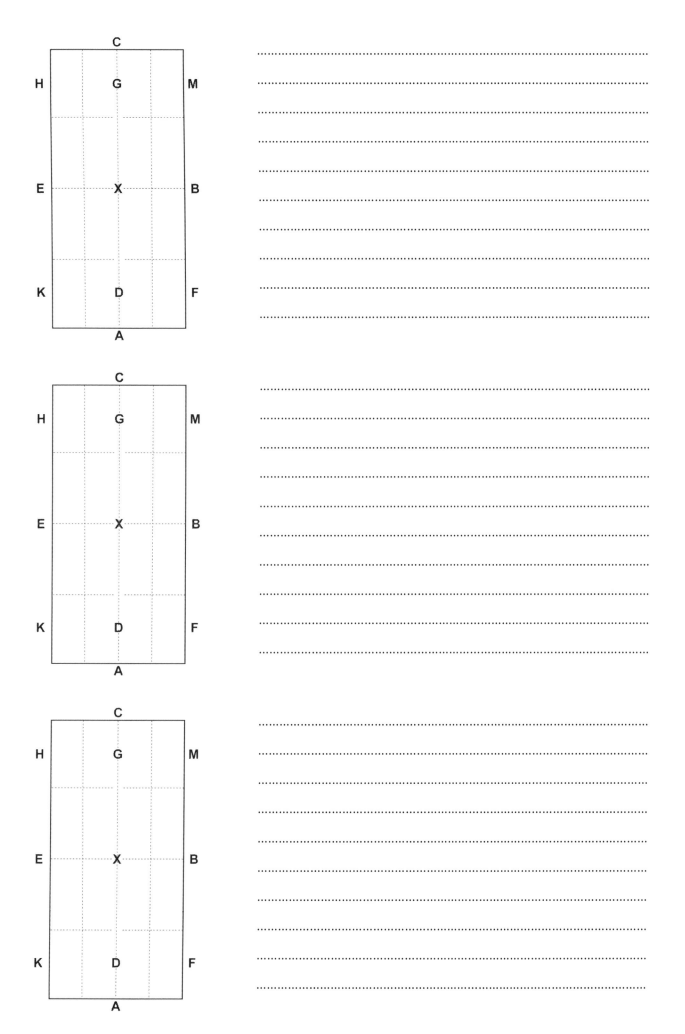

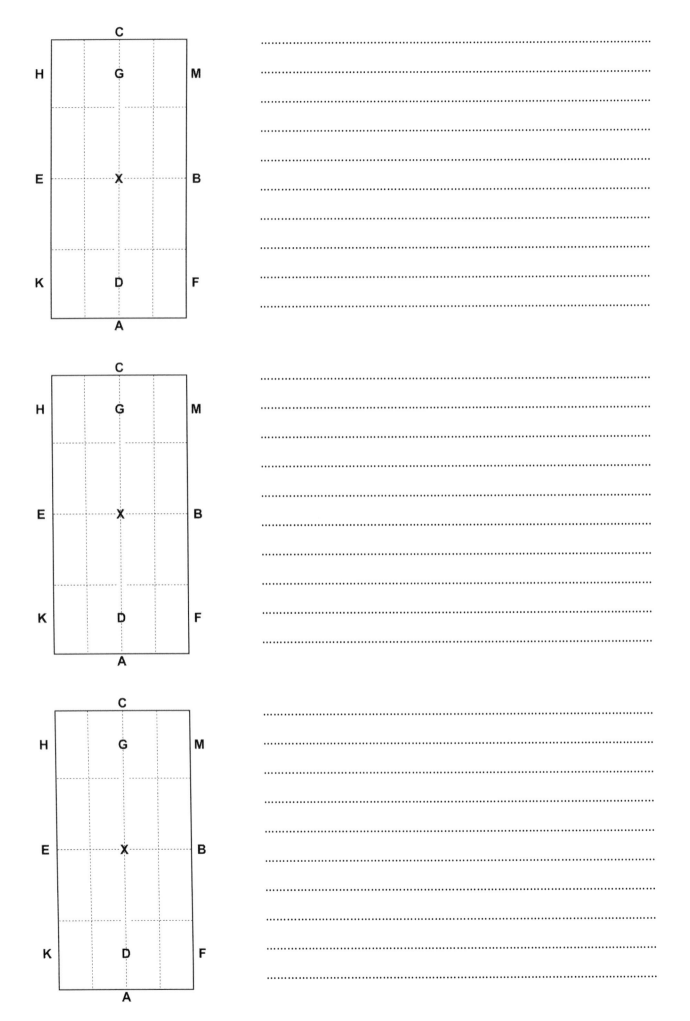

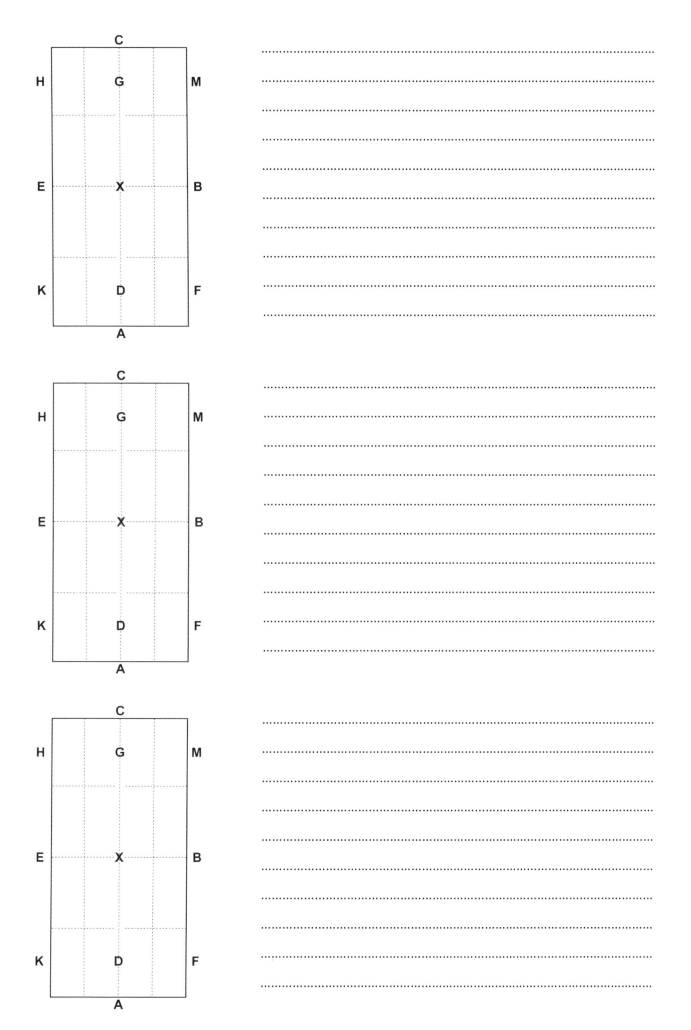

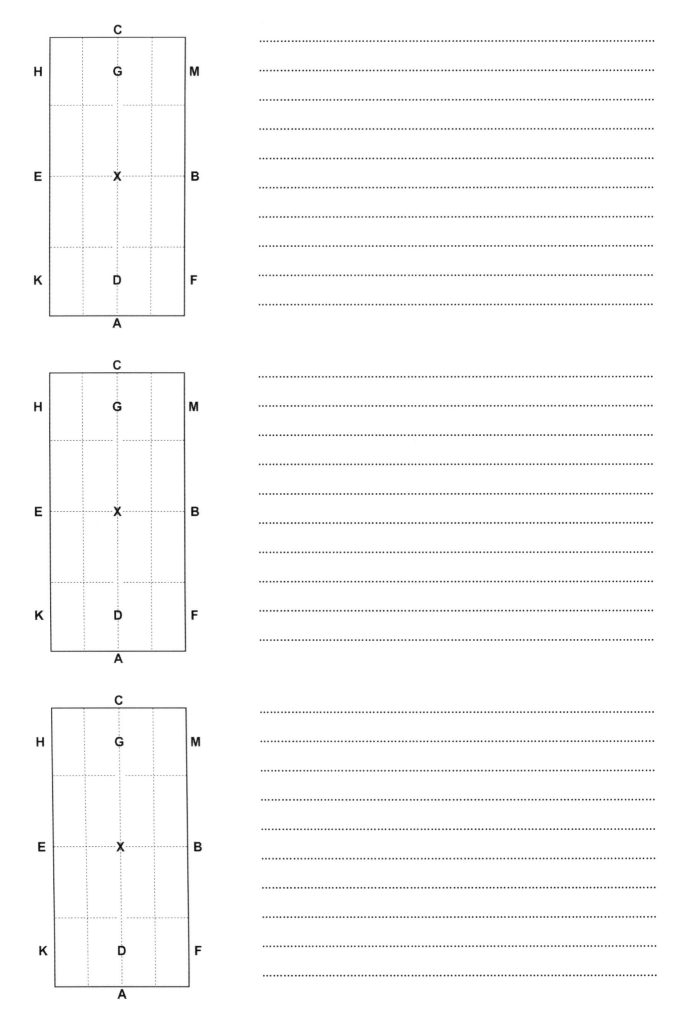

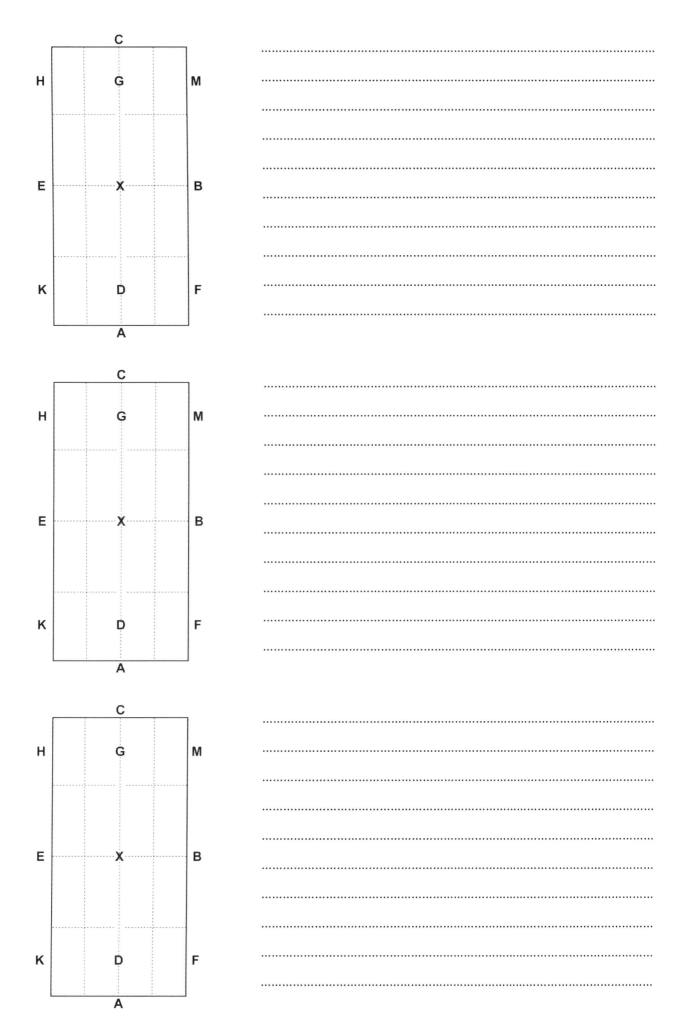

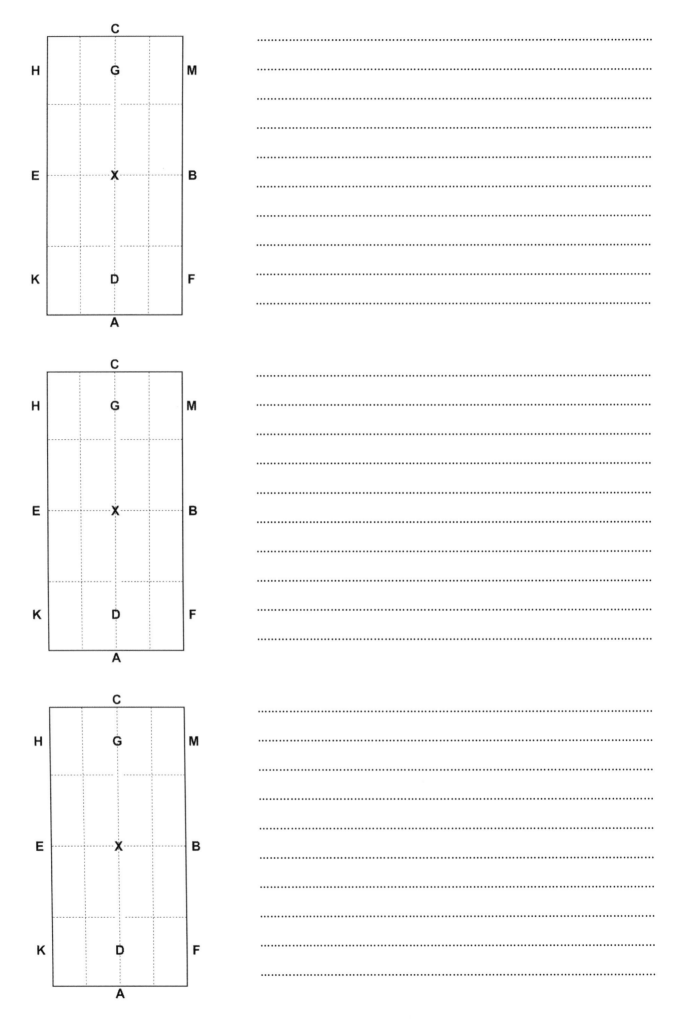

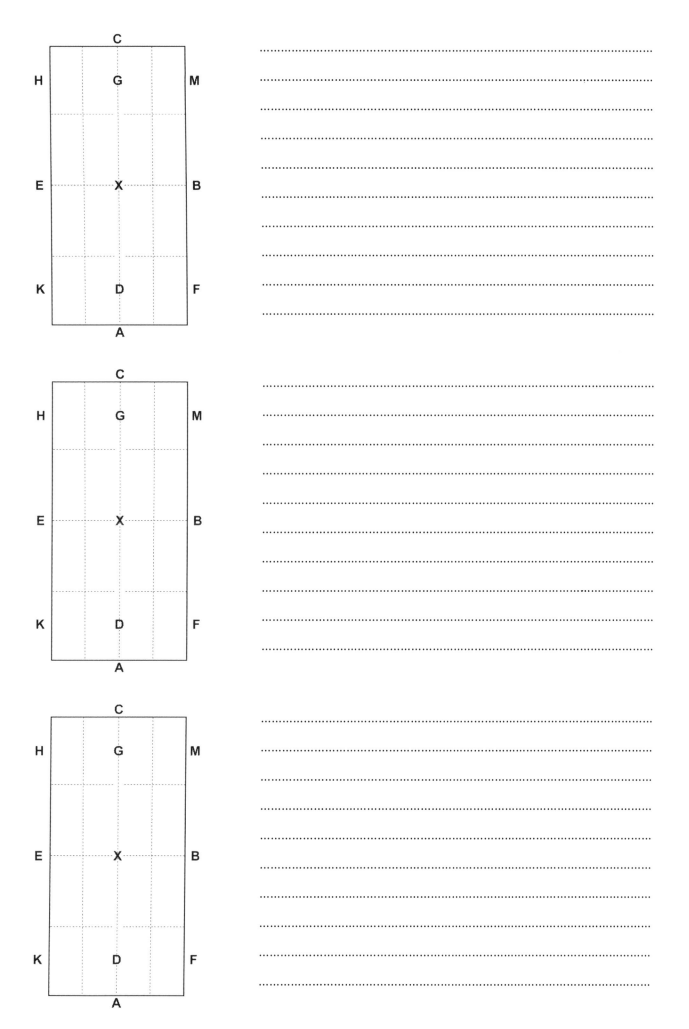

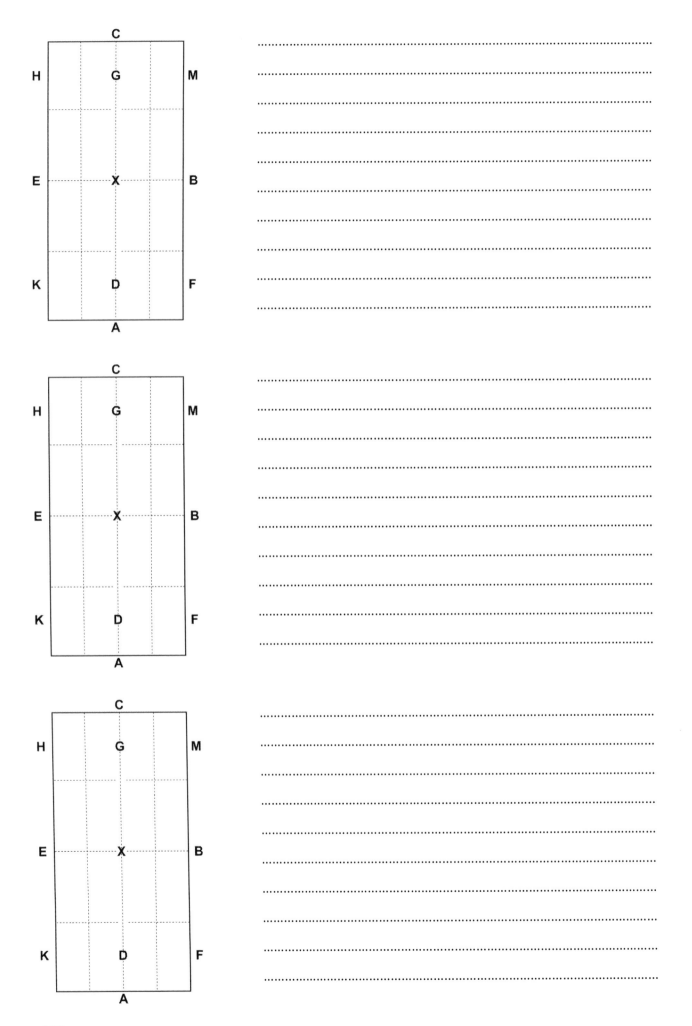

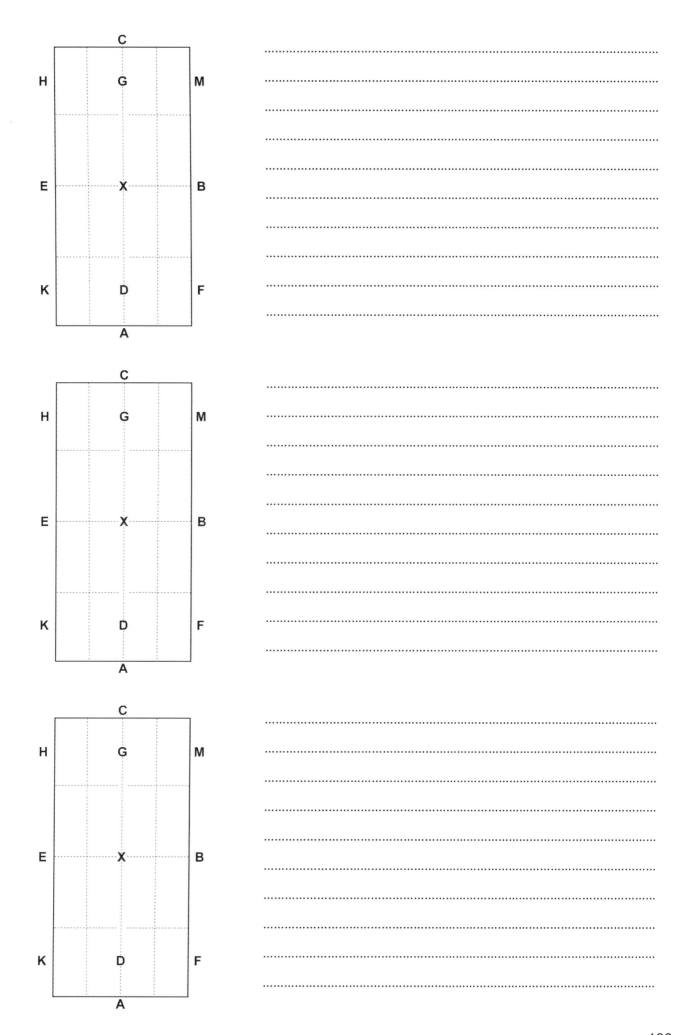

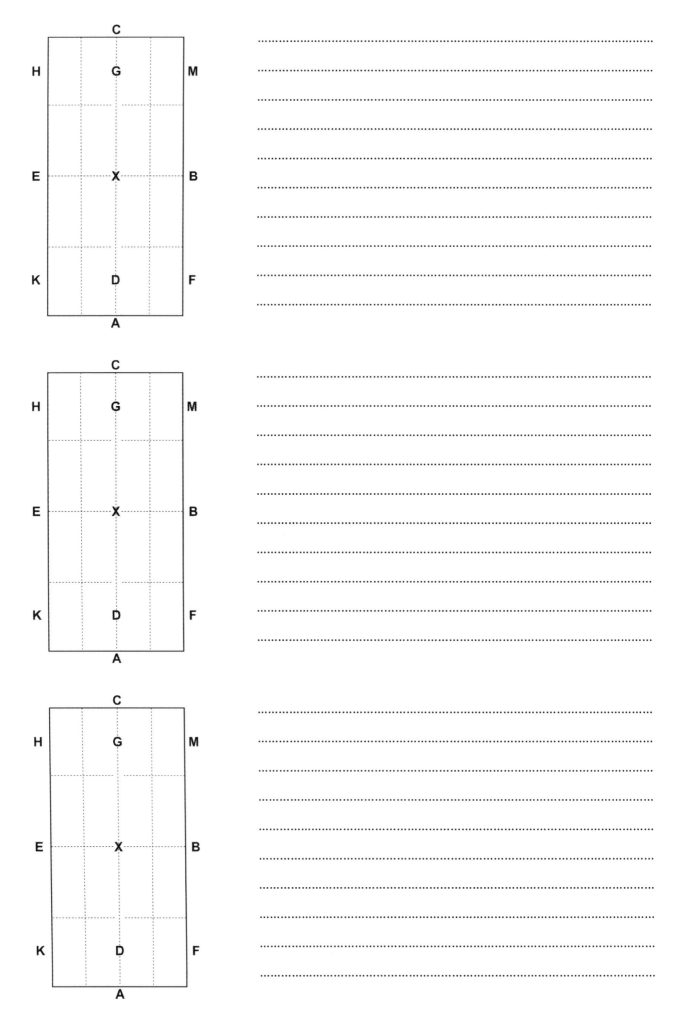

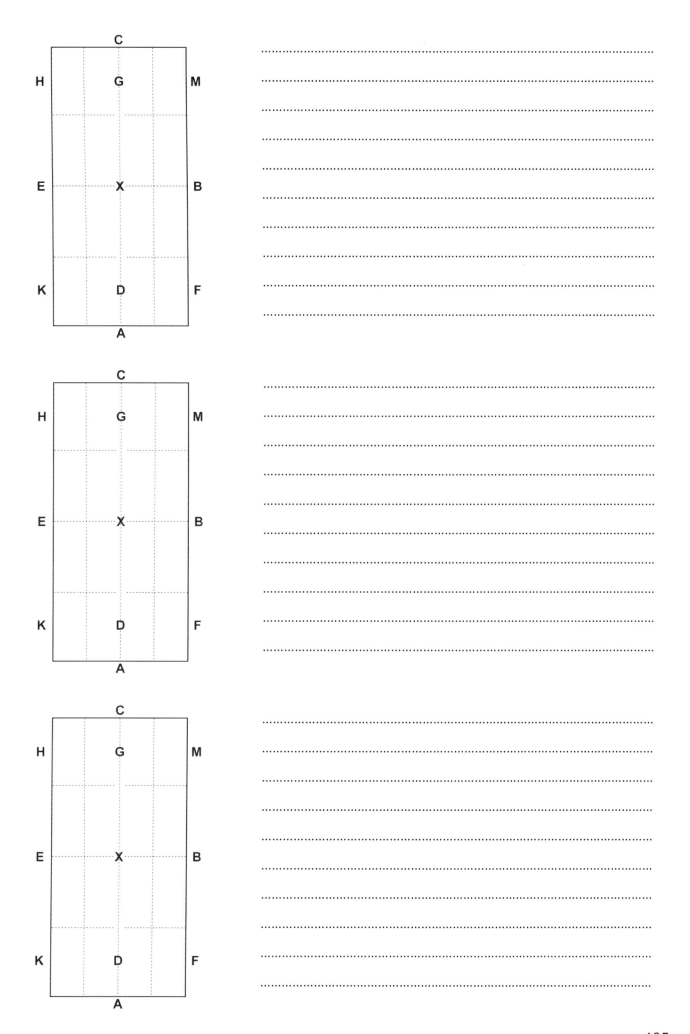

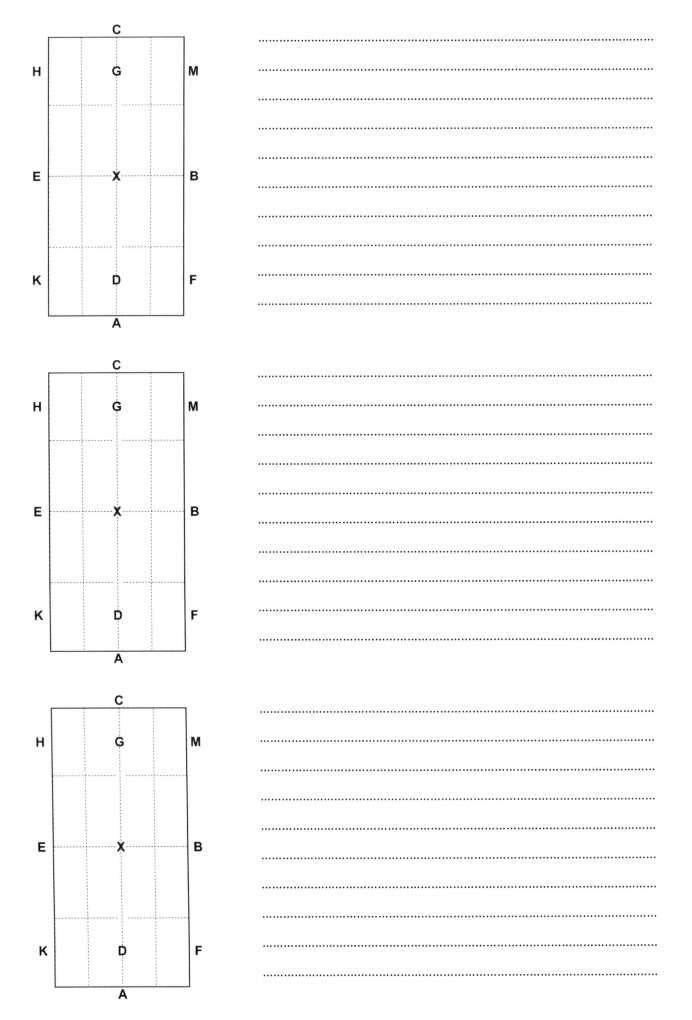

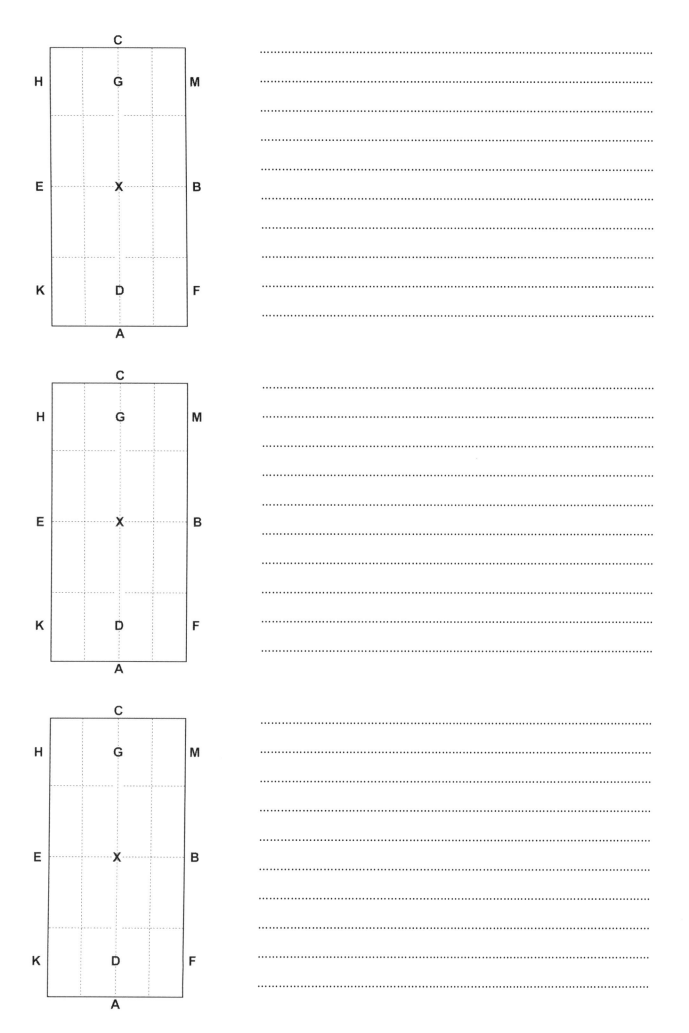

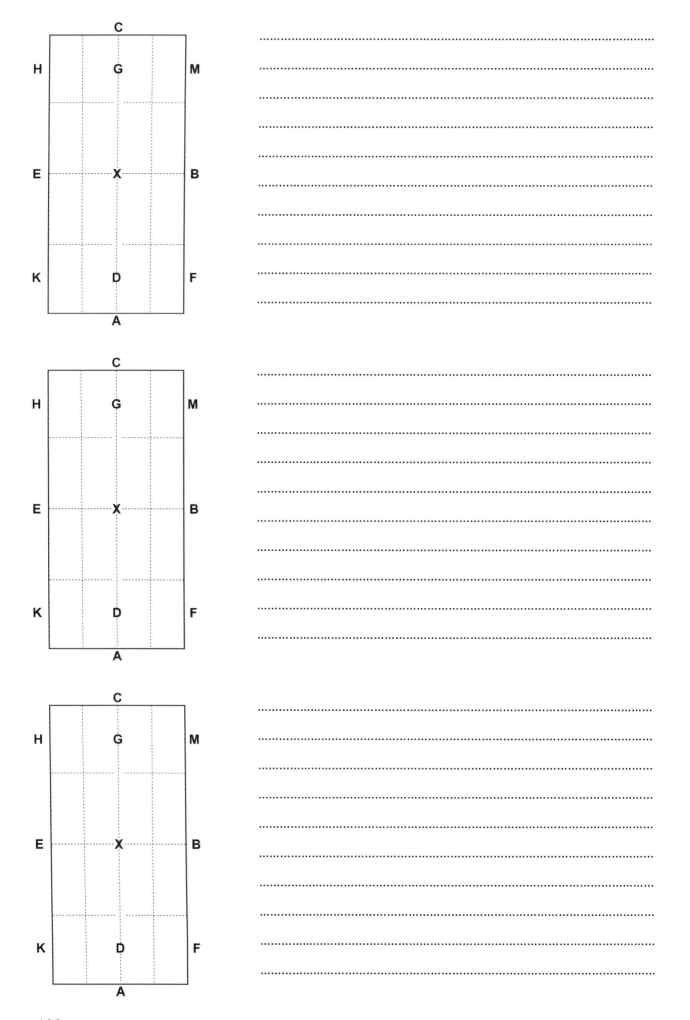

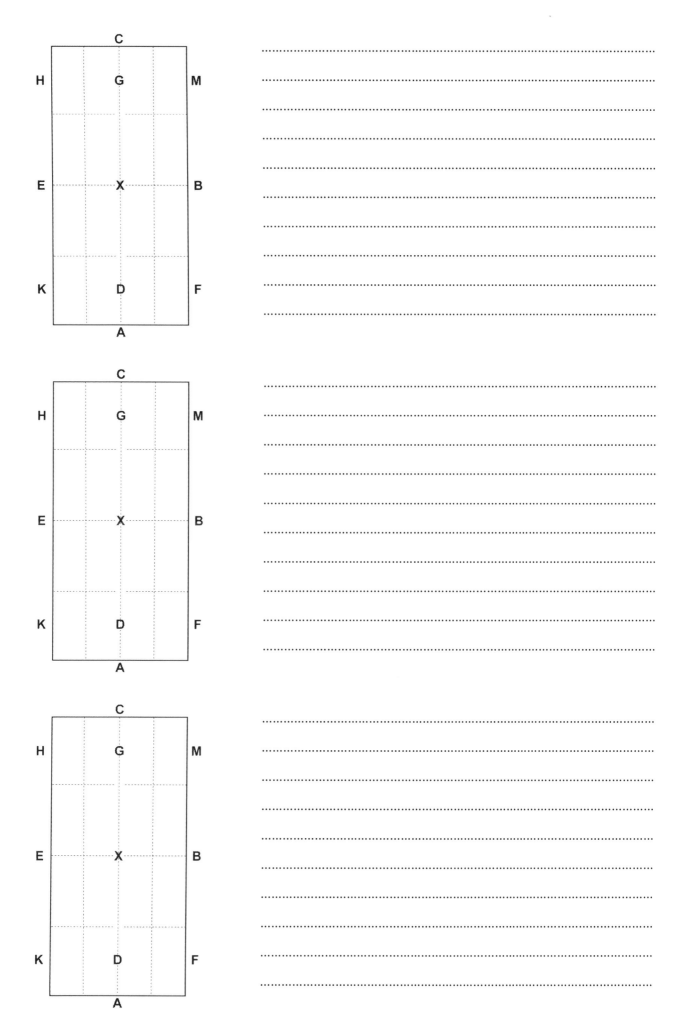

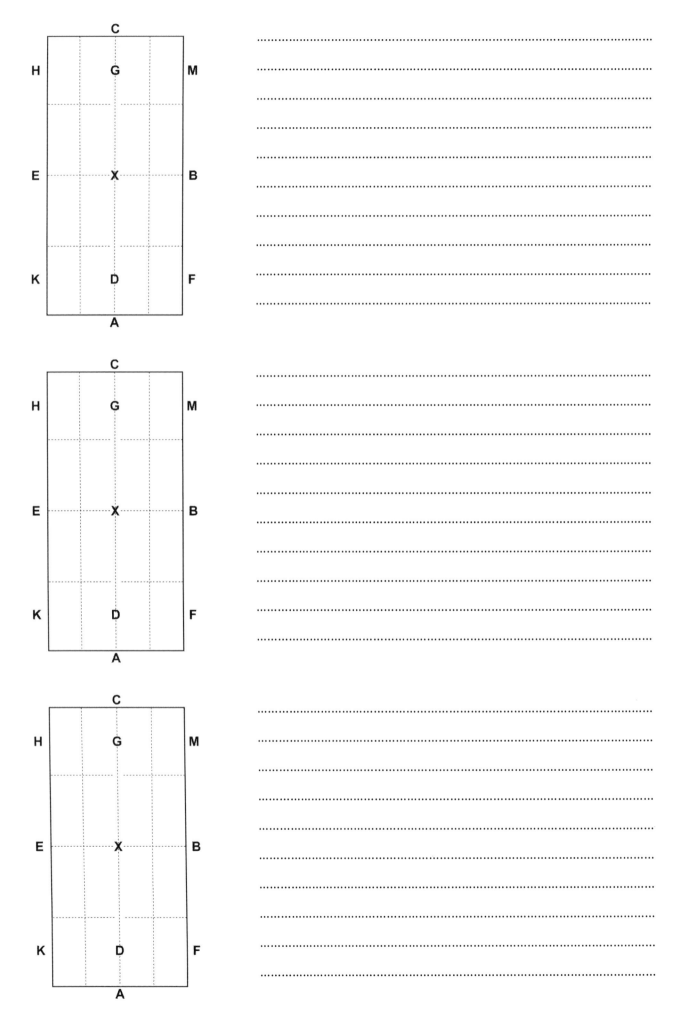

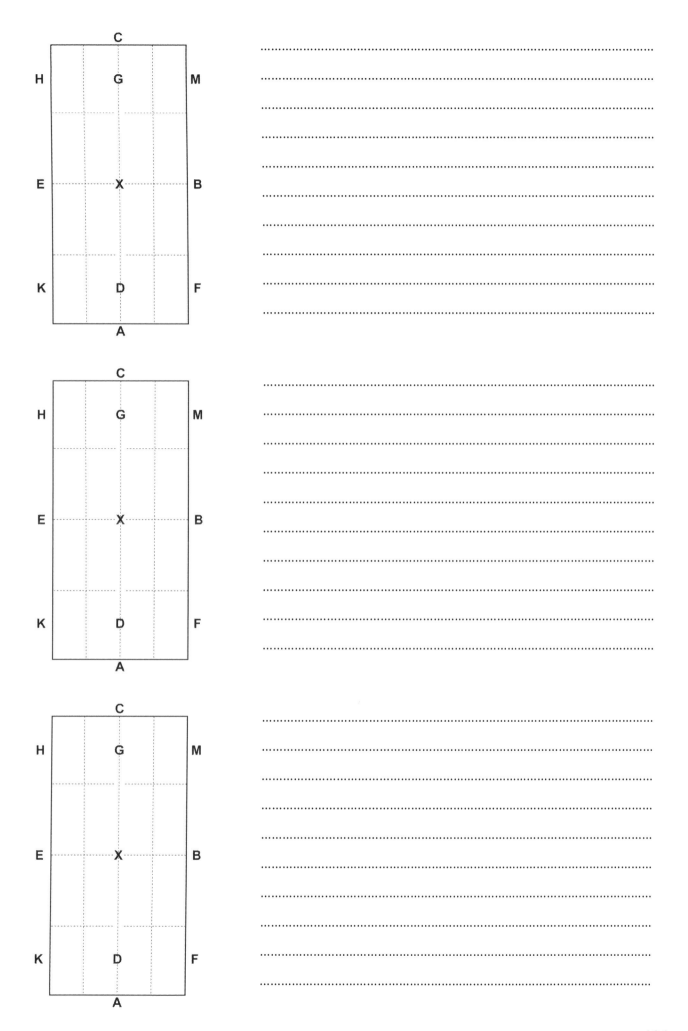

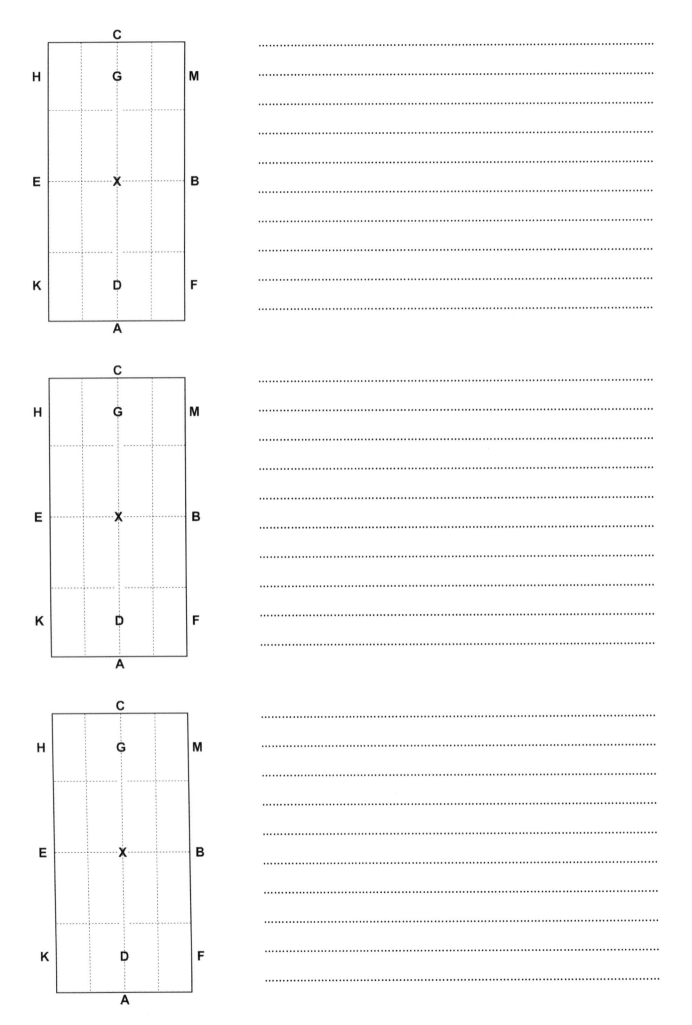

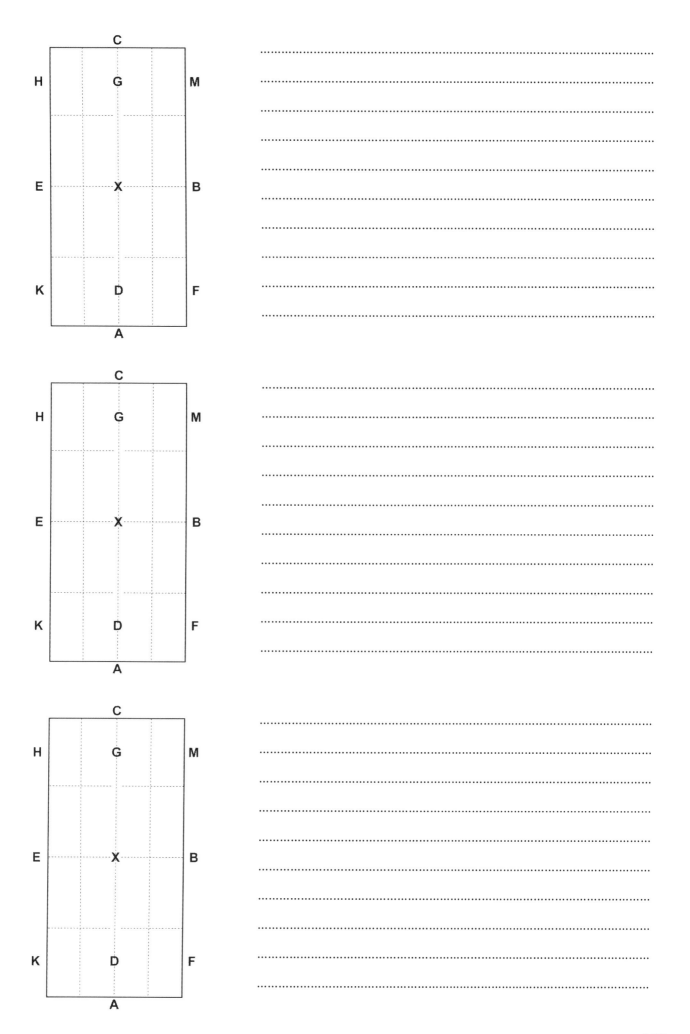

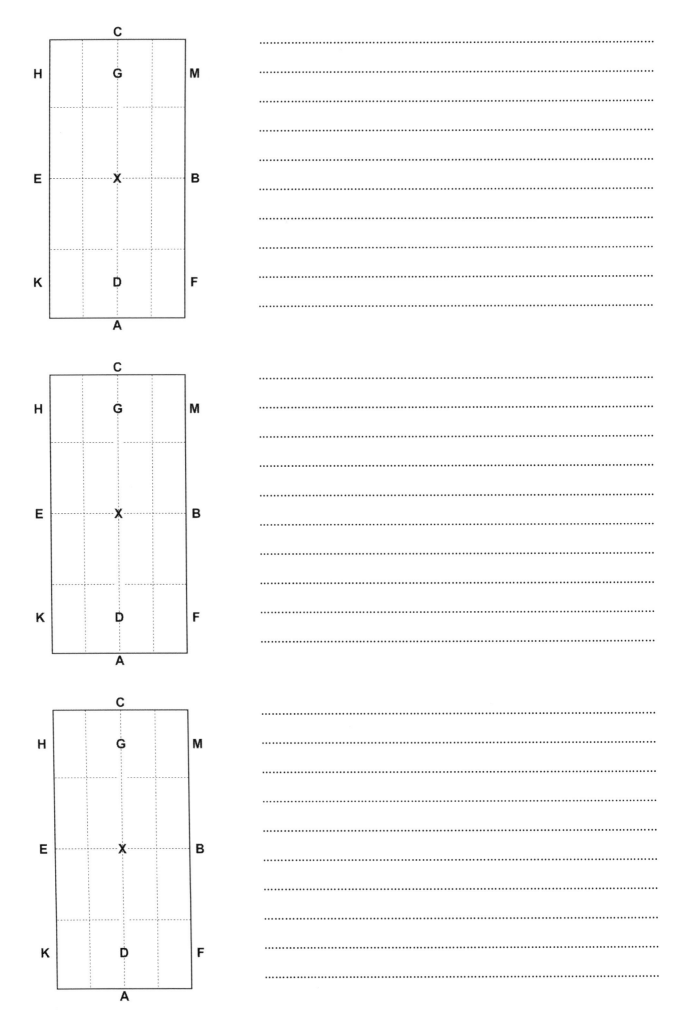

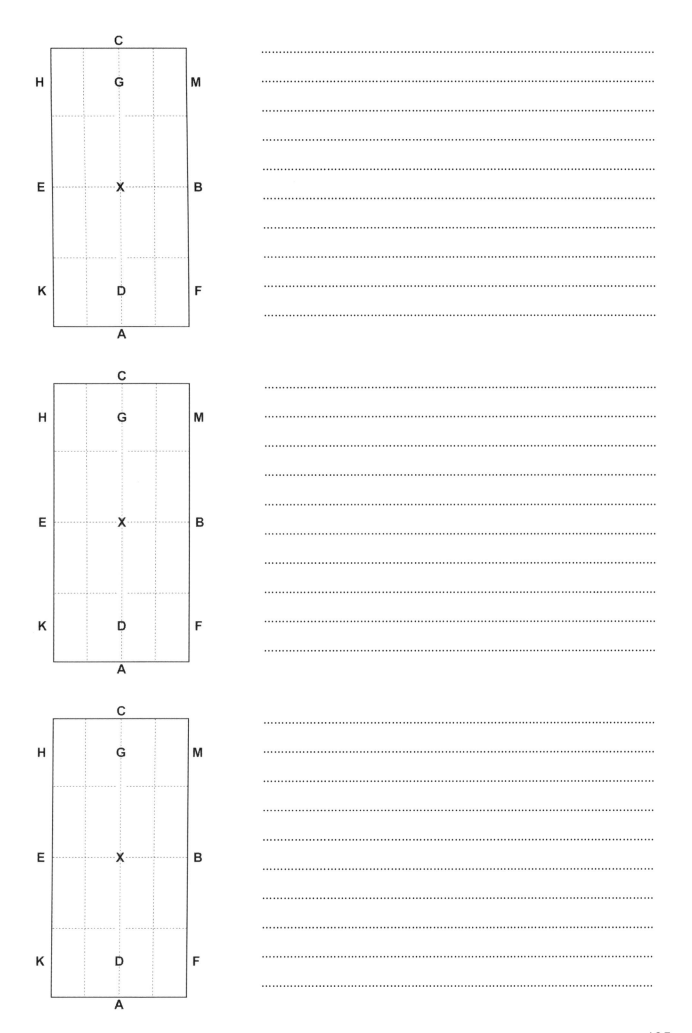

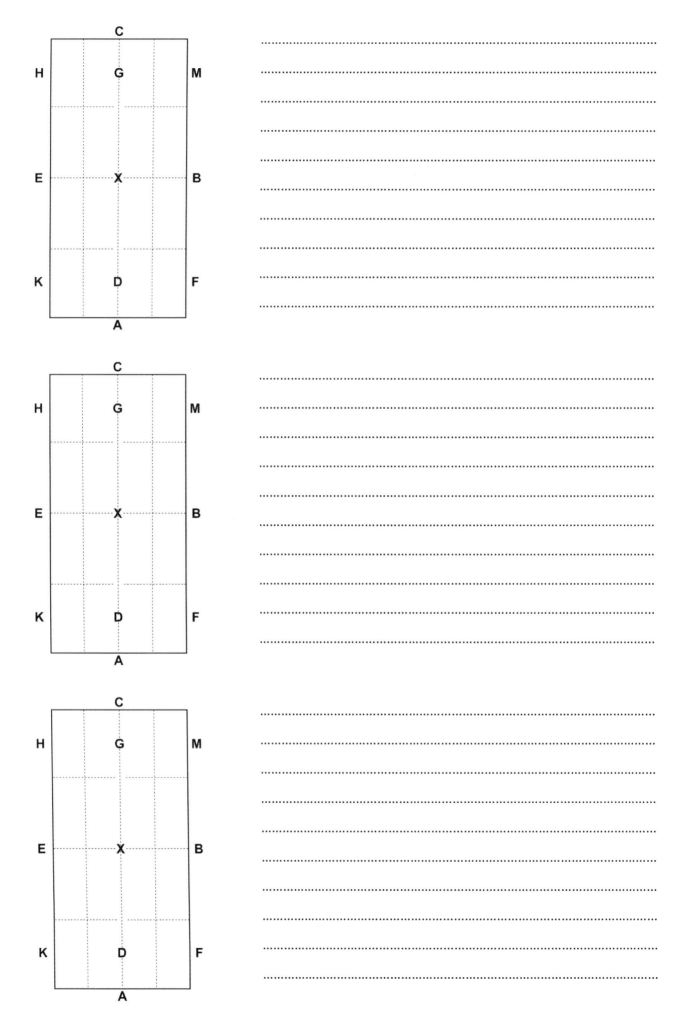

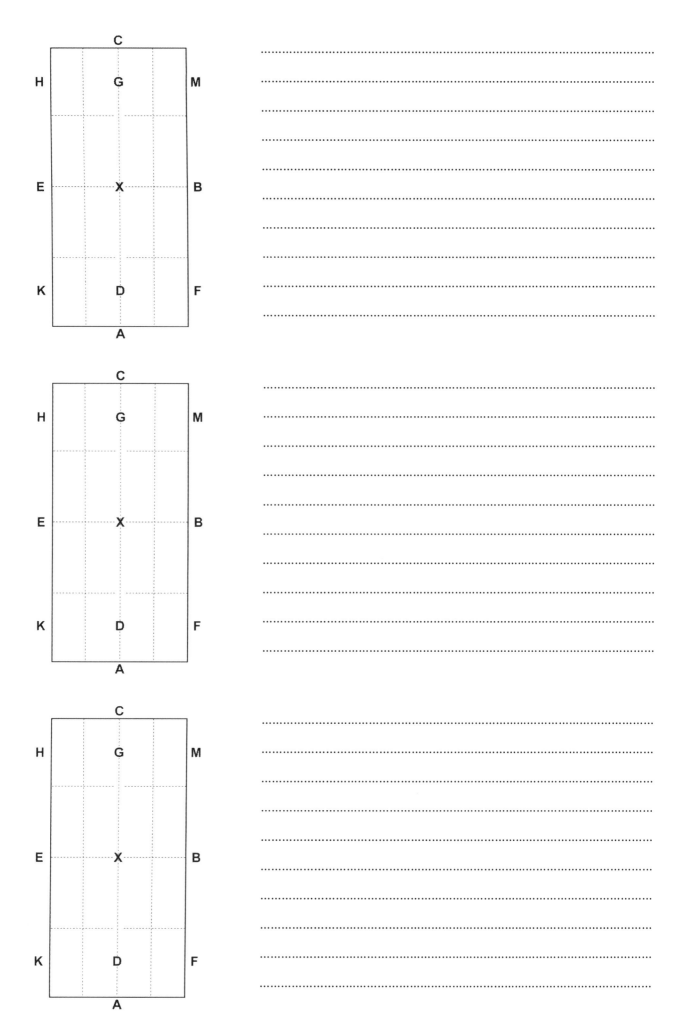

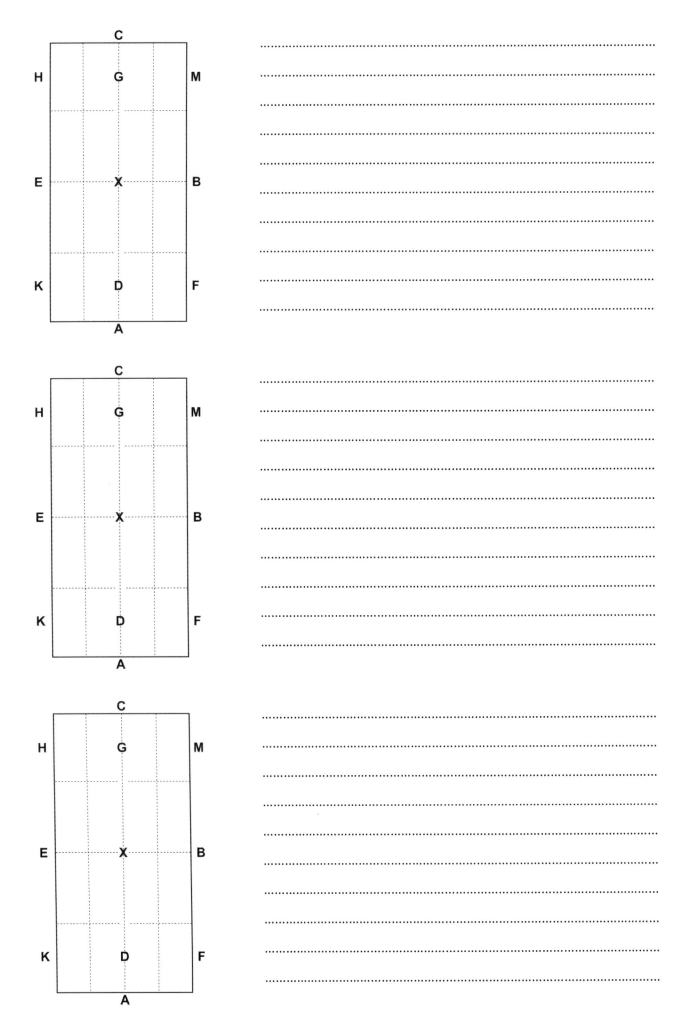

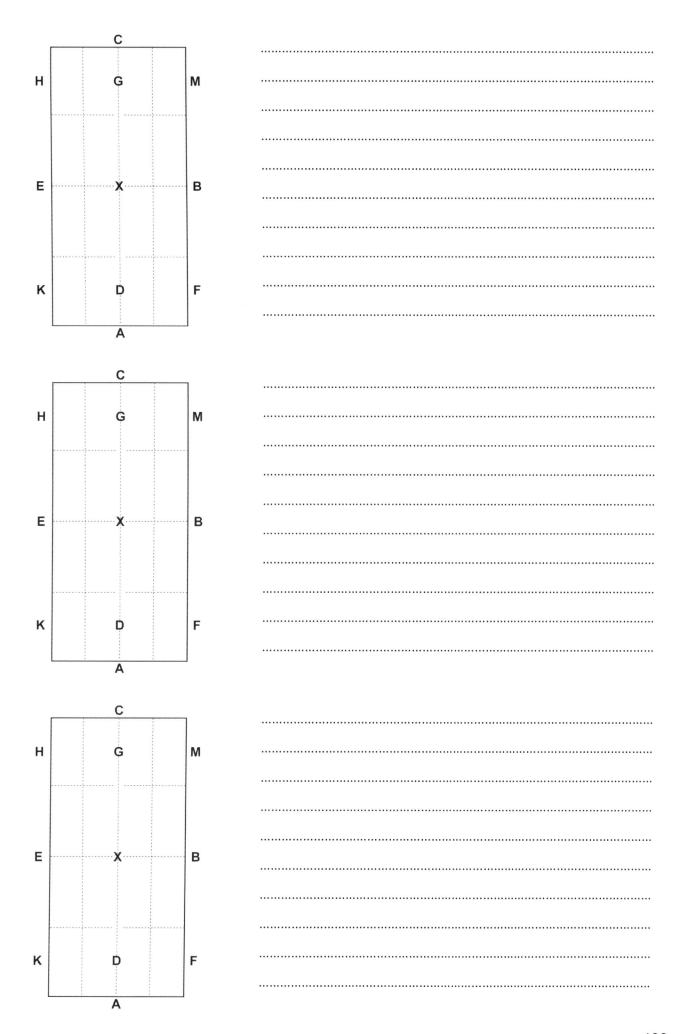

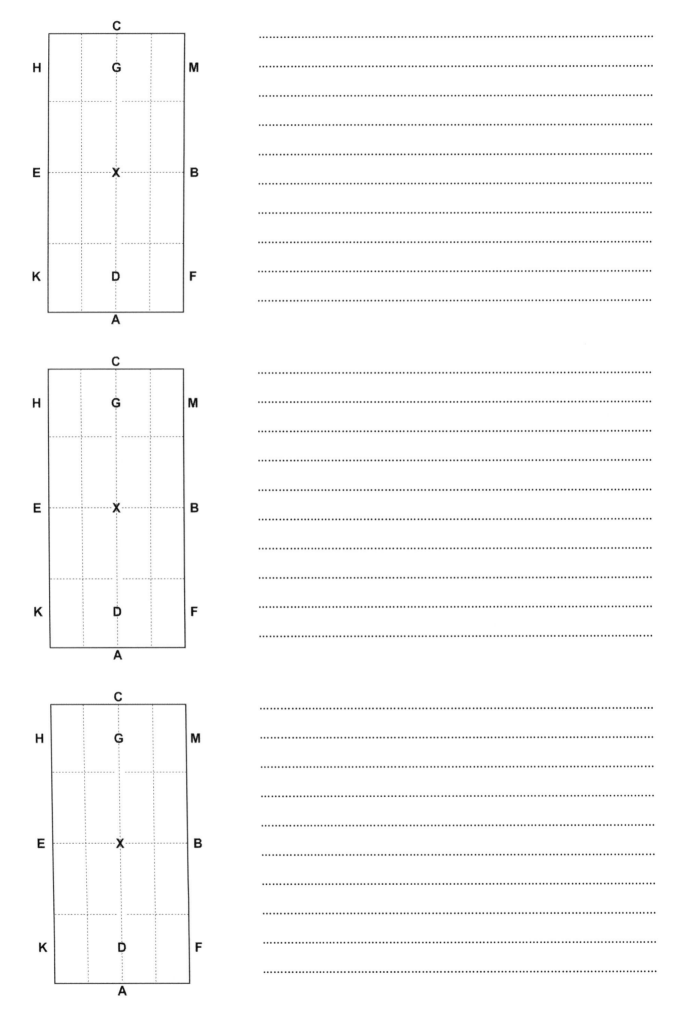

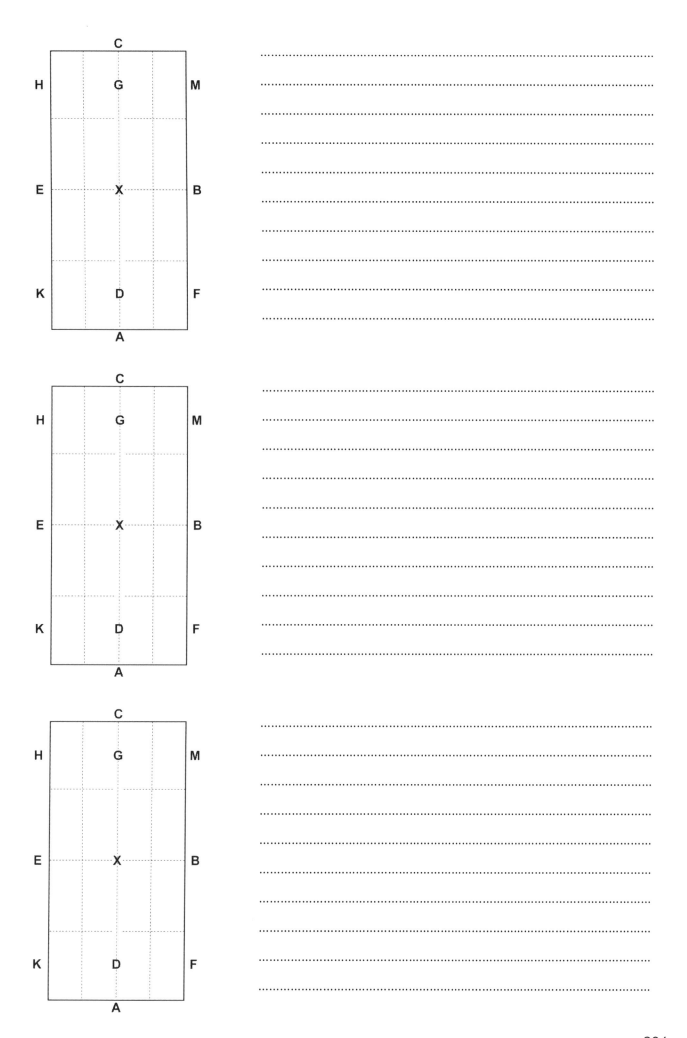

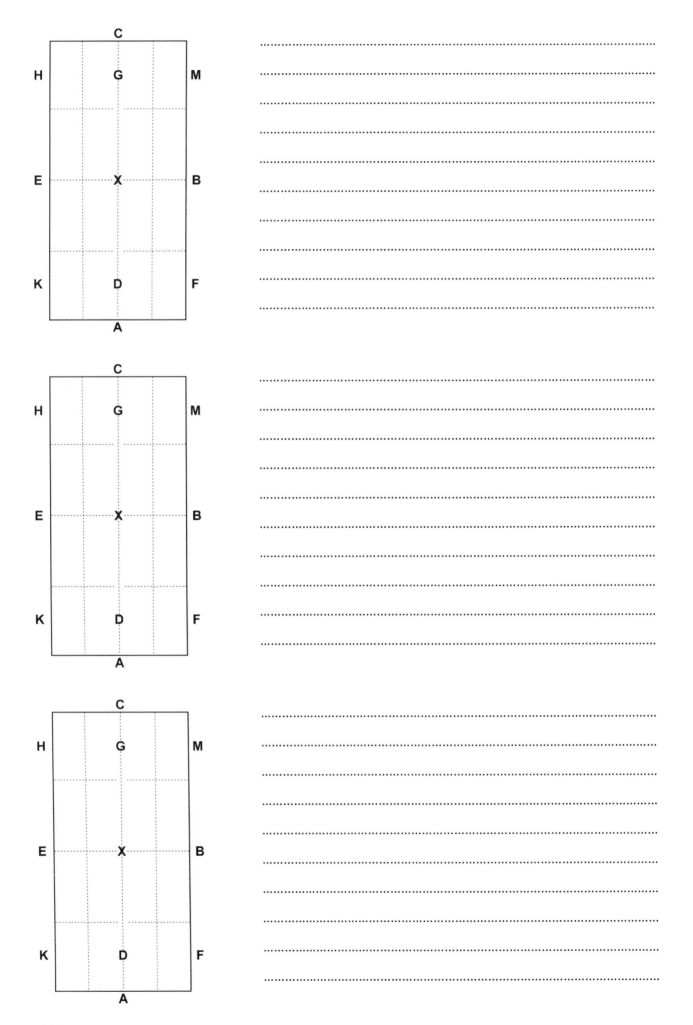

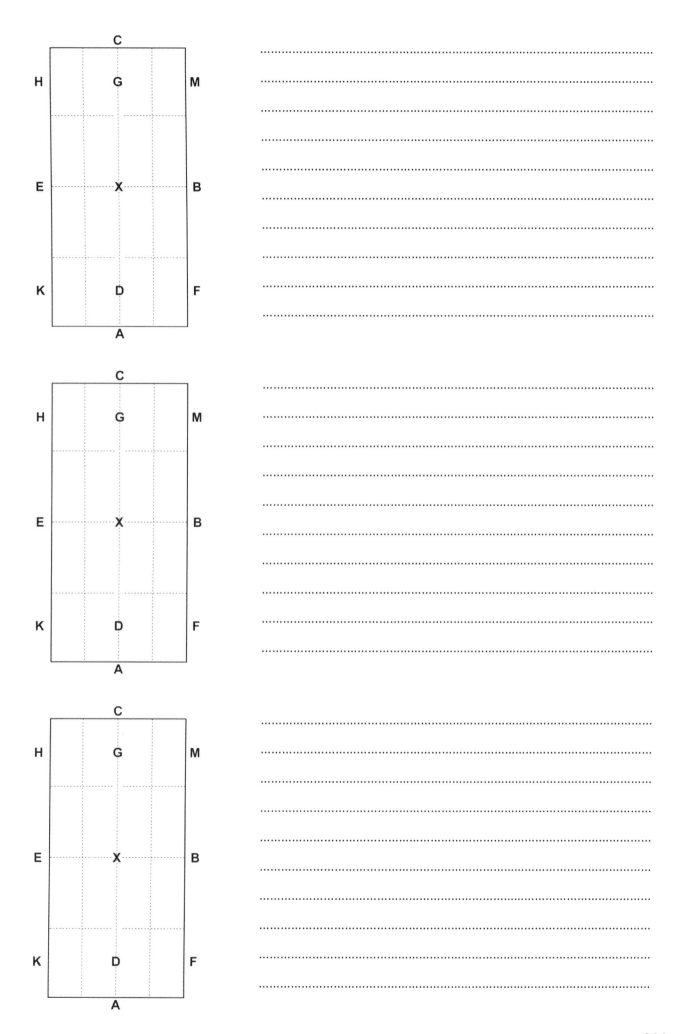

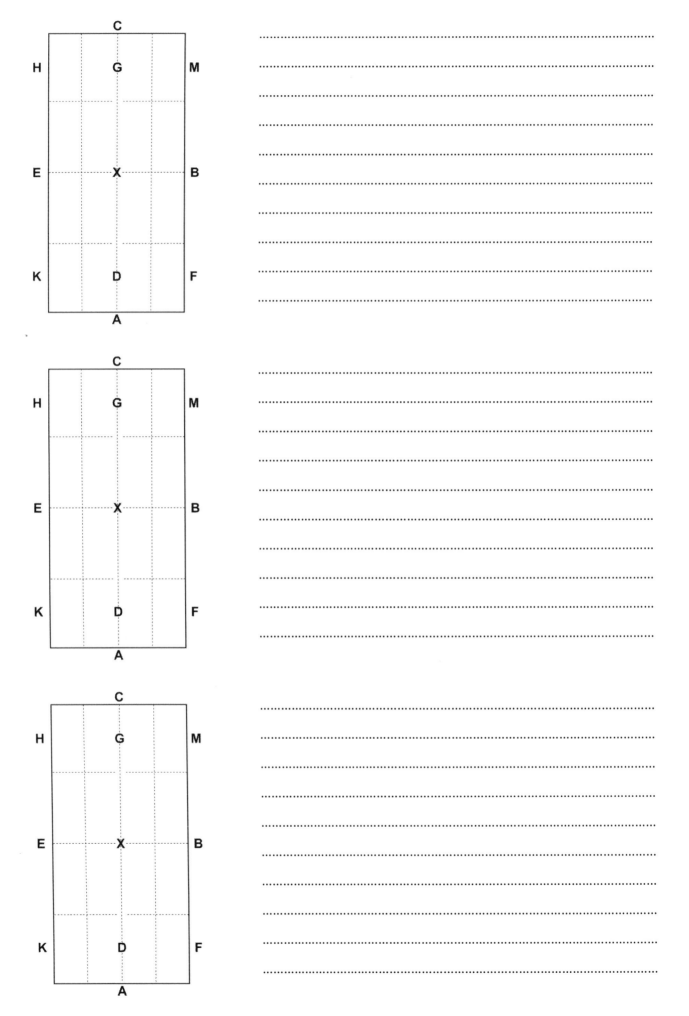

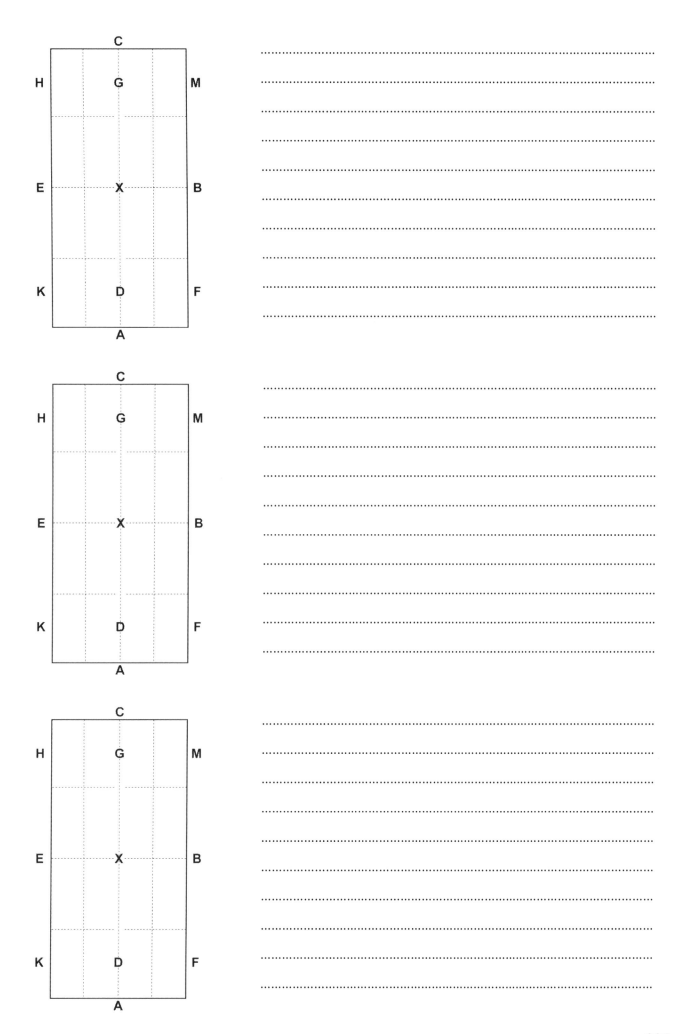

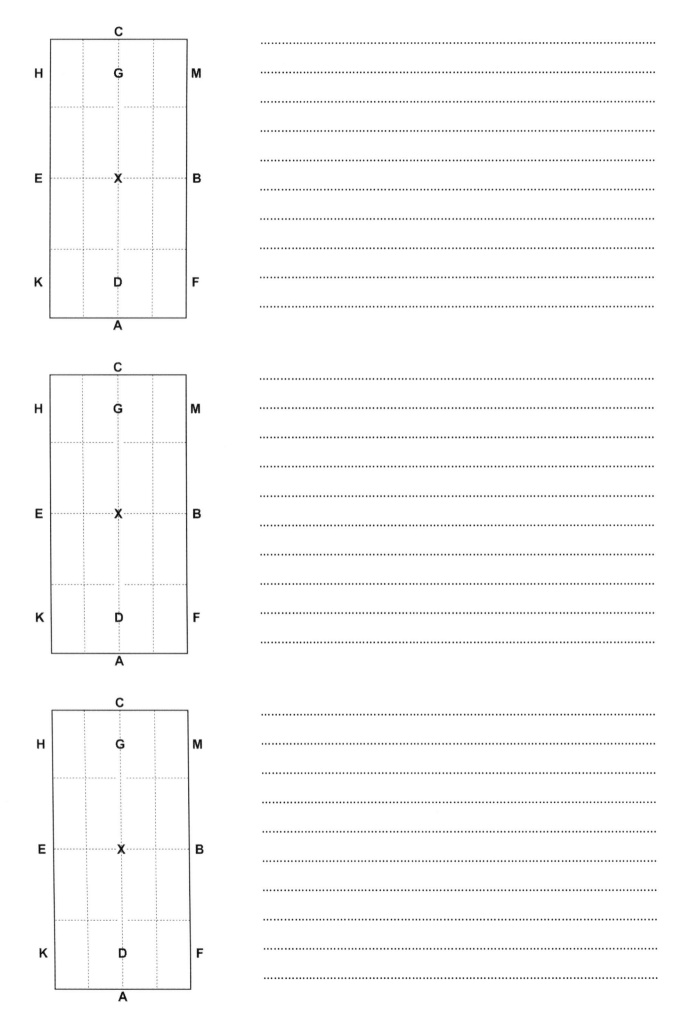

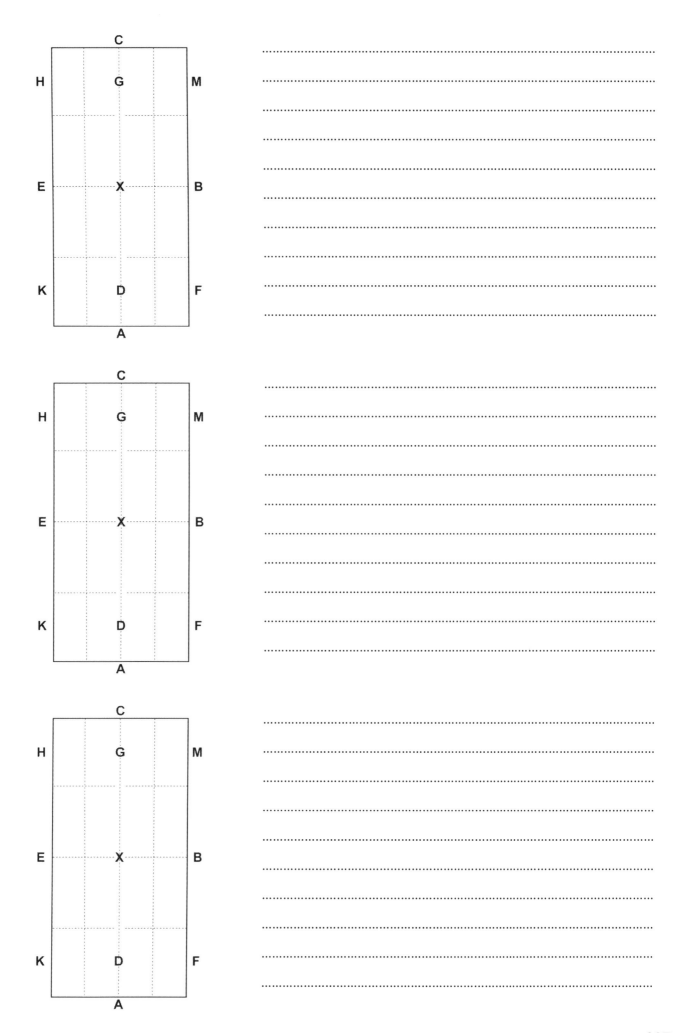

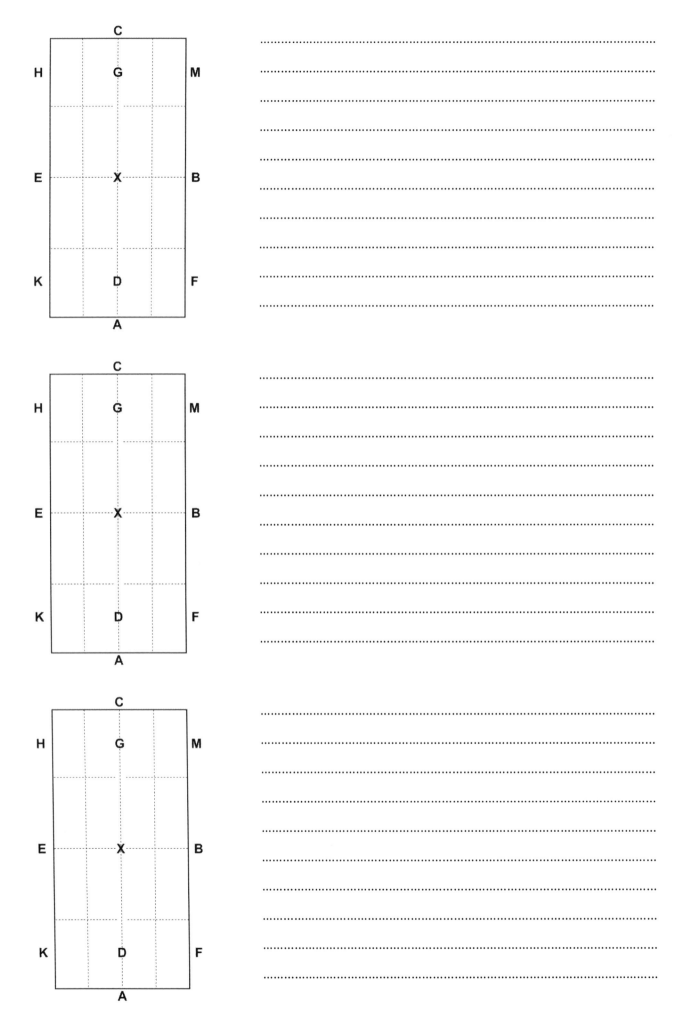

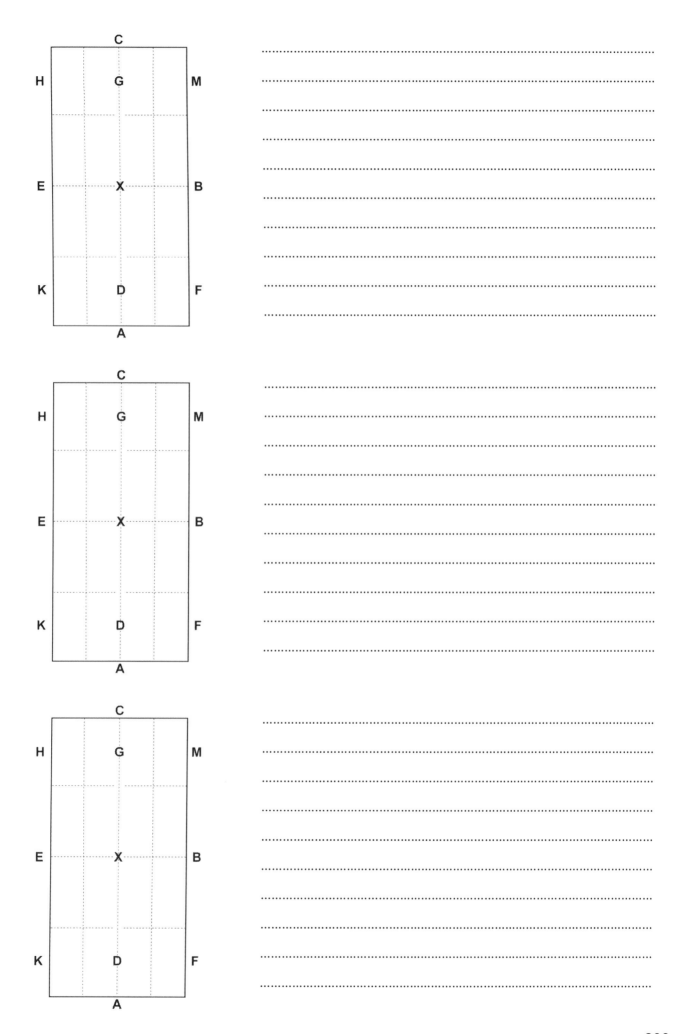

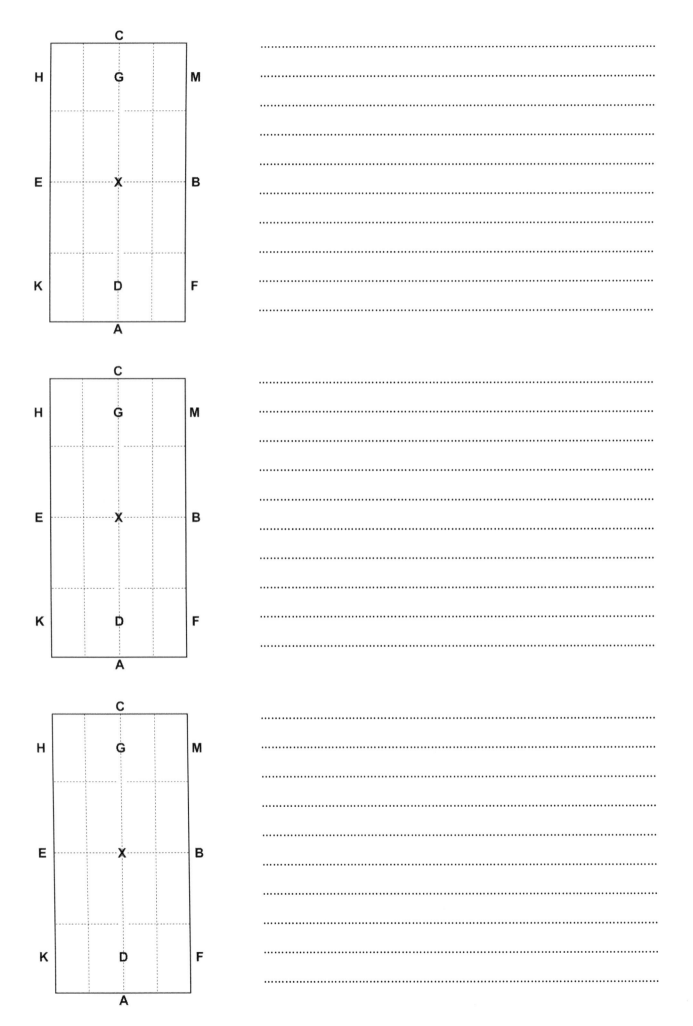

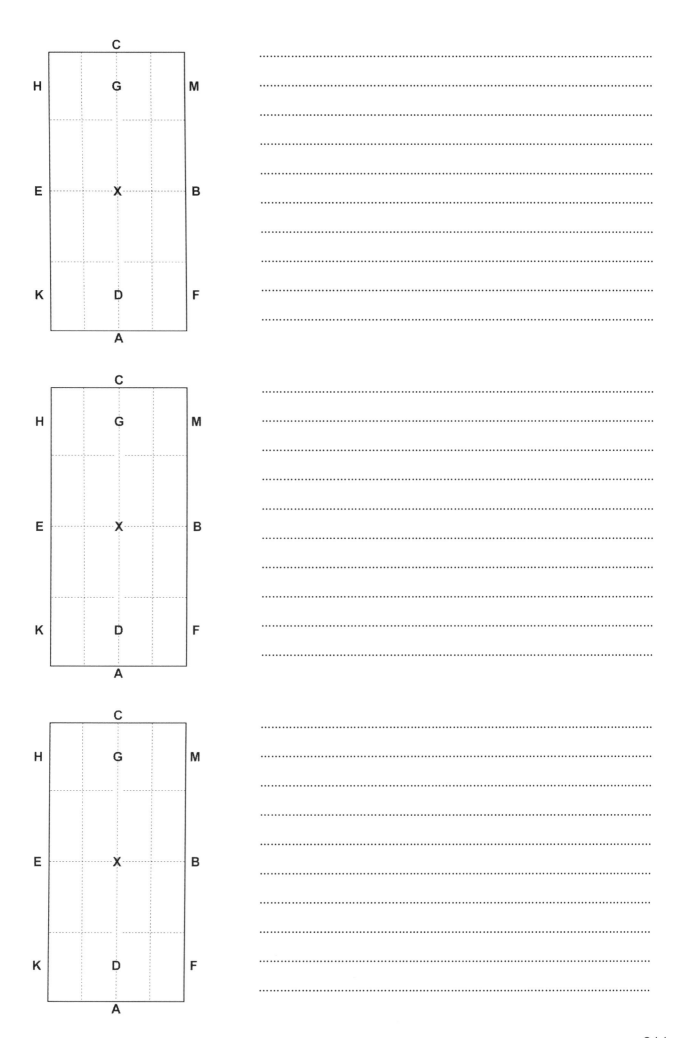

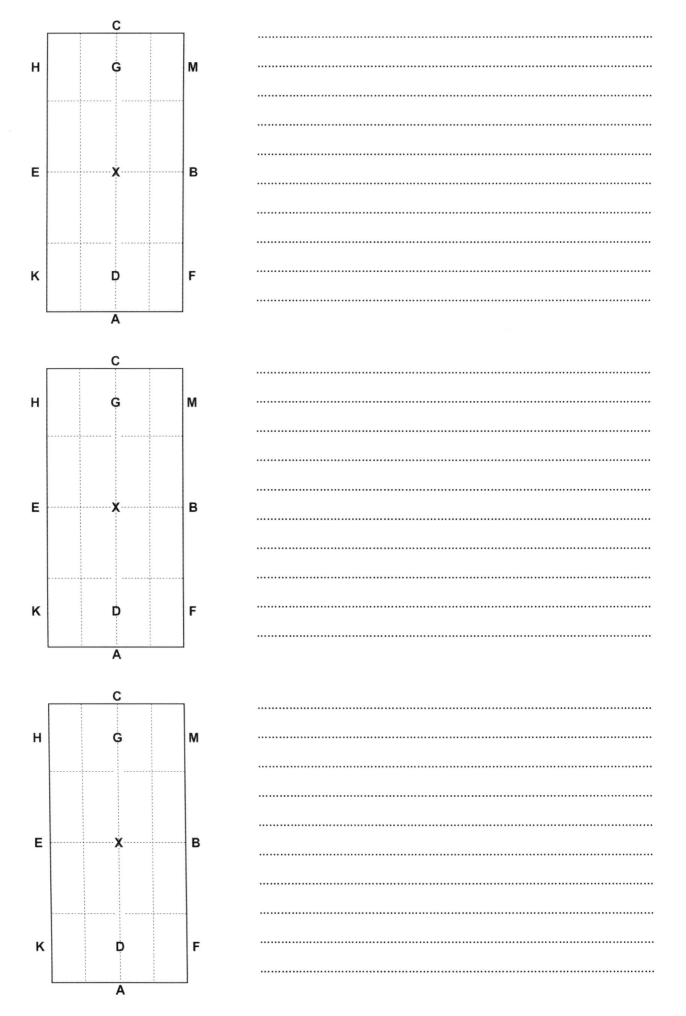

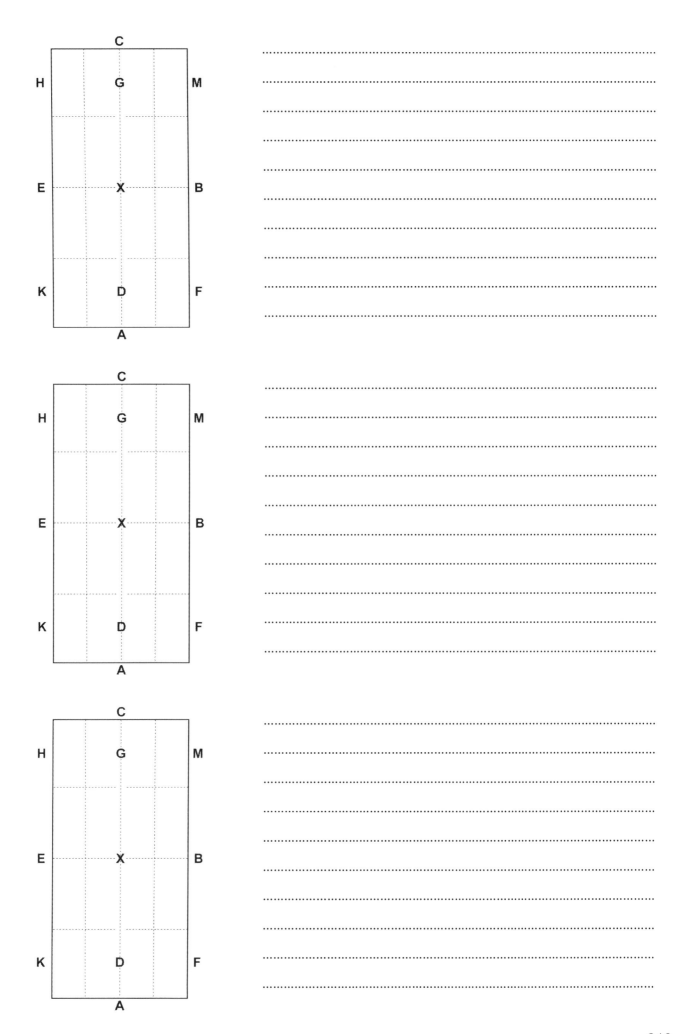

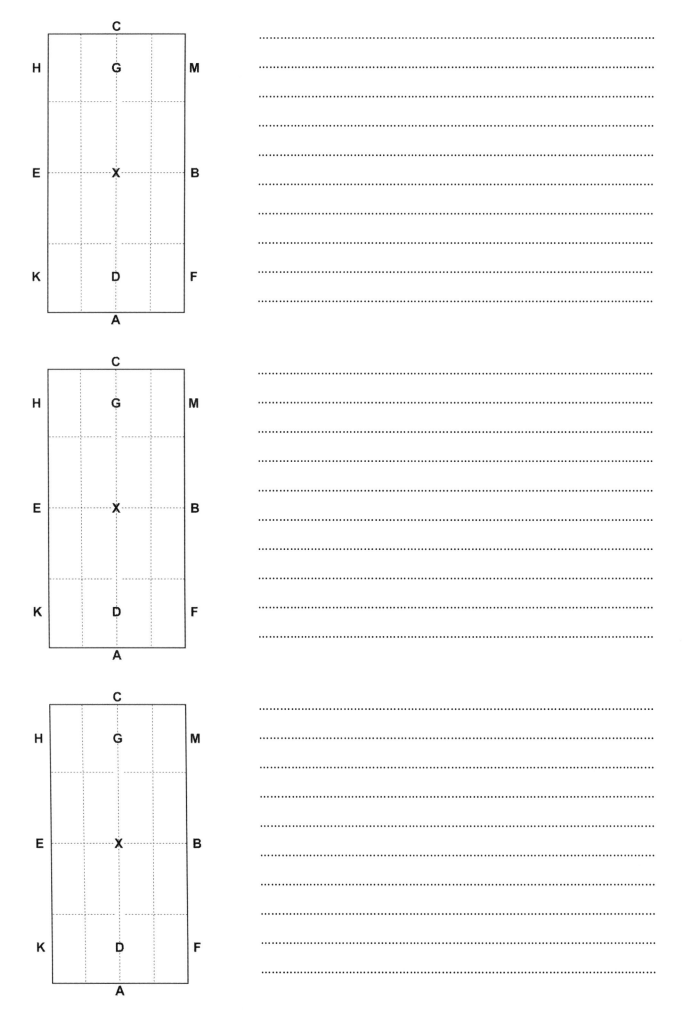

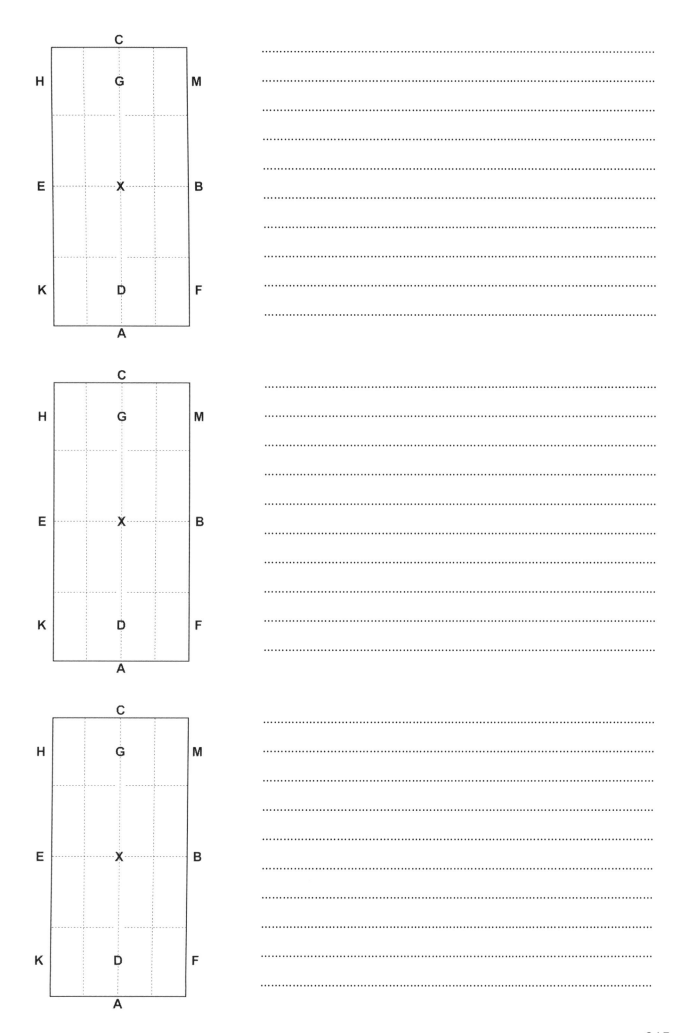

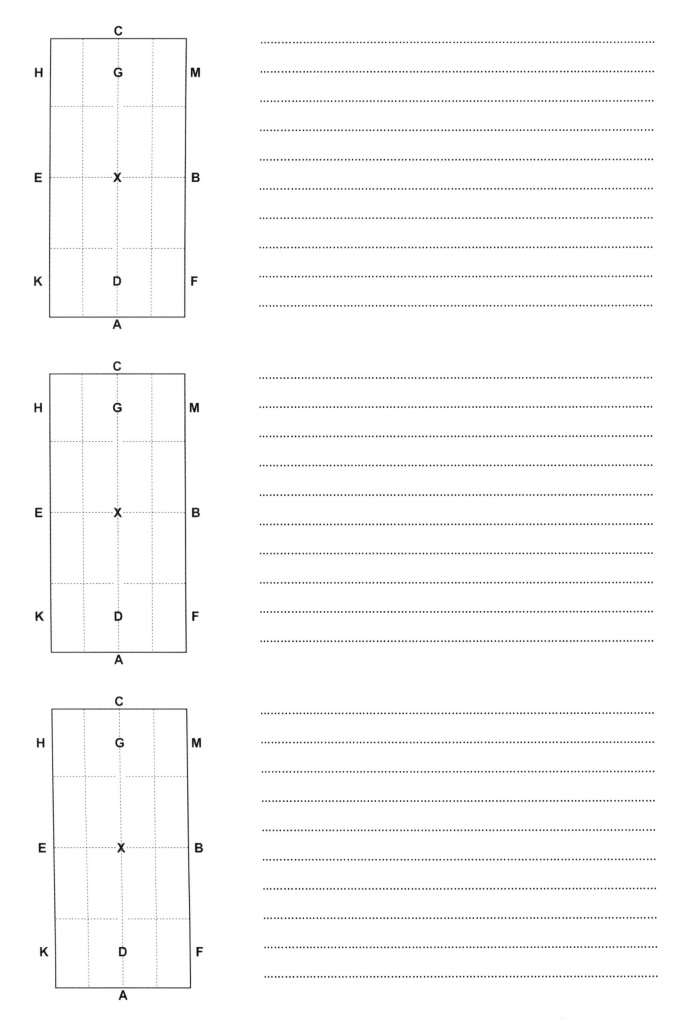

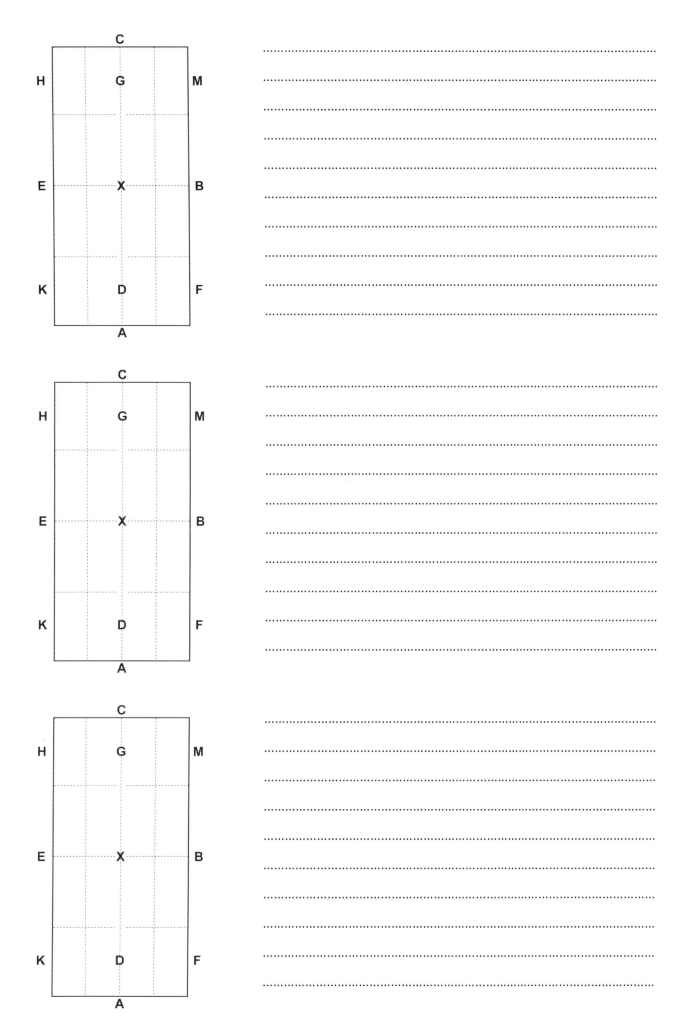

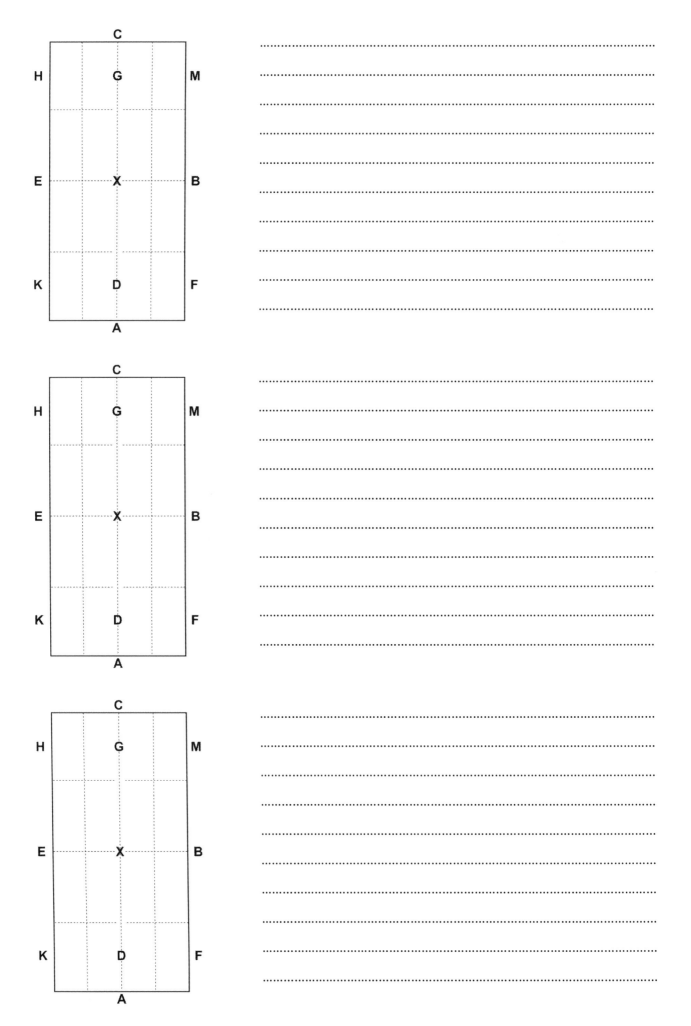

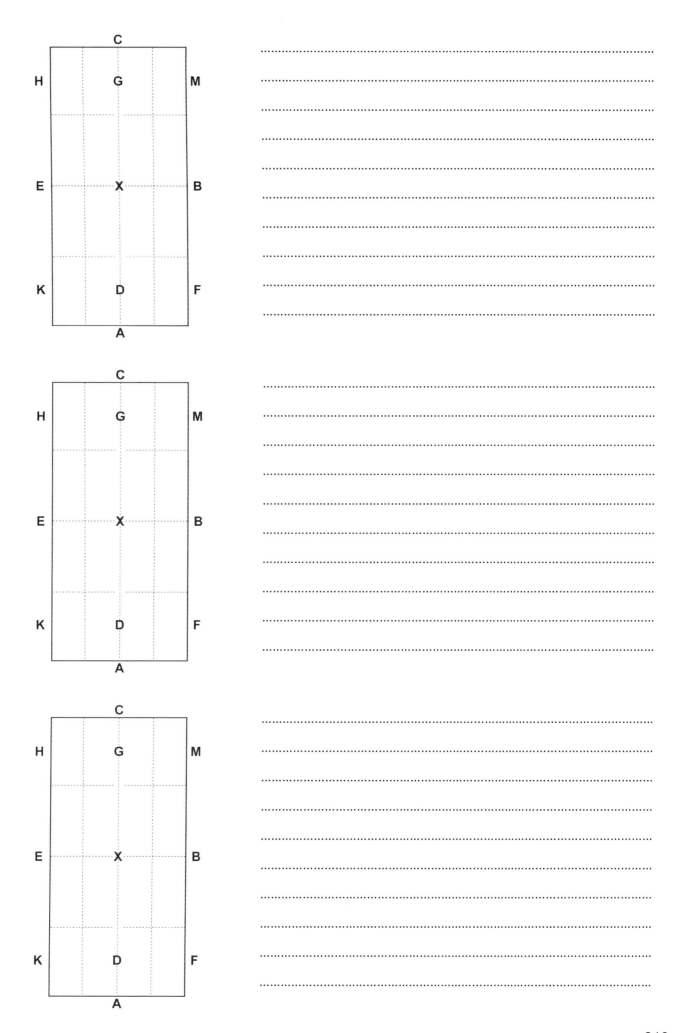

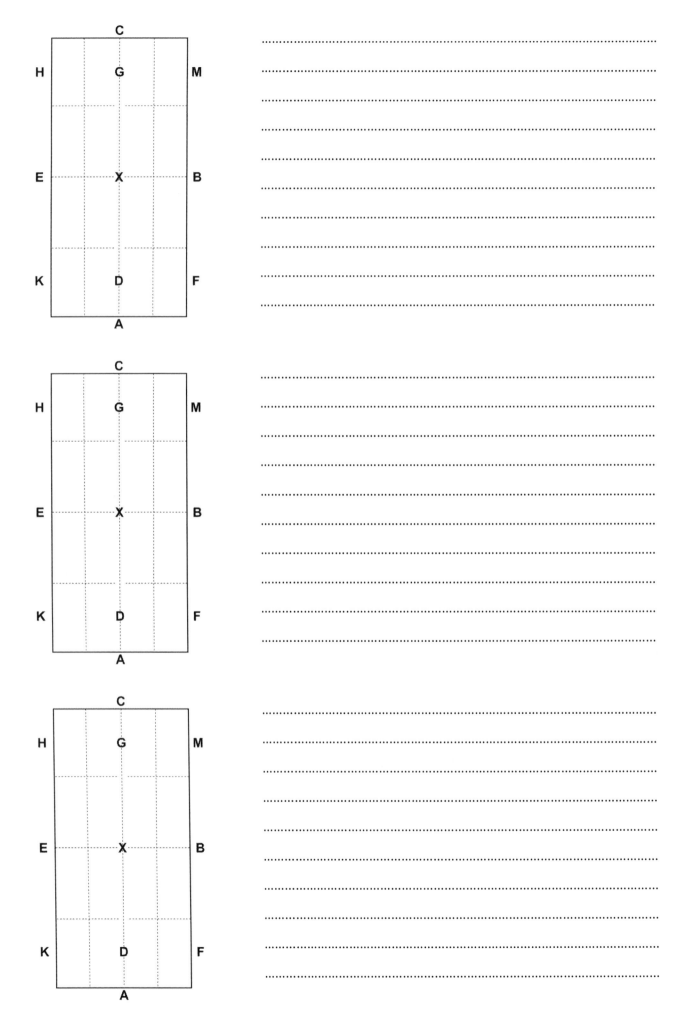

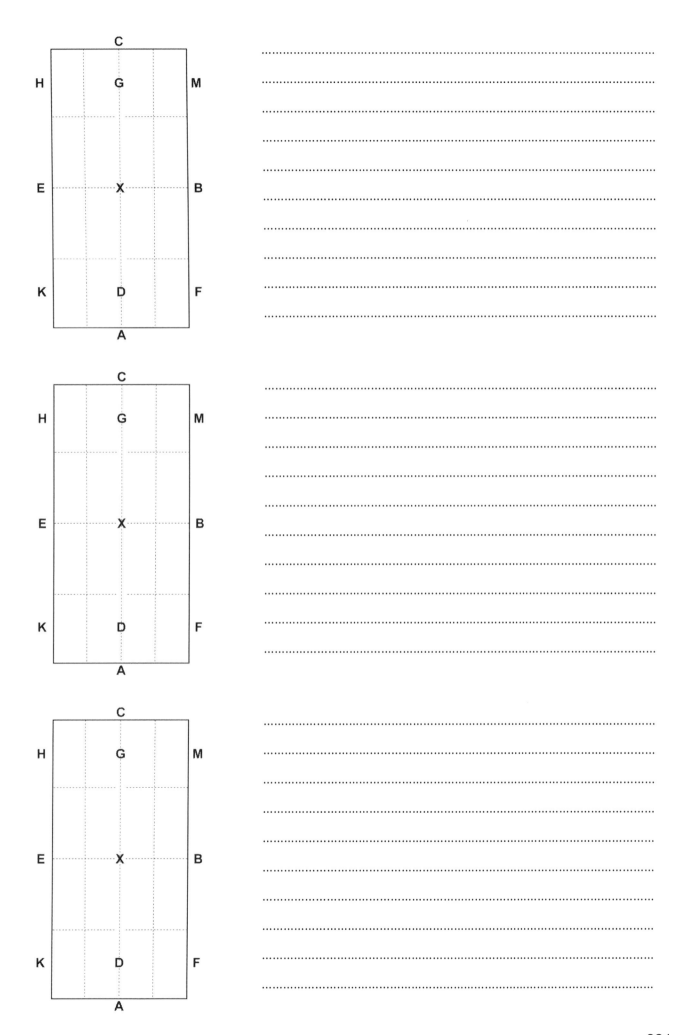

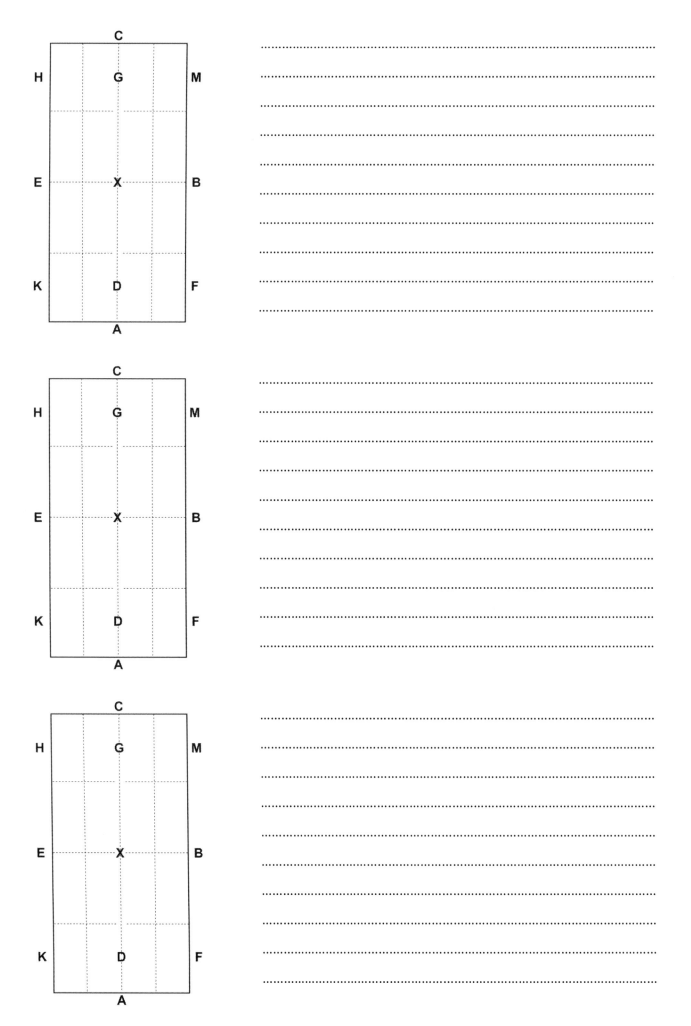

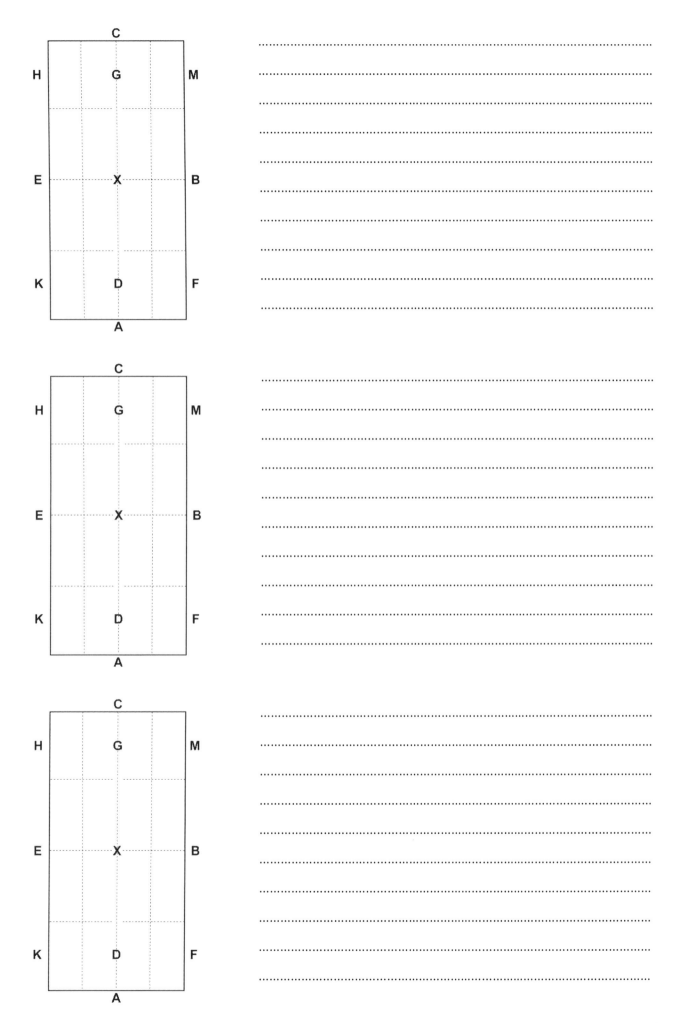

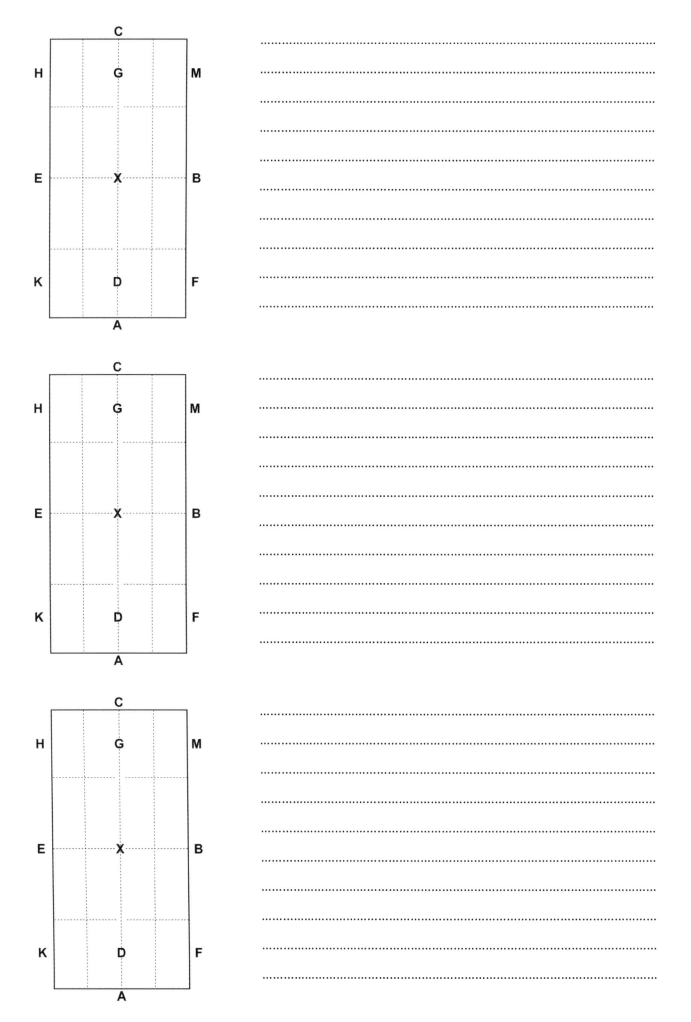

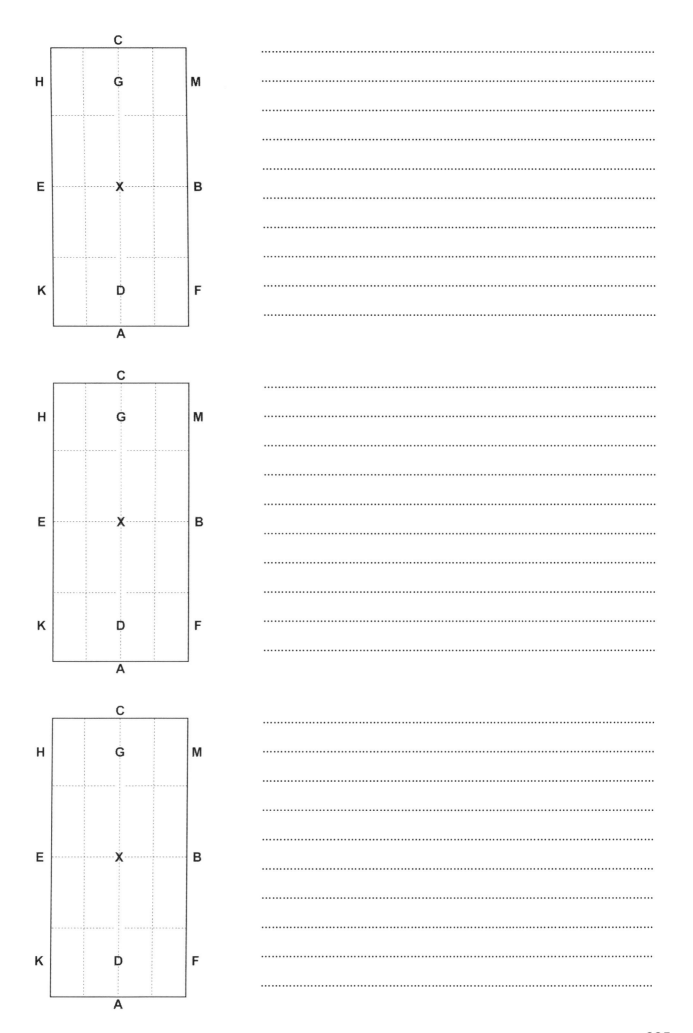

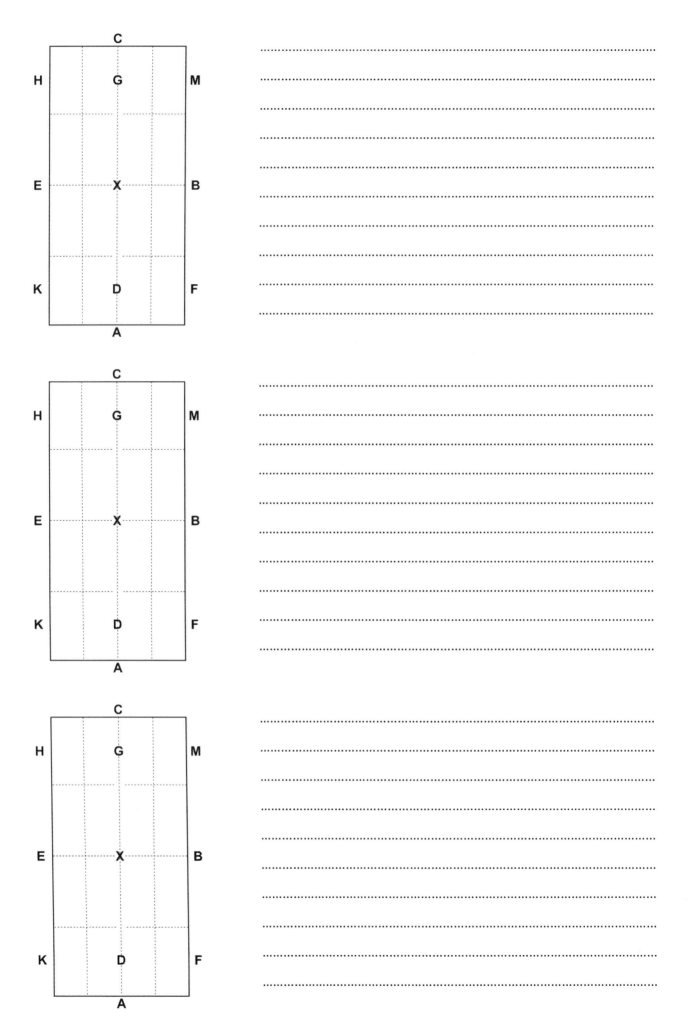

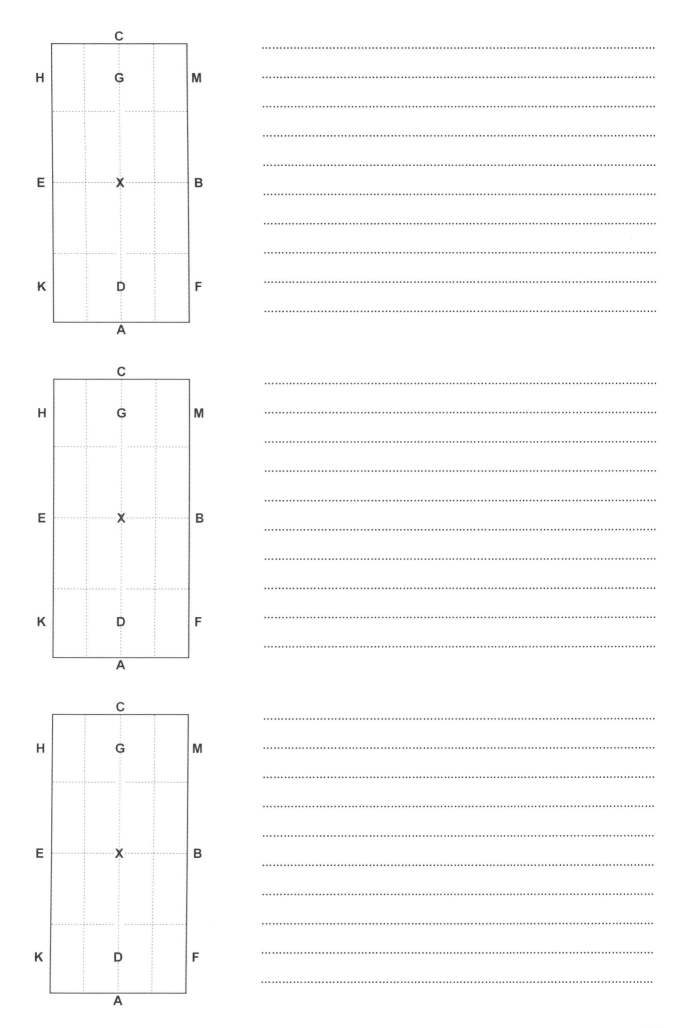

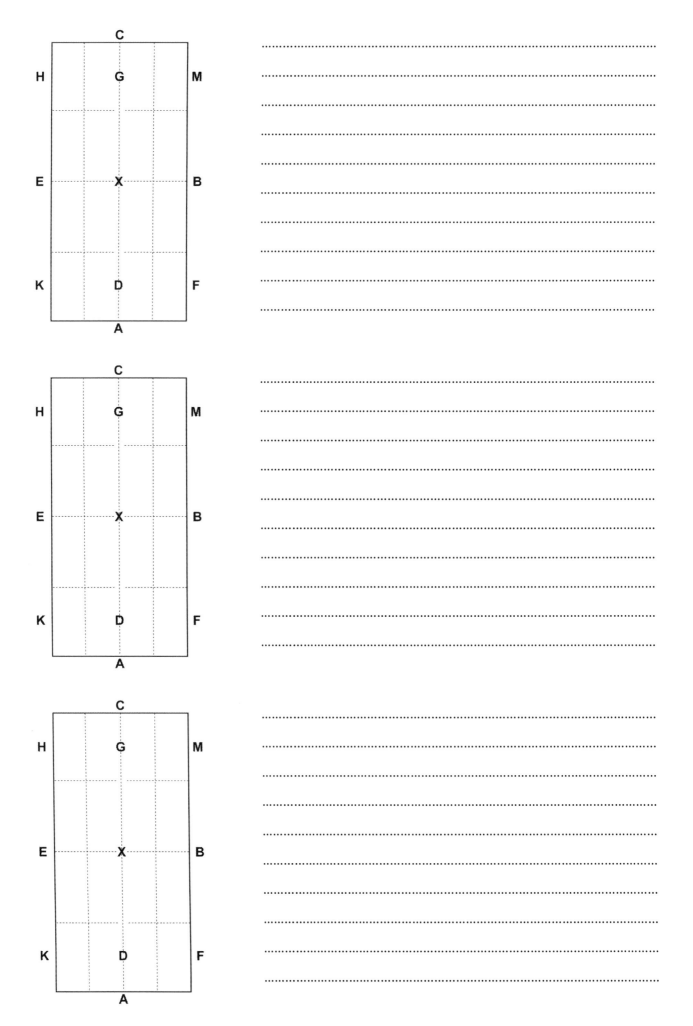

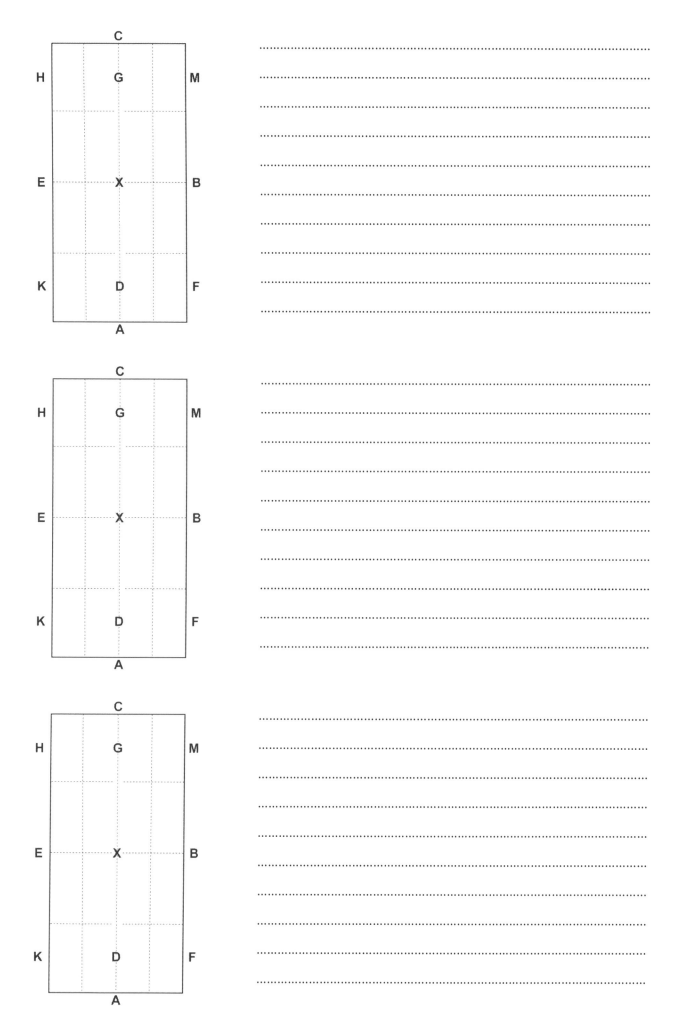

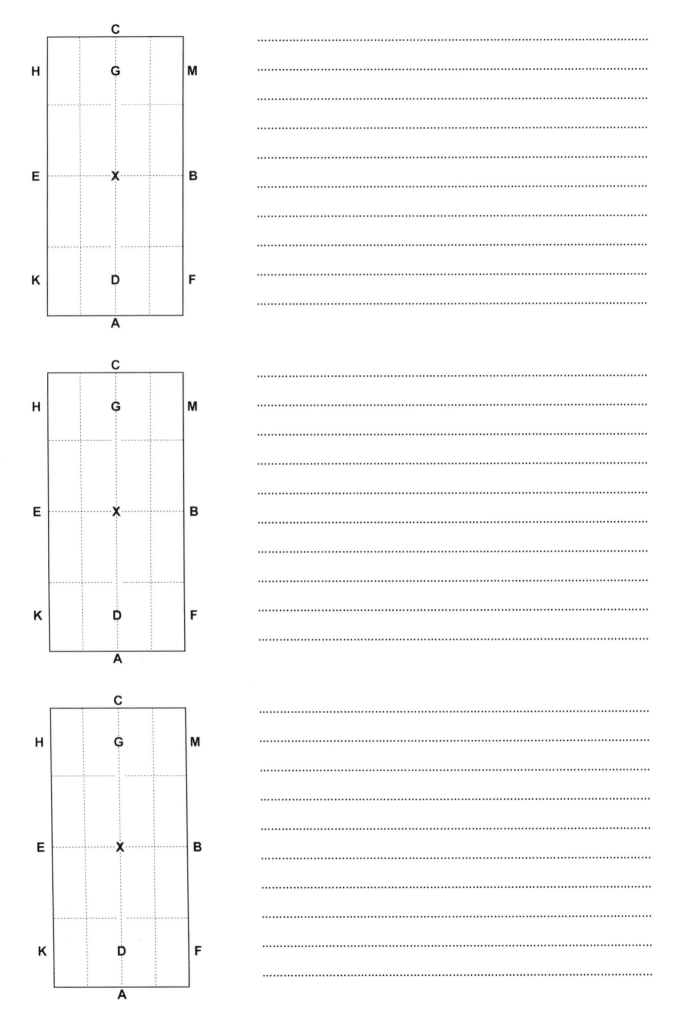

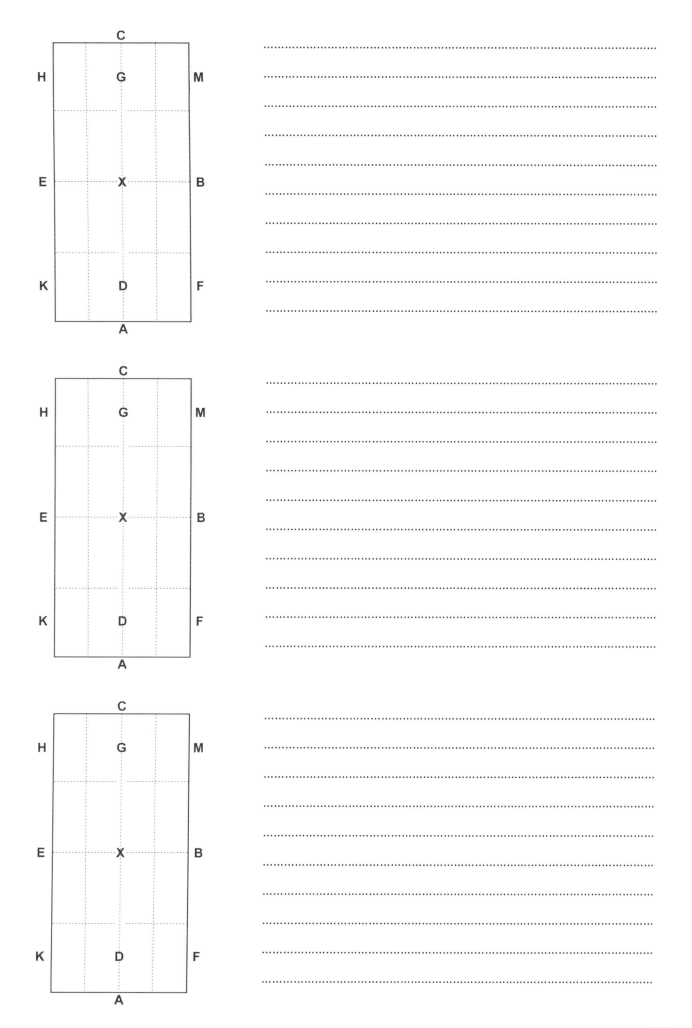

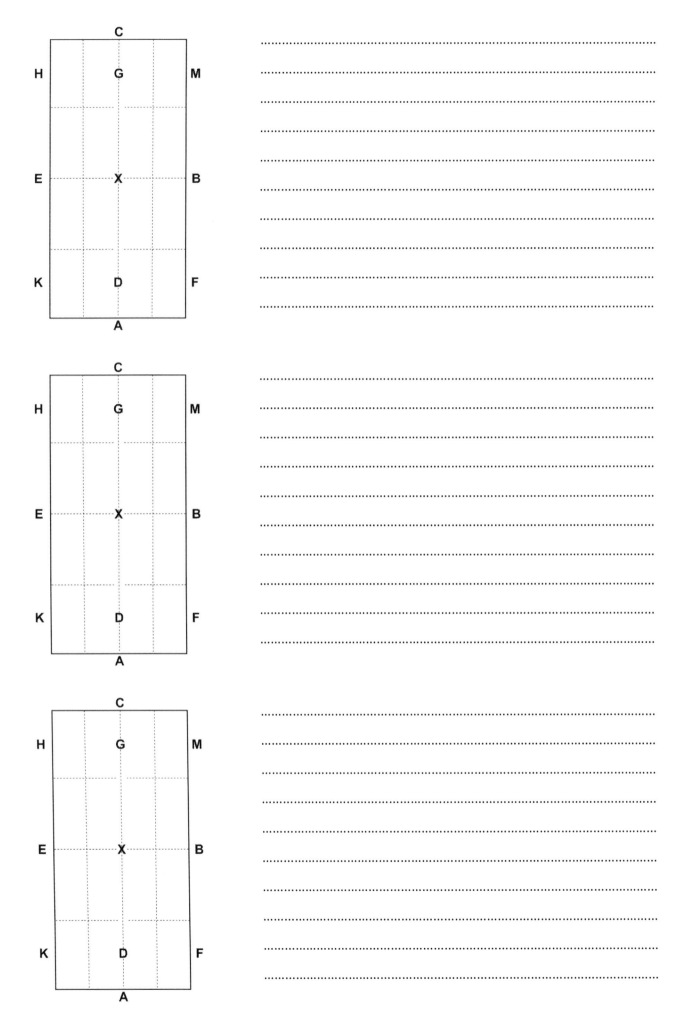

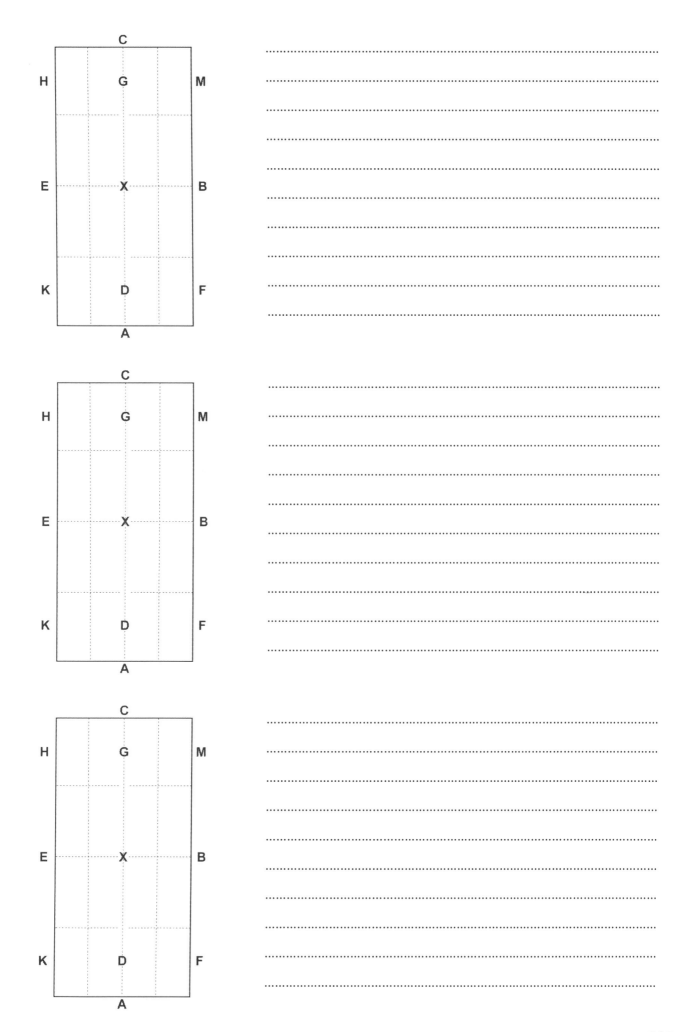

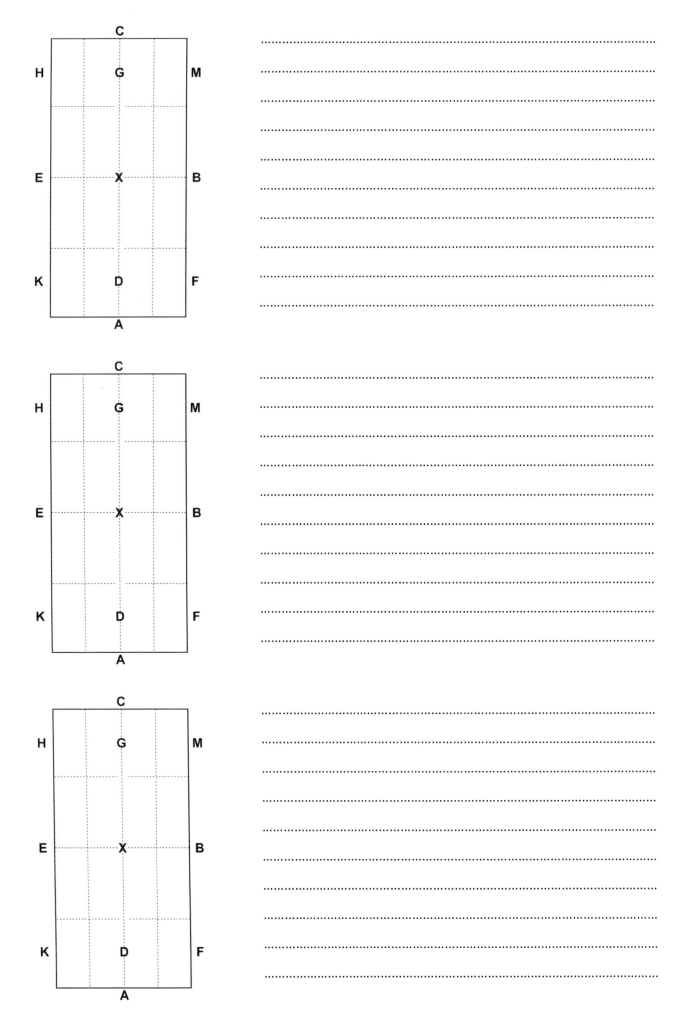

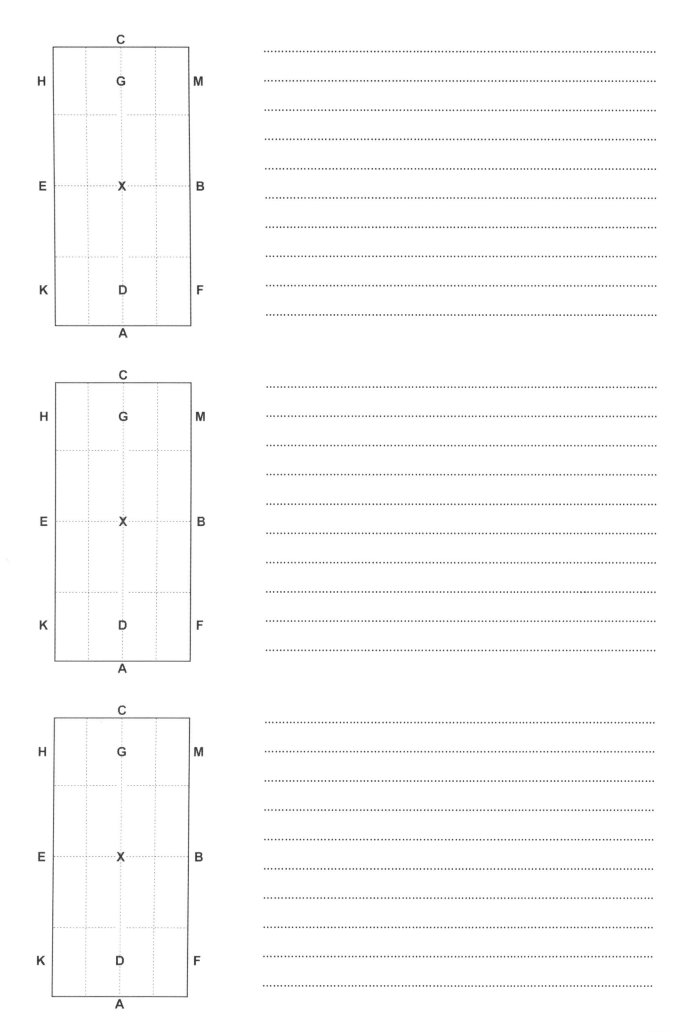

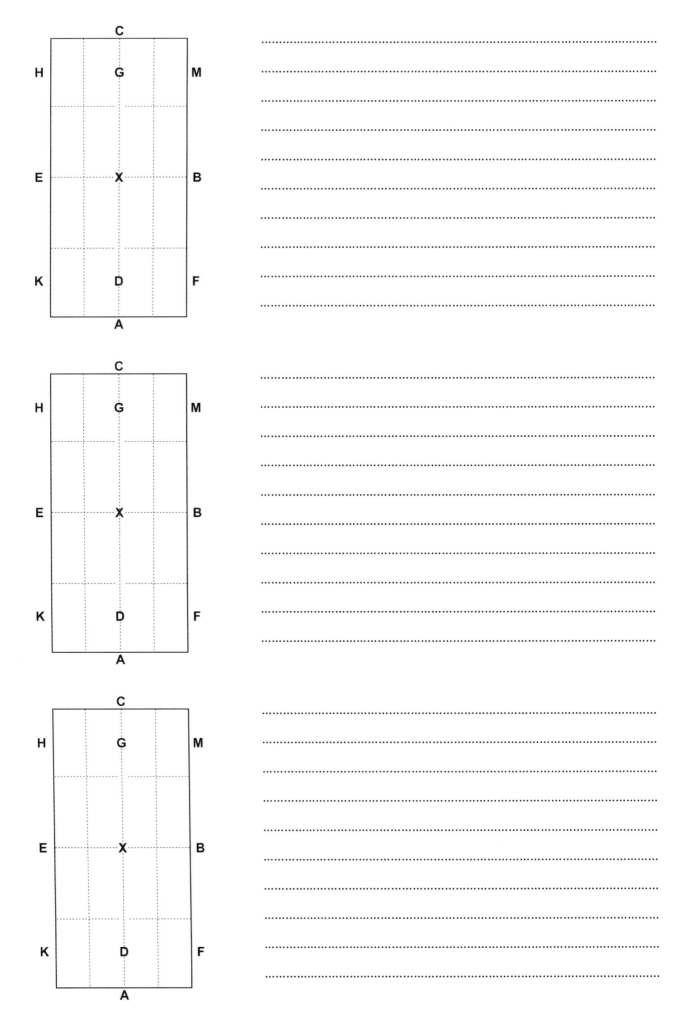

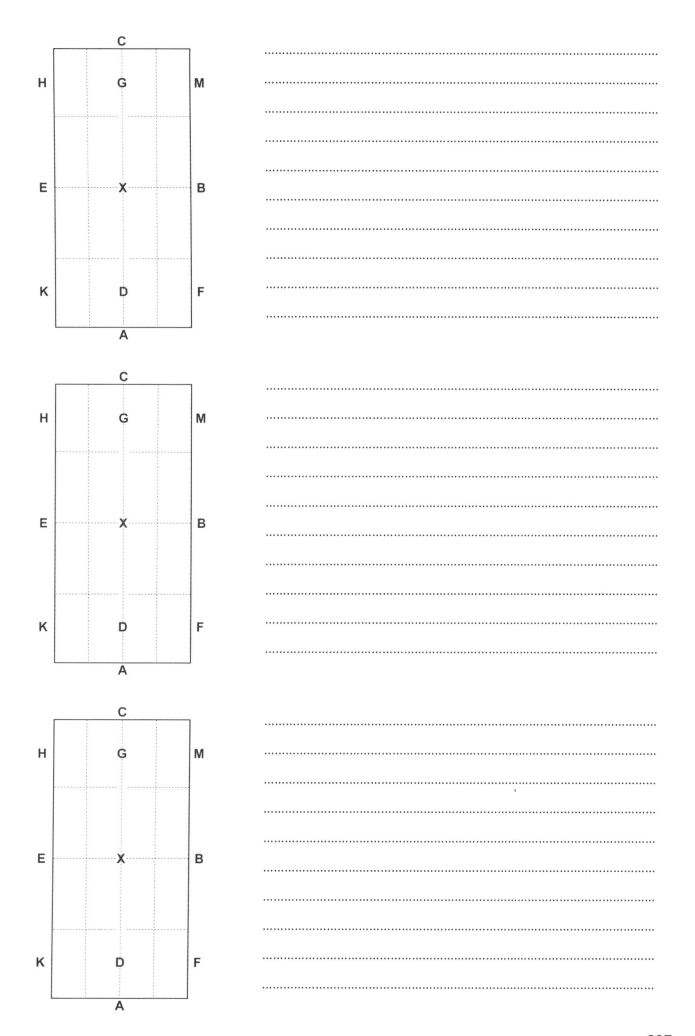

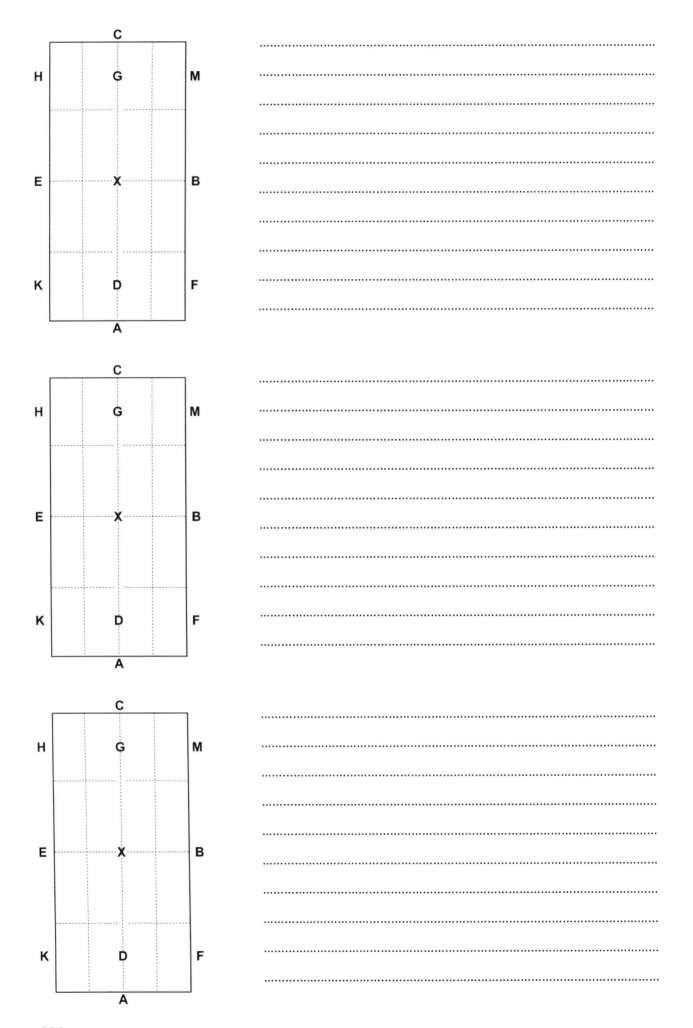

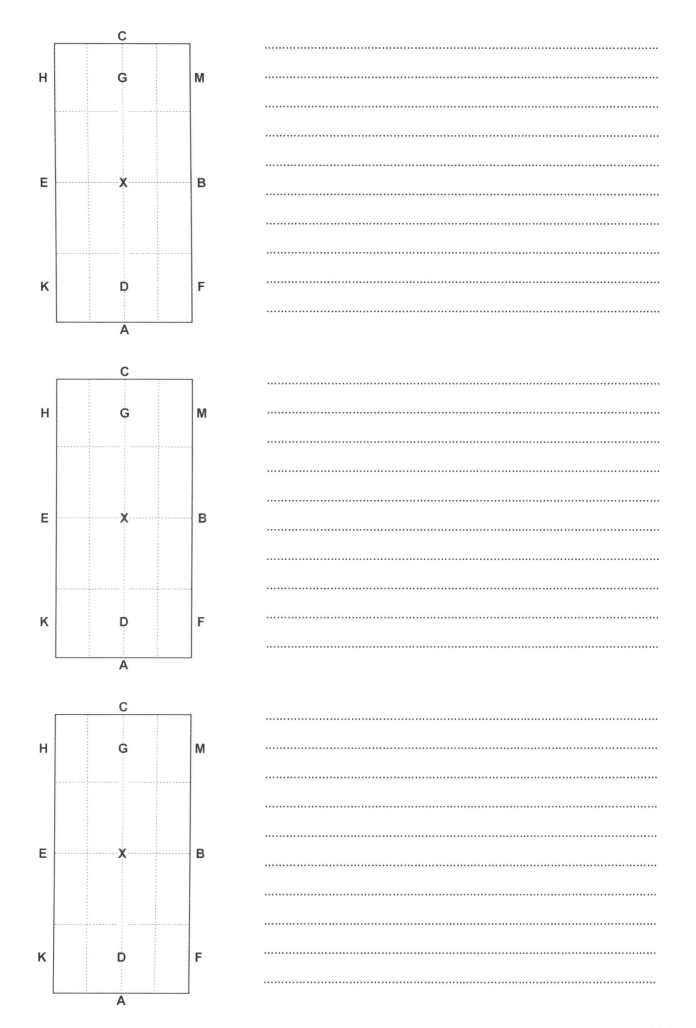

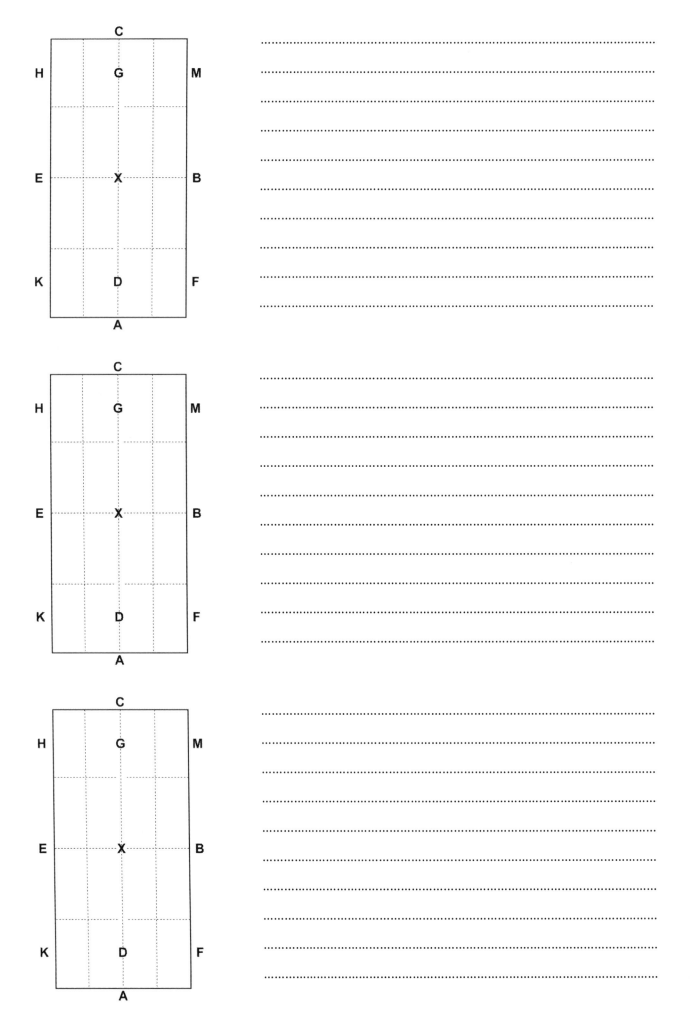

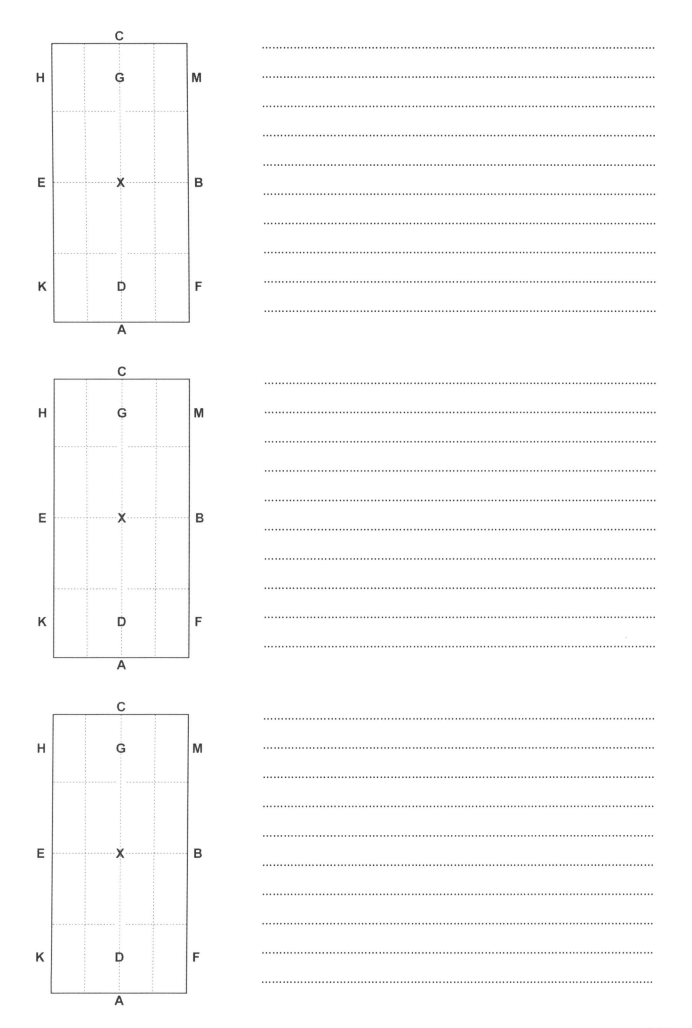

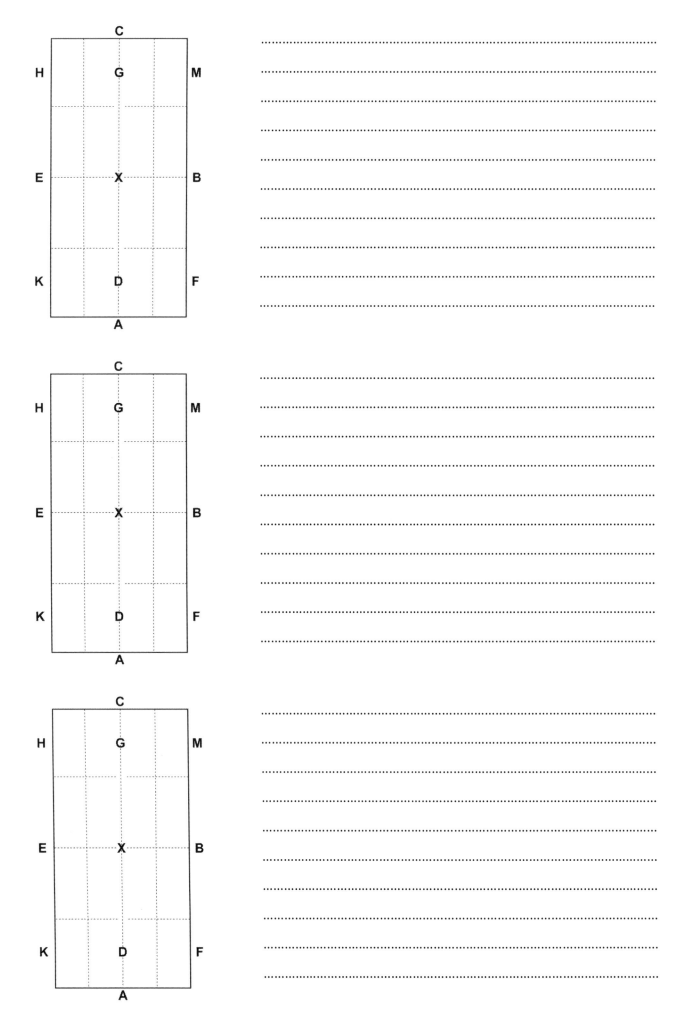

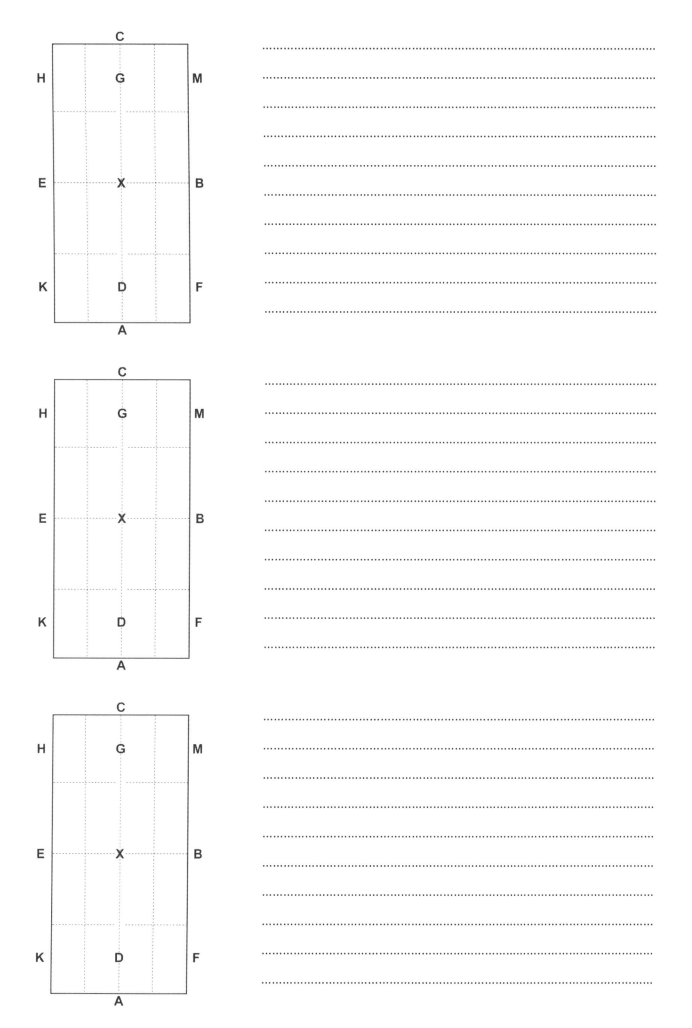

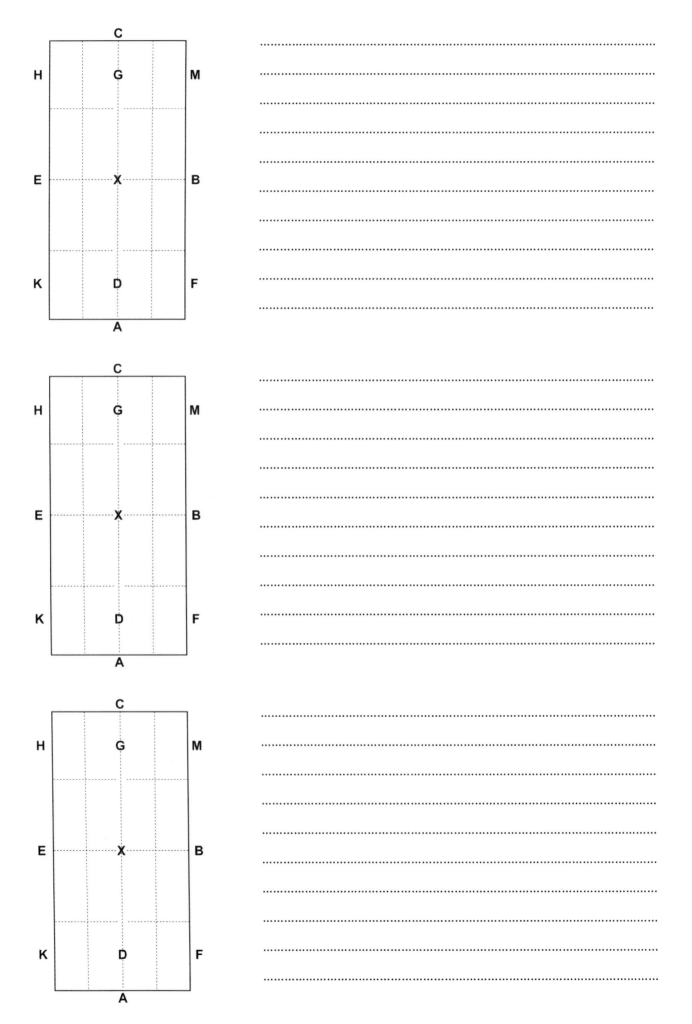

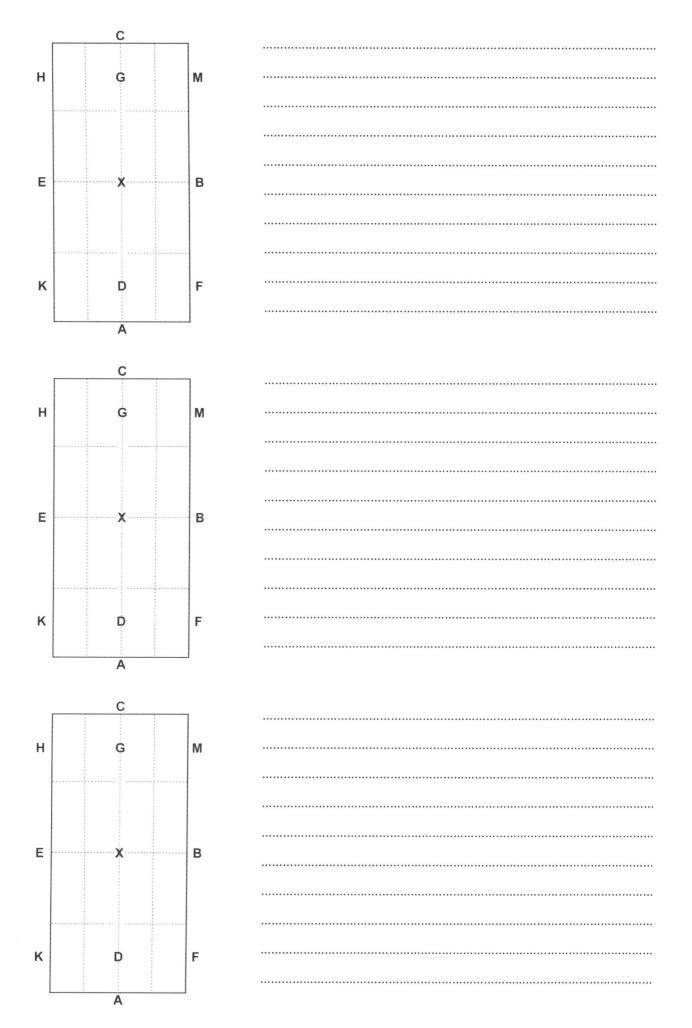

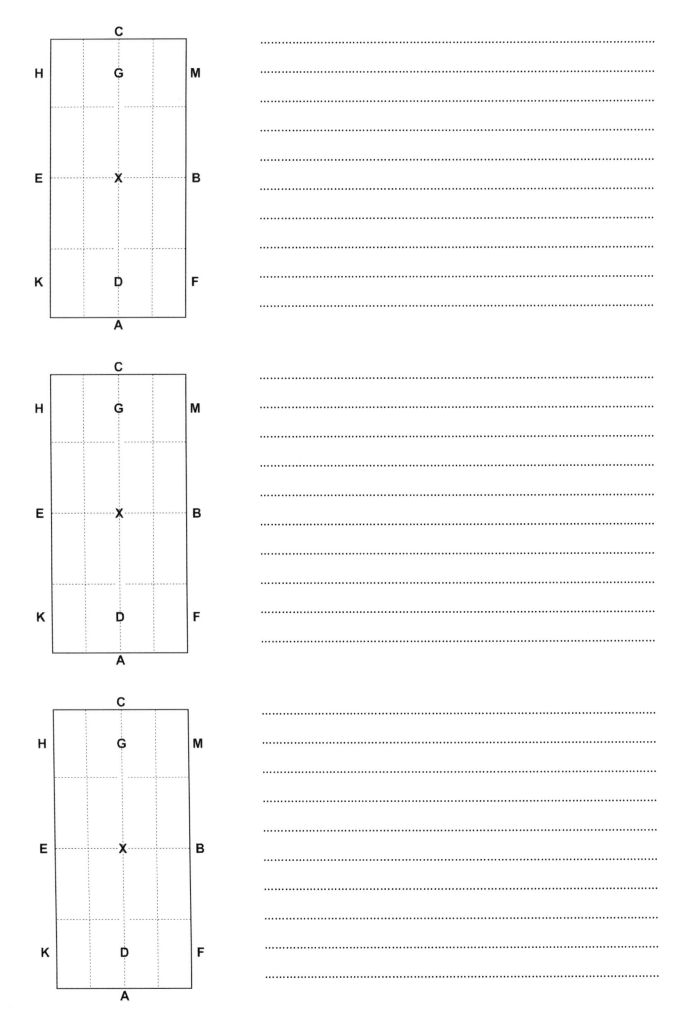

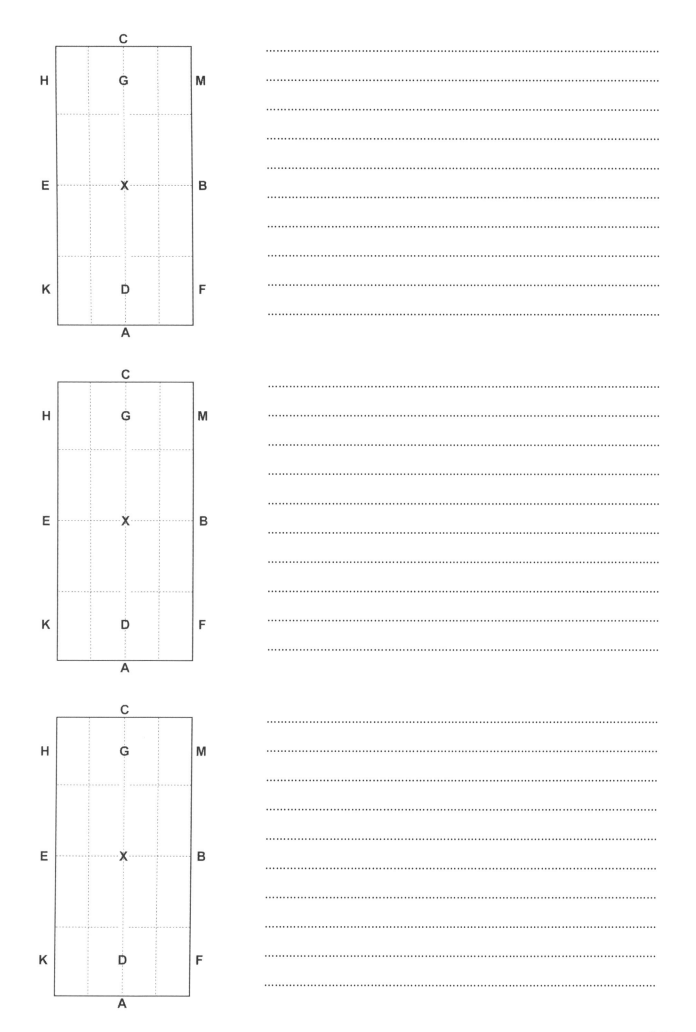

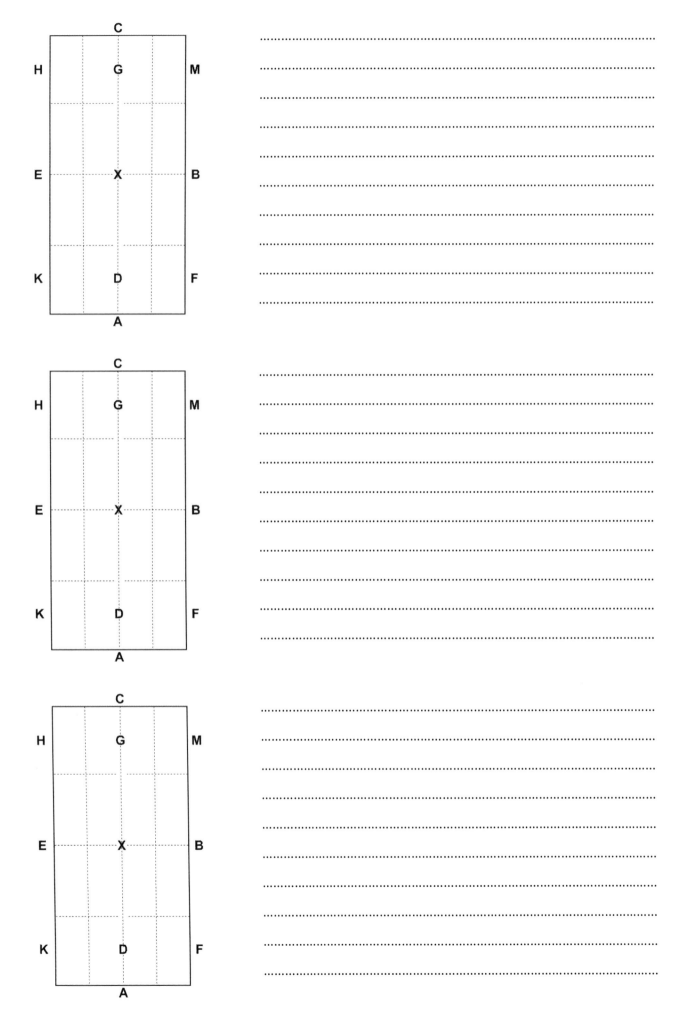

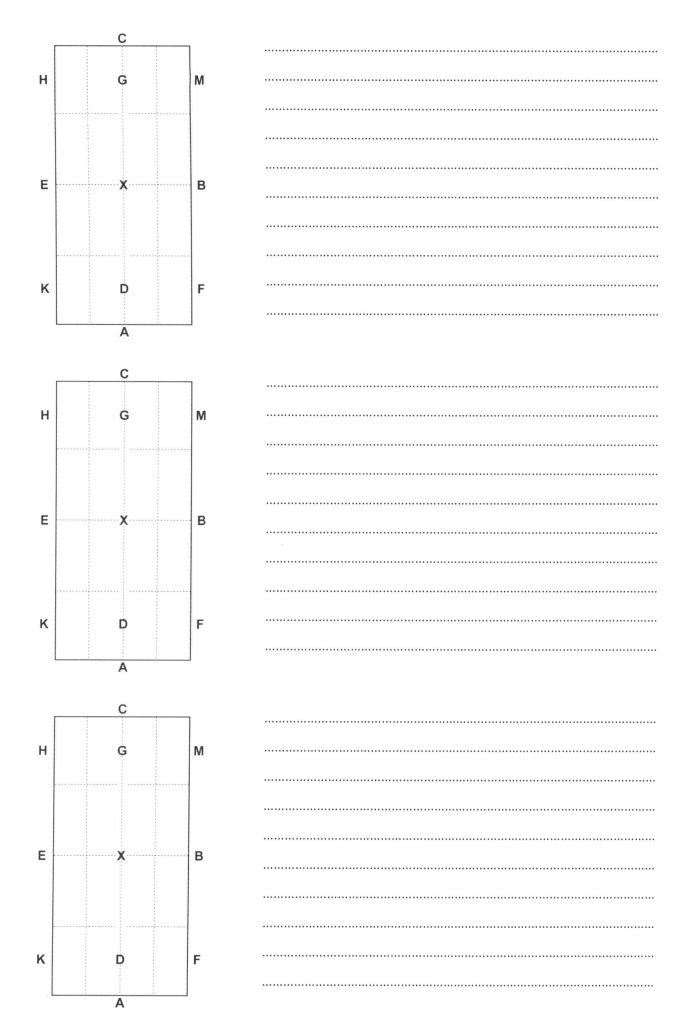

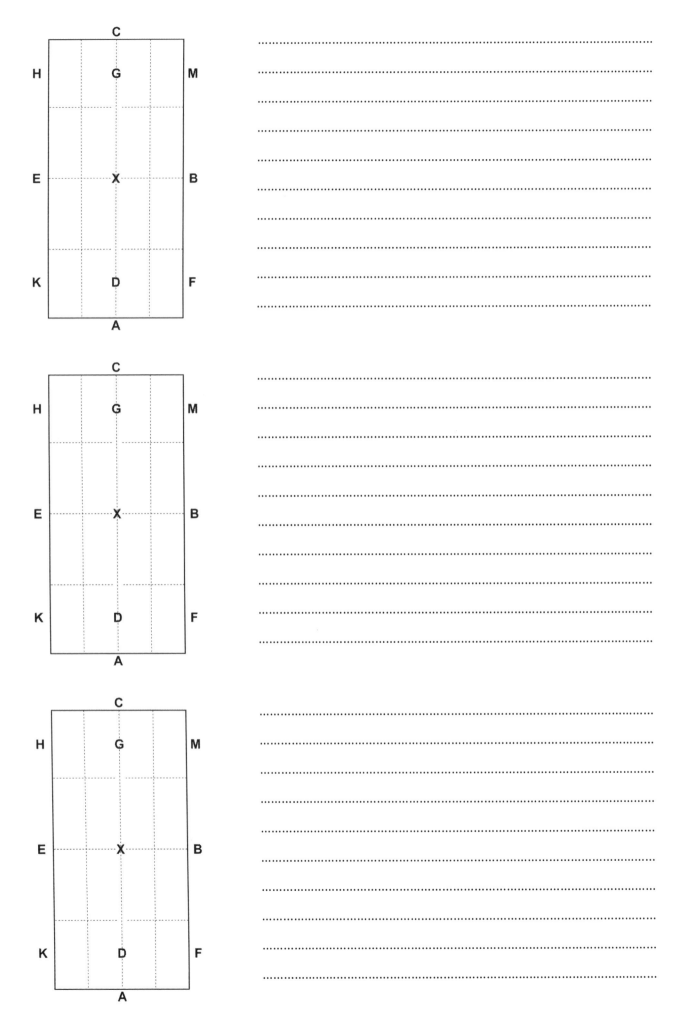

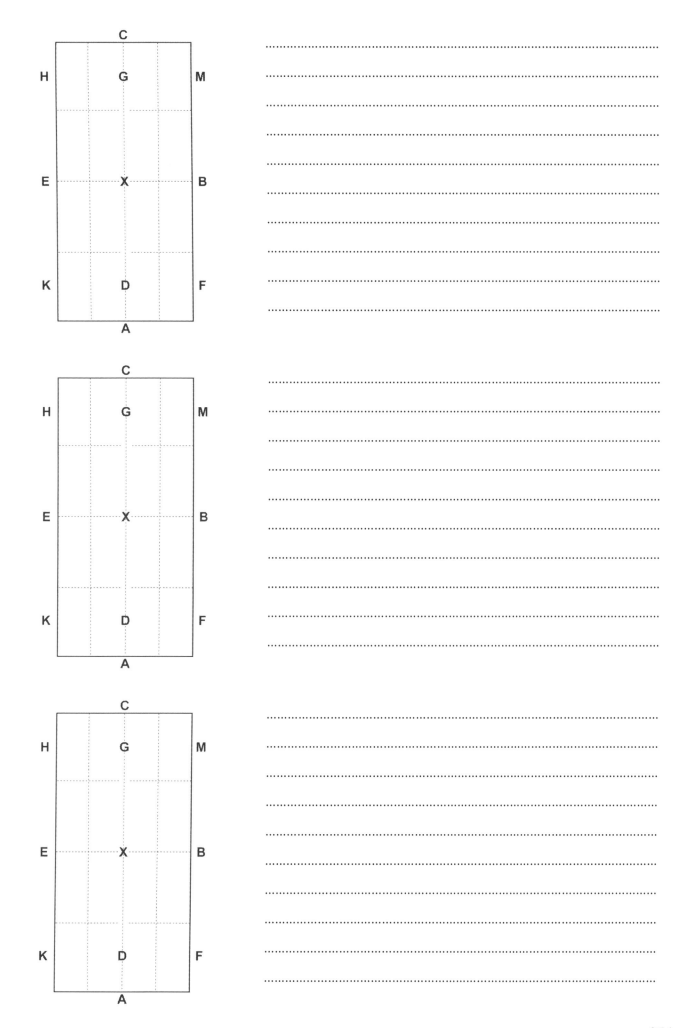

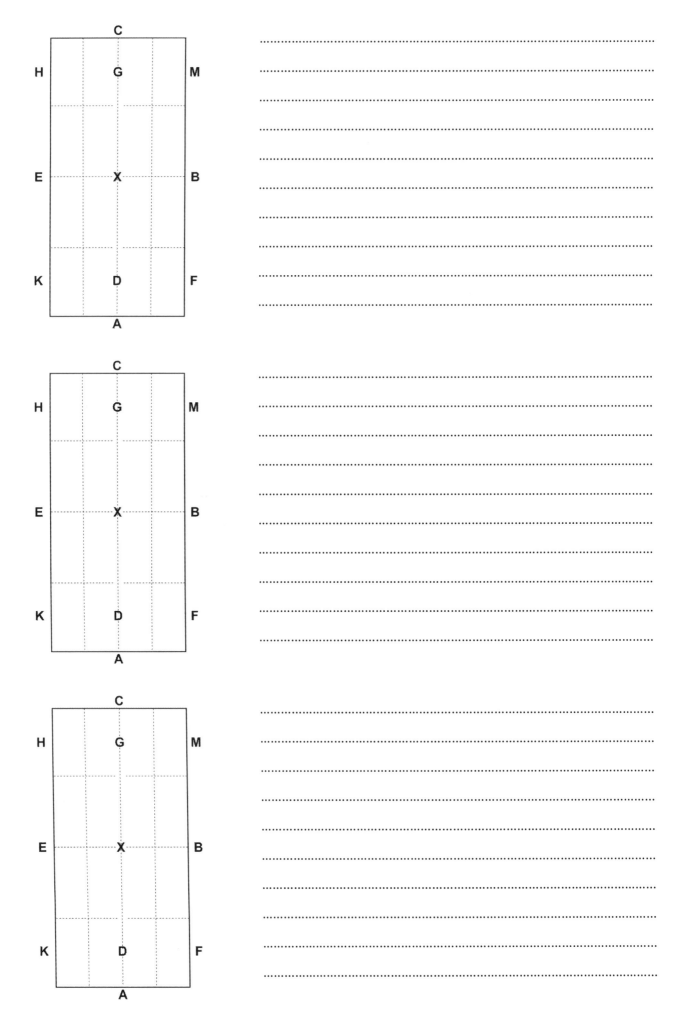

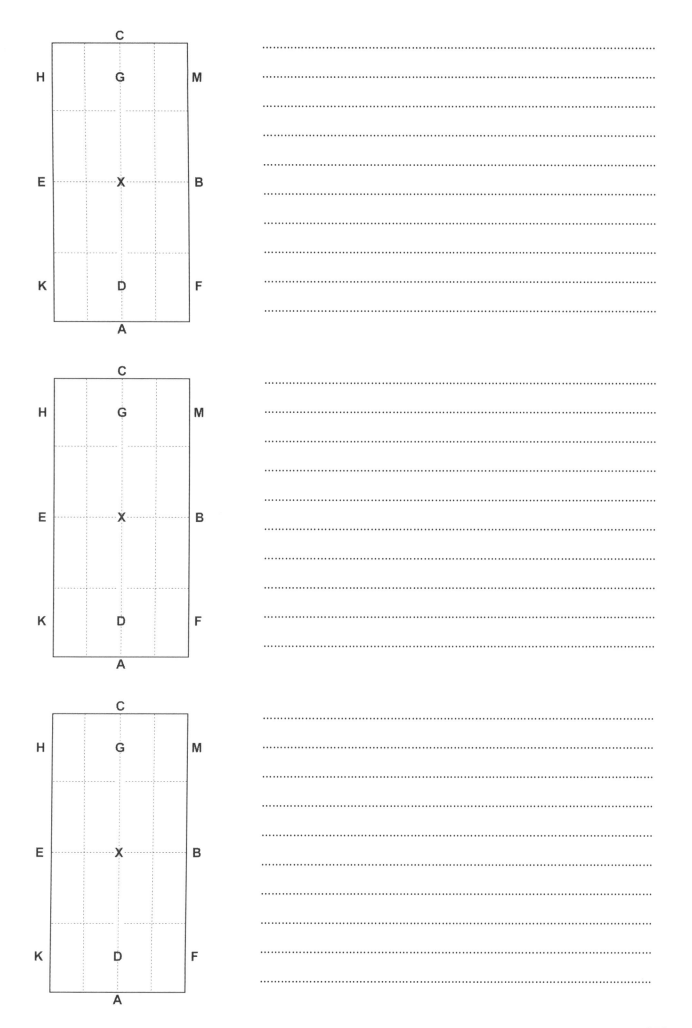

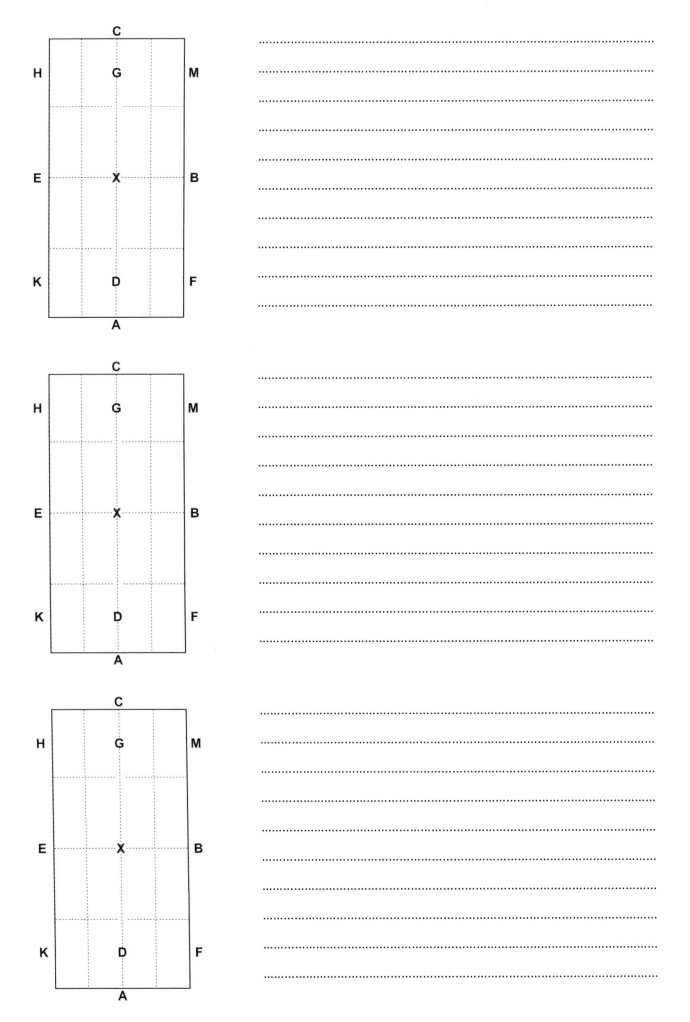

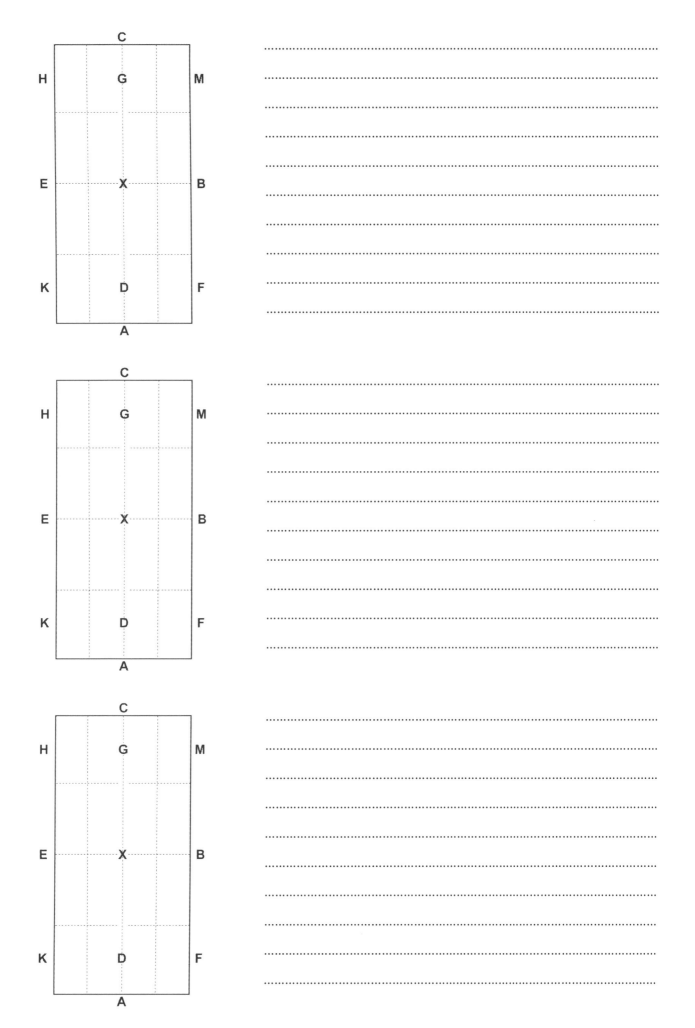

Made in United States
Troutdale, OR
12/12/2024